3-

INSIDE CLASSIC ROCK TRACKS

Songwriting and recording secrets of 100 great songs, from 1960 to the present day • Rikky Rooksby

INSIDE CLASSIC ROCK TRACKS

RIKKY ROOKSBY

A BACKBEAT BOOK
First edition 2001
Published by Backbeat Books
600 Harrison Street,
San Francisco, CA 94107
www.backbeatbooks.com • email: books@musicplayer.com

An imprint of The Music Player Network
United Entertainment Media Inc.

Published for Backbeat Books by Outline Press Ltd,
115J Cleveland Street, London W1T 6PU, England.
www.backbeatuk.com

ISBN 0-87930-654-8

Printed in the United States of America

Art Director: Nigel Osborne
Editorial Director: Tony Bacon
Design: Paul Cooper
Editor: Paul Quinn
Production: Phil Richardson

Origination by Global Colour (Malaysia)
Print by Tien Wah (Singapore)

01 02 03 04 05 5 4 3 2 1

For Rhonda

“I took a music appreciation course, but the teachers were against anything except classical stuff. Well, I wasn't going to sit there and let any guy tell me that pop music is bad. I love both.”

BRIAN WILSON

“Those 12 notes are so mysterious, and each time I sit down at the piano I can't wait to see where they're going to take me today. It still fascinates me. Each generation, from Scott Joplin forward, has found its own ways of playing with those 12 notes. The possibilities are endless.”

LAMONT DOZIER

“My theory is that every time the industry gets powerful, and corporate thinking dominates what the music is, then the music really pales.”

PAUL SIMON

INSIDE CLASSIC ROCK TRACKS

CONTENTS

1960s

1970s

1980s

1990s

endmatter

INTRODUCTION

INTRODUCTION

Listening to music is such an instinctive part of human nature, you might think the last thing you need is a book to tell you how to do it. But this book is for those of you who want to listen a bit more closely – to get a fuller picture of the music you're buying at the moment, or the records you have loved over the years.

It's a book about *active* listening, rather than just *passive* hearing. Nowadays we're increasingly exposed to music in passing, as background noise, or in brief soundbites, in commercials and the like. *Inside Classic Rock Tracks* is for people willing to take the time to sit down (or maybe even lie down, with headphones on) and get to know some great songs really well – whether it's to glean insights into the writer or producer's craft, or just to enjoy a fuller listening experience.

The book focuses on a personal selection of 100 songs – from almost as many different artists – all written and recorded between 1960 and the turn of the 21st century. It puts them under the microscope to recover their secrets, and asks questions like: How does this song work? What is the music doing? How was it all put together? What are the lyrics about? What the hell is that weird noise? Is there a reason why a certain song has a particular emotional effect? And what aspects of these recorded performances might the listener easily miss?... You may be surprised how even in songs we've heard 100 times there will be elements we overlook.

Ever wondered why so many people buy new versions of old songs, or original recordings re-issued on technologically-improved media? Chasing familiar music through successive formats is largely about recovering the initial thrill of hearing it for the first time – when you fall in love with a song and can't get it out of your head or off your hi-fi. It's also about hearing more of it. New audio formats feed this desire (at the same time as, of course, feeding the coffers of record companies). Hear it again, they whisper, but this time, hear it properly. *Get closer to the original.*

But there is another way of doing this, and not through technology. It involves using your ears and your mind. The power to recover these details is in you, not your hi-fi.

IS POP MUSIC WORTH LISTENING TO SO CLOSELY?

Since the early 1950s consecutive generations have grown up being told that popular music is not 'serious' music (and what's more it makes you hysterical, immoral, drug-crazed, Satan-worshipping, and will stunt your plants). Since it is produced largely for commercial purposes, the argument goes, it is obviously insincere and disposable... The inadequacy of this view is demonstrated by the majority of tracks in this book.

Of course you can always find examples of musical insincerity and commercial crassness if you look for them, but this book chooses to take a generally more positive approach. It hopes to prove, moreover, that the 'disposable' criticism thrown at popular music says as much about the listener as it does about the songs. The more you listen, the more you will hear.

It was largely because of the 'throwaway' tag that, during the late 1960s and early 1970s, some kinds of popular music aspired to the status of 'serious music'. In so far as this made a rock audience more willing to consider that an album might require repeated playing, this was a good thing. But it also led to dubious developments like rock operas, concertos for group & orchestra, and concept albums. The single was considered *passé*. Length and profundity were confused. *The Wall* or a side of *Tales From Topographic Oceans* is not 'deeper' music than 'She Loves You' or The Sex Pistols' 'God Save The Queen'.

All good music, of whatever genre, repays active listening. The best popular music may well be great to dance to, or entertaining, or for enhancing a mood; but more than this, it contains plenty to listen to – if you know what to look out for.

In popular music the *sound* of the recording is an integral element – the way a song is recorded can bring it excitingly to life or, if done badly, kill it stone dead. Even if we don't realise it, the sound is part of what we love about our favourite singles and albums.

So it's worth taking a few minutes here – especially for the non-musicians reading this – to consider some of the elements that may go into the creation of a classic popular recording: what instrumentation is used, and the interaction between players; how it has been recorded, produced and mixed; and of course how the basic song itself is constructed and arranged.

INSTRUMENTATION – THE COLOUR OF SOUND

Part of active listening is simply consciously registering the instruments on a recording. Most people only notice a small amount of the instrumentation: they listen first to the voice – the most immediate and human element; and if there is a lead instrument – a prominent riff or solo by an electric guitar, trumpet, saxophone, for example – they will focus on that, in-between the singing. Everything else is background. This is a reality lost sight of by many professionals in the industry.

Stories about 1970s bands taking two weeks to get a drum sound are the stuff of legend. The fact is, a great many listeners only hear a drum kit as a bashing noise that keeps the beat. I once asked a guitar student, who was finding it hard to play in time with a track, to focus on the snare drum. Back came the question – "Which is the snare drum?" If the producer spent a whole morning adjusting the EQ on that snare, the effort was wasted on *that* listener.

The snare is normally the mid-to-high-pitched, punchiest-sounding drum-beat, usually the loudest part of the kit. In most post-1950s popular music the snare provides the driving 'backbeat', normally alternating with the bass drum. The bass drum (or 'kick') is the lowest-pitched drum sound – the one that hits you in the pit of the stomach on a loud metal or dance track – usually stressing the first beat of a bar, and providing a solid rhythmic foundation to the music. The hi-hats – a pair of small cymbals operated with a footpedal as well as played with sticks – is often like a metronome on a track (especially prominent on early Seventies soul, disco or rock): they can be closed for a tight sound or opened for a 'splashy' effect. A ride cymbal can be used for the same time-keeping purpose. Crash cymbals are mainly for accents or dynamic effects. Side drums and tom-toms are incorporated into 'fills' – often spontaneous additions to the basic rhythm which a drummer inserts to increase excitement, or link two sections of music.

That's a basic drum kit, to which can be added any number of percussion instruments – from cowbells to congas – or it can even be replaced completely by modern digital drums, which can be programmed to introduce almost any kind of sound to widen the percussive palette.

Listening to characterful drummers like Ginger Baker, Ringo Starr, Mitch Mitchell, Keith Moon, John Bonham, Budgie, Stewart Copeland, and Lars Ulrich is a pleasure in itself (a number of tracks included in this book spotlight great drum parts).

But rock's most important instrument (the one which really differentiates it from pre-rock and post-rock music) is the electric guitar – right from the clean(ish), reverberating twangs of Scotty Moore (Elvis's first guitarist), or Duane Eddy, or The Shadows, through the overdriven blues-tone of Jimi Hendrix, Eric Clapton, Peter Green or Paul Kossoff, to the gargantuan, earth-rippling thrash-chords of Metallica, Anthrax, Nirvana, or Oasis.

It used to be possible to educate your ears to recognise the individual sound of many different models of guitars, amplifiers and effects units (names like Gibson, Fender, Rickenbacker, Gretsch, Marshall, Vox, Hi-Watt, Ampeg, WEM, Electro-Harmonix, Colorsound... may or may not mean anything to you), but these days there are so many combinations and permutations in use it's much more difficult to be sure. And of course, as with drums, digital modelling can recreate almost any guitar or amplifier sound, past or present. Besides, a large part of a good player's tone comes as much from the head and fingers as from the equipment – witness Hendrix, Hank Marvin, Marc Bolan, Neil Young, Edward Van Halen *et al.*

There are other guitar sounds you might hear – such as 12-string guitars, acoustic or electric, bring a chiming quality to a record (like The Byrds' 'Mr Tambourine Man'); or a guitar played with a 'bottle-neck' or 'slide' (typical of George Harrison, and much blues); or with a 'capo' tightening the strings high on the neck (as on many Simon & Garfunkel tracks); or in an altered tuning (popular in folk-oriented rock – see John Martyn, Richard Thompson, and also Jimmy Page).

The bass is often one of the harder instruments to hear, for the untrained ear at least – but if it was removed from the mix the difference would be noticed immediately. The traditional upright 'double' bass was always notoriously difficult to record, due to limitations of microphone and amplification technology; the electric 'Fender' bass (as it was originally known, because that's who invented it) was a giant leap forward – played like a four-string electric guitar, and as loud as your amplification allows.

How audible a bass is depends on how loud it is in the 'mix' (see below), as well as its tonal properties (bright slap bass is easier to hear than other types), whether it has any effects on it, and how much else is going on. There's no problem hearing Jack Bruce's bass on the live recording of 'Crossroads' by Cream because there are only three instruments. Funk and soul-style bass, including much of Motown, often used a less bright, more 'middly' tone, but was very prominent in the mix, and central to the music.

Keyboards could either be another lead instrument – augmenting or replacing guitar – or used as a subtle atmospheric 'pad' to fill out sonic gaps in the background. The acoustic piano and reed organ of the early years were largely superseded by analogue and then digital synthesisers, which could emulate most types of keyboard, or even orchestral sounds (again making it harder to identify exactly what you're hearing).

Sampling – taking instrumentation from an existing recording – has introduced a further complication (quite apart from the legal and ethical implications of re-using someone else's work). Well-known samples may be easy for the keen listener to spot, but the drive to find ever-more obscure old records to sample from makes it difficult to tell if what you're listening to is being played or re-processed. One giveaway is that sampling grabs all the related sonic information from a record, along with the chosen instrument or riff – for example, the original 'reverb' (see below), not to mention vinyl crackle.

Which brings us to the recording process itself.

RECORDING – HOW A SONG IS CAPTURED

Recording means committing a song to tape, or to a digital medium such as hard disk. In the early days of recording all the musicians on a session would play together: they would be positioned in a studio at appropriate distances from the microphones to achieve a satisfying balance of sound. The performance would be captured complete with the colouration of the room and the microphones, and any mistakes. Such single-take recordings often have a raw excitement and atmosphere which is rewarding in its own way (listen to an early Elvis song, from the Sun Studio Sessions, or to Howlin' Wolf).

The development of multi-track recording, through the ingenuity of Les Paul and others, fundamentally changed this. It became possible for musical parts to be recorded separately – which meant extra instruments could be added later, or the song could be recorded as an instrumental and the vocals added afterwards. It also meant that a smaller group of musicians could make a bigger sound. The number of tape 'tracks' available for such 'over-dubbing' grew from two, in the early 1960s, to three, then four, then, by 1970, eight and 16 separate tracks. Bouncing back and forth could create even more tracks, but sound quality deteriorated by doing this. Nowadays, in the digital era, there is essentially no technical limit on track numbers – only a financial or temperamental one (it's down to money and inclination).

The second recording stage is 'mixing'. In the early years this was a straightforward process of deciding the relative volume of the individual tracks, and creating a final 'master' from the multi-track recordings; but it gradually became much more of an extension of the recording process – a chance to further shape and refine the final sound. Since the 12-inch single trend began in the 1980s, the idea of one definitive mix of a song has diminished, as famous re-mixers/producers are encouraged to create their own, sometimes radical, interpretations of a track.

Mixing can even be considered a compositional technique, since it's during a mix that the artist/producer might decide to omit a solo, or drop out the rhythm section for a third verse, or repeat something. This is one of the reasons why (aside from time and money) no-one would dare to go back and re-master, say, Hendrix's *Electric Ladyland* from the original multi-track – there are too many artistic decisions that would need to be recreated in the process of mixing that were originally made by Hendrix and producer Eddie Kramer.

There are other reasons why some classic sounds can never be recreated. For one thing, the equipment has changed over the years: many of the great recording studios of the 1960s and 1970s have been demolished, or stripped of their gear – some of which resurfaces in modern studios attempting to recreate those classic, pre-digital sounds. As a side-note, a particularly worrying phenomenon for music lovers is the seemingly inevitable deterioration of magnetic tape (assuming the original still exists at all), and the indifference of some record companies to their tape vaults. The compilers of the recent deluxe *What's Going On* wrote that there are 'drop-outs' (holes in the sound) on one of the tracks, caused by decaying tape.

When Jimmy Page sat down with George Marino to remaster Led Zeppelin's back catalogue they noted a loss in high frequencies, owing to the age of the tapes, and made digital copies before going any further. How many tapes haven't been so lucky? Some of R.E.M's 1980s multi-tracks had to be rescued from a garbage skip. The original multi-track of Love's *Forever Changes* (1967) is currently missing...

Rescue and restoration operations can have added benefits for the listener – not only in terms of cleaned-up sound, but also the occasionally fascinating insights to be gained from the issuing of unheard demos or rejected takes (as with the tracking sessions for 'God Only Knows', or the Foundations mix of 'What's Going On', or, for sheer entertainment, the take of John and Paul giggling their way through 'And Your Bird Can Sing' on The Beatles *Anthology*).

PLAYING WITH MUSICAL SPACE

During the mixing process, the artist and/or producer (the person employed to help turn a musician's basic ideas into a listenable finished product) makes creative decisions about where to place particular sounds in a roughly 180-degree stereo field of sound (unless they're working in 360-degree Surround-Sound, or they're from the Phil Spector/back-to-mono school).

Moving signals left or right is called 'panning', and helps separate instruments and spread the overall sound. There are certain ground rules about panning: the current consensus is that drums and bass should be in the middle (equal amount of signal to left and right), as should the lead vocal. Any other lead instruments, especially solos, tend to be central or just off-centre. Harmony instruments can be panned left or right in varying degrees to widen the sound.

In the 1960s these rules were still being formulated. Many classic Motown recordings have drums and bass squashed into one side. Cream's 'I Feel Free' has all the instrumentation in one speaker and all the vocals in another. Many Beatles tracks almost sound like different songs if you flip between one speaker and the other while listening. In this respect it is interesting to compare stereo and mono mixes of the same recording, as is possible with the *Pet Sounds Sessions* box-set and *Hitsville Motown Singles 1959-71*.

The aural equivalent of the visual field's up and down is frequency. A piece of music contains instruments which produce high, middle or low frequencies, or mixtures of these, with their own different pitch ranges. In a recording these are chosen to compliment one another and to paint a sonic picture that has a wide band of frequencies. Crudely put, frequency alteration is like fiddling with the bass and treble functions on a hi-fi. Such frequencies can be further changed during the recording and mixing process, and also during the creation of a production 'master' (the final stage before multiple CD or vinyl copies are run off). It helps you to work out what's going on in a record if you think about which instruments are playing the high notes and which the low.

Producers and sound engineers develop the ability to hear the effect of a broad band of frequencies, to pinpoint where several instruments are bunching at the same frequency, and cut or boost frequencies to make the instruments distinct.

If panning gives us the left, right and centre of the stereo image, and frequency gives us up and down, there is also the matter of 'near' and 'far'. In a recording not all the instruments seem the same distance from us: the voice will often be close up; orchestral instruments such as strings may sound further away. This is partly a matter of volume, but certain 'effects' applied to the sound can influence how they are perceived. There are too many of these to go into in this particular book, so we'll just look at the most fundamental of these, namely reverberation, or reverb.

Reverb devices were originally intended to compensate for the fact that many recording studios have acoustically dead rooms. In fact they are designed this way to prevent adverse sound 'reflections' blemishing a recording. Everyone knows that you sing in the bathroom because it sounds better than in the lounge: the average lounge/sitting room is full of soft things – sofas, carpets, curtains, rugs, cushions, pets – that soak up sound. Hard surfaces (like bathroom tiles, sinks, tubs) reflect sound and make a series of little echoes, too fast for the ear to hear as separate events. This is reverb. Churches, cathedrals and large halls are renowned for their long reverberation times, making choirs sound fuller and more ethereal.

There is a whole sub-technology devoted to reverb – from early devices involving sheets of metal with springs attached, and specially-built acoustic chambers, to small modern digital units which recreate the sound of different environments, and allow for sophisticated editing.

Reverb should not be confused with echo or delay – a distinct repeat of a voice or instrument, mostly used for rhythmic effect, and much less common nowadays than it was in the 1950s and early 1960s, when a fast 'slapback' echo typified the rock'n'roll sound.

The type and amount of reverb put on a record is very much a matter of taste and fashion. Some purists think you can't beat the primitive but very effective reverb Sam Phillips employed at Sun Studios in the 1950s. In the 1980s many producers and bands liked to get big sounds by using long reverb times. The late 1990s have seen a return to a 'drier', less reverberant mix, in which voice and instruments seem in-your-face, very near to the listener.

This change in taste is partly a consequence of the increased use of computers in music. Many recordings, especially in the dance field, are composed, recorded, edited and mixed entirely within the digital domain – and since they've never been in an acoustic environment, reverb is almost irrelevant. Madonna's *Music* album shows some of this 'drier' recording approach.

THE SONG ITSELF

Again, for those of you who aren't trained musicians, a few musical pointers on the compositional components of a song might be helpful at this stage. For instance, it makes a difference if you can distinguish a major from a minor chord – a contrast that's fundamental to Western and other music. This is not as daunting as it might seem: very young children are often instinctively aware of it, without any knowledge of musical theory. Essentially, major chords sound happy in comparison to minors – or, put another way, minors sound sad; although I would hesitate to ascribe absolute emotional meanings to either, partly because their effect is relative to each other, and dependent on context.

Even though, as Motown's Lamont Dozier has pointed out, there are only 12 notes available to play with, there's an almost infinite number of possible combinations. Just as in painting, where there are only three primary colours, but thousands of variations and shades – so blue could be light-blue, dark-blue, sea-blue, sky-blue, indigo – in the same way the basic colour of a straight major or minor chord can be modified by the introduction of other notes. So a simple chord like A major – made up of the notes A, C# and E – might become A7, Amaj7, A6, Asus2, Asus4, A7sus4, A9, Amaj9 etc, just by adding or taking away certain notes. The same is true for minor chords.

Chords are the building blocks of harmony. Most chords and notes are chosen by songwriters because they fit together pleasingly, or sound 'right' together – they're usually in the same 'key'. When they are not, they can produce deliberately striking effects (take the third chord in the verse of David Bowie's 'Absolute Beginners' – an Amaj7 instead of A7 in the key of D).

Unless you're a musician trying to learn to play the song, it doesn't really matter if you can't recognise the actual chords. For listeners, it's more important you're aware there's something unusual happening, and how the impact of the music can be changed by shifts in pitch or harmony (or indeed tempo – the speed or rhythm of the music).

Certain chords and harmonies create the moods associated with particular styles of music: the 'smoky night-club' sophistication of some jazz is a result not only of instrumentation but of altered and extended chords that change frequently; early rock'n'roll depends on the dominant 9 chord (in the key of A, this uses the notes A, C#, E, G, and B), as do many James Brown records; MOR (Middle-Of-The-Road/easy listening) and ballads often depend on the lush-sounding major 7 (in A: A C# E G#). Conversely, most Heavy Metal (HM) bands will never use a major 7 because to them such chords are too sweet or wimpy – instead, HM is typified by 5th chords, which are neither major nor minor (for example, in the key of A, playing a chord made up just of the notes A, E and A).

The effect of chords can be extended further by inversions (same notes, different one at the bottom) – very common among piano players and more inventive guitarists. These contribute to the distinctive sound of songs by people like Brian Wilson or Elton John.

For a further explanation of chords, keys and scales, and a glossary of the musical terms you may come across during the discussion of the 100 tracks, see the *Appendix*. If you would like to try it for yourself, and want know more about some of the theoretical aspects of songwriting, seek out a copy of *How To Write Songs On Guitar* (Backbeat, 2000).

ABOUT THE 100 CHOSEN TRACKS

This book is not a 100 greatest songs list, nor is it a compilation of greatest artists, or greatest recordings, or biggest selling records. It's true that a lot of great singers and bands are included here, and many of these tracks are justly renowned – most have been chart hits or belonged to chart albums. But I have sprinkled a few lesser-known gems among the hits, which I hope you will get to know, and even the odd song of dubious merit, or one where the appropriate response is necessarily complex: the idea is to provoke some interesting questions about how we evaluate such pieces of music.

Inside Classic Rock Tracks is unashamedly biased towards song-based music. The dance genre as a whole – music essentially created first and foremost for the dancefloor – is not explored in any depth. That's for another book. As the title suggests, the emphasis here is on rock music – though in its widest sense: from instrumental beat-groups, folk-rock and orchestrated MOR pop to psychedelia, soul, glam, punk and metal.

Each entry provides a multi-layered analysis and response to the track in question, as well as a brief look at the wider musical context of that track in its day. It discusses how the track was recorded, instrumentation, arrangement, production, musical features (chords, key-changes, etc), and lyrics. Each entry also has an element of critical evaluation – informed opinion on why a track works, or doesn't.

The tracks selected may not all be to your personal taste, but I believe all 100 are worthy of your attention, for a variety of reasons. When getting to grips with unfamiliar music, we shouldn't reject it on the basis that it isn't some other type of music: if you are into heavy rock there is no point finding fault with a Carpenters record because it doesn't bang heads in the same way as *Black Sabbath IV*. Similarly there's no point in faulting Black Sabbath for a lack of melodic finesse or pretty vocal harmonies. Heavy metal and MOR seek different musical ends: recognise what a style of music is supposed to do, and then respond to it on that basis.

The broader matter of whether some types of music might be 'better' than others is an interesting one, not least because of the assumptions it brings to the surface, but too big a question to be dealt with here.

If read sequentially, *Inside Classic Rock Tracks* provides a chronological potted history of the development of the popular song from 1960 onwards. Alternatively, you can dip in wherever you like and follow the *Links* at the end of each entry, connecting the song to other tracks by similar artists, or those featuring a comparable musical technique.

Songwriters or record producers suffering from a creative block could open the book at random, read the entry (particularly the *Creative Tips*), hopefully pick up a spark of inspiration, and use it as a starting point for a new track of their own. At a time when chart music is in the grip of formula and conservatism, this book also serves as a timely reminder of what popular chart music can be – artistically and commercially. These tracks throw down the gauntlet to a new generation of songwriters and performers.

All the observations in this book were obtained through active listening: I did not have special access to any original multi-track tapes – like you, I had only a hi-fi and a pair of headphones to tease out these secrets and write these commentaries. If any artists, producers or songwriters mentioned feel I've missed a significant overdub, undertone, or other detail, why not pass on the inside knowledge for the benefit of a future edition...?

Meanwhile, let's begin our musical journey through 40 years of aural delights and surprises. It starts with the power of two voices in close harmony...

RIKKY ROOKSBY, 2001

1960s

1	The Everly Brothers	*Cathy's Clown*
2	Roy Orbison	*Running Scared*
3	The Tornados	*Telstar*
4	The Springfields	*Island Of Dreams*
5	The Beatles	*Please Please Me*
6	The Ronettes	*Be My Baby*
7	The Beach Boys	*Don't Worry Baby*
8	Cilla Black	*Anyone Who Had A Heart*
9	Dionne Warwick	*Walk On By*
10	The Walker Brothers	*Make It Easy On Yourself*
11	Bob Dylan	*Positively Fourth Street*
12	Tom Jones	*Thunderball*
13	The Who	*The Kids Are Alright*
14	The Beach Boys	*Good Vibrations*
15	The Marvelettes	*The Hunter Gets Captured By The Game*
16	The Four Tops	*Seven Rooms Of Gloom*
17	Pink Floyd	*See Emily Play*
18	Procol Harum	*A Whiter Shade Of Pale*
19	The Herd	*From The Underworld*
20	Love	*A House Is Not A Motel*
21	The Jimi Hendrix Experience	*All Along The Watchtower*
22	The Rolling Stones	*Street Fighting Man*
23	The Casuals	*Jesamine*
24	Bob & Earl	*Harlem Shuffle*
25	Fleetwood Mac	*Man Of The World*
26	Pink Floyd	*Astronomy Domine (live)*
27	Glen Campbell	*Wichita Lineman*
28	Janis Joplin	*Little Girl Blue*
29	Thunderclap Newman	*Something In The Air*

TRACK 1

CATHY'S CLOWN

THE EVERLY BROTHERS 1960

"As a teenager, I had Hank Williams Syndrome. I created emotional havoc to make myself miserable, then I could write miserable songs. Catherine [Coe, his high school girlfriend] never treated me badly at all. It was me who broke up with her." (DON EVERLY)

The Everlys remain one of the great male duos in popular music. Don and Phil's voices were so finely matched you might have been hearing a singer harmonising with himself. A string of immaculately sung hits secure the Everlys an illustrious page in the book of (teen) love. Signed to the Cadence label in 1956, their first success came with 'Bye Bye Love' in 1957, a song which 30 other artists had turned down. This started a run of hits that included 'Wake Up Little Susie', 'All I Have To Do Is Dream', 'Claudette', 'Bird Dog', 'Till I Kissed You', and 'Walk Right Back'. Many of their songs were written by the husband and wife team of Boudleaux and Felice Bryant, though 'Till I Kissed You' came from Don Everly.

Their harmony vocals and acoustic guitars were country in origin, but guitarist Chet Atkins helped with arrangements in the studio to give the Everlys a stronger beat. It's widely forgotten just how large the Everlys' presence loomed in that innocent period between the death of Buddy Holly and 'Love Me Do', when rock'n'roll's first wave ebbed and the charts were full of bland pop songs. The Everlys could turn out impeccable ballads – as their cover of 'Let It Be Me' shows – but they also carried the country rock torch on tracks like 'Rip It Up' and Orbison's 'Claudette'. It's easy to imagine Eddie Cochran singing 'Wake Up Little Susie', a song that got them into trouble because the lyrics were considered too suggestive; and the laconic asides in the verses of 'Bird Dog' are as effective as the voice-of-authority in 'Summertime Blues'.

Having cut 38 tracks for Cadence, in 1960 the Everlys signed the first million-dollar contract with Warner Brothers. The first fruit of this was 'Cathy's Clown', written after a tour when the duo were home in Nashville, under pressure from the label to come up with a hit single. The song spent five weeks at number 1 in the US and nine weeks at the top in the UK (they had already topped both charts in 1958 with 'All I Have To Do Is Dream').

WRITER	Don Everly / Phil Everly
PRODUCER	Wesley Rose
RECORDED	RCA Studio B, Nashville
DURATION	2.22
RELEASED	Warner Brothers, April 1960
CHART	US 1 UK 1

'Cathy's Clown' is a song of powerful hooks and significant structural contrasts which directly relate to the lyric content. It has two sections – a verse which starts with the hook of "Here he comes...", and a bridge where there is only a single voice and a strong contrast in timing: try counting 1-2 during the verse in time with Buddy Harman's drums and then maintain that count through the bridge to hear the effect.

The rhythmic contrasts in 'Cathy's Clown' hold a vital songwriting secret. Unlike much chart music in more recent times, the function of rhythm here has nothing to do with dancing – it is entirely emotional, the expression of an inner conflict within the speaker, and his determination to triumph over circumstance. The martial drum rhythm is the sound of someone being dragged to an execution by public ridicule, and trying to put up a brave face.

The harmony is conventional enough. The verse uses a powerfully assertive G D / I-V change (chords I and V are the pillars of the major key) with Em and C. The bridge has the slightly softer G C / I-IV change, with Em C D – the placement of the Em chord is fabulous (under the words "treating me" and "hears them passing by"). The number of chord changes in the bridge is also different to the verse. As for the main vocal hook, part of its power stems from the way the top voice is static while the lower moves down – this means the intervals between them change, as opposed to the usual method of harmonising in parallel thirds.

Lyrically, it's a song about self-respect, anxiety about masculine identity, and the universal fear of being humiliated, by being seen as a clown in public. With the words, "Here he comes", the Everlys express the point-of-view of the social group; in the bridge the perspective changes to that of the protagonist, confessing his feelings and talking to himself – "I've gotta stand tall / You know a man can't crawl". – and the harmonic and rhythmic change reinforces this. In the second bridge he reproaches Cathy to show he still cares.

In the production and arrangement, nothing is wasted. Listen for the general reverb on the track, and the electric guitar chord that whipcracks on beats two and four in time with the fierce snare-rolls. The bass is slightly to the left, drums centre, piano on the right, prominent in the bridges; you'll also hear faint strummed acoustic guitar. Towards the end of each verse the guitar on the left plays two four-note motifs, placed in-between the vocal phrases. Listen for the drummer's use of the ride cymbal in the bridges. The sound of the record is probably shaped by a certain amount of spill from the various players into each other's mikes.

LINKS

The Everlys' use of melody and vocal harmony had a powerful influence on The Beatles (see track 5), as well as on acoustic duos from Simon & Garfunkel to The Proclaimers.

CREATIVE TIPS

Rhythm can be an emotional element, not just a beat, or for time-keeping – double/half-time is a good way of creating the illusion of tempo changes without altering the underlying tempo... Harmony vocals don't always have to be in parallel... Lyrics can combine a group view with an individual's perspective.

TRACK 2

RUNNING SCARED
ROY ORBISON 1961

"On 'Running Scared', most of the high notes were falsetto. We had 30 musicians, and [producer] Fred Foster said, 'How come I can't hear the [vocal] ending? We're going to lose the record if you can't give us a little more.' He said, 'Run it by us one more time', and I did it in full voice. I didn't even know I could do that at the time. I didn't know there was a difference between full voice and falsetto. I could feel the difference, but I didn't understand the technical differences. Then the power of the voice came. It was a gradual thing, and it came with confidence." (ROY ORBISON)

Born in Texas in 1936, Orbison was originally a rockabilly singer, working at the Sun label in the magic year of 1956. He went to Nashville to concentrate on songwriting after the Everlys had a hit with his composition 'Claudette', and signed for a short period with RCA. But it was his third single for the Monument label, 'Only The Lonely', a big hit in 1960, that ushered in four years of chart success, with songs like 'Crying', 'In Dreams', and 'Running Scared'.

In 1963 he headlined a British package tour that included The Beatles, and went on to

have 16 Top 20 hits in the UK; but by the mid-1960s Orbison was left stranded by the seismic shifts in popular music. His career was further blighted by tragedy – his wife was killed in a motorcycle accident in 1966 and two of his three children died in a house fire in 1968. In the Seventies he signed a new deal and resumed touring; in the late 1980s he found renewed success as a member of the Travelling Wilburys, curtailed by his untimely death in 1988.

To modern ears some Orbison hits can sound overblown, but early in the Sixties, at a time when pop was synonymous with 'fluff', Orbison's songs aspired after a grandeur few records could match. Many of them come on like mini-operas, chunks of reverb-laden drama that heave their way to some staggering climax after a mere two-and-a-bit minutes, and then crash into silence. The effect was amply assisted by Orbison's powerful and wide-ranging voice – which, as the quote on the previous page shows, he pushed to new limits on this track.

'Running Scared', allegedly written in five minutes, is a lovely exercise in the principle of asymmetry. The lyric focuses on a single crisis, summed up in the line "If he came back / which one would you choose?". The speaker is running scared of the possibility that this former flame is going to return and steal his baby. To dramatise this fear, 'Running Scared' uses a simple eight-bar rising chord sequence of I-II-III-V-I in A major, set to a Bolero-like rhythm; the track is cleverly arranged so that an air of mounting tension and anxiety is created by the gradual introduction of more instruments.

WRITER	**Roy Orbison / Joe Melson**
PRODUCER	**Fred Foster**
RECORDED	**RCA Studio B, Nashville**
DURATION	**2.10**
RELEASED	**(US) Monument, April 1961; (UK) London, May 1961**
CHART	**US 1 UK 9**

The eight-bar phrase occurs four times: first time through it is largely carried by Orbison's vocal and a strummed acoustic guitar panned right; second time the right channel introduces another guitar, kick drum and bass – the reverb from these instruments and voice is clearly audible panned to the left; the third time, a string section enters on the left, balancing out the stereo image; and the fourth time this is strengthened by backing voices.

This fourth time through is truncated to only seven bars, which moves the song unexpectedly quickly into what appears to be a bridge section. For the first time the song goes to chord IV (D major), and at the same time the lyric states that what has been up to this point only his fear is now a reality: his rival has appeared, and the moment of truth approaches. The music stays on the D chord, with a pair of two-bar vocal phrases neatly answered by a one-bar string phrase. Brass continues the Bolero motif from the verse.

The musical ambiguity captures the ambiguity of the situation – is this man subordinate to the speaker in the lady's affections? Is the D chord merely chord IV in A major (his key), or have we changed key to the new reality of D major? It isn't clear until, after a few more bars, the D chord gives way to E (chord V) and then A major, on which chord (and key) the song resoundingly finishes, just as the lyric declares, "she turns and walks away with me". The ending is sudden. What we thought was a bridge isn't at all: there is no return to the verse.

CREATIVE TIPS

Experiment with structure so your song has a true climax right at the end... Always look to see if you can cut a bar at transition points between one section and another, to make the change occur slightly earlier than the listener is expecting.

LINKS

For the symbolic value of contrasted keys, see 'Wichita Lineman' (track 27). On his final album, the posthumously released Mystery Girl, *Roy Orbison covered songs by Elvis Costello, U2, and Cyndi Lauper.*

"Orbison's songs aspired after a grandeur few records could match"

TRACK 3

TELSTAR

THE TORNADOS 1962

"As soon as you set foot in the room you were up to your ankles in lengths of quarter-inch tape, with tape boxes lying all over the place. That was the first thing that struck you – all this tape." (FRIEND TED FLETCHER, ON JOE MEEK'S STUDIO)

The 1960s was really a decade of two parts: 1960-63 and 1964-69. In Anglo-American politics the former is marked by the Kennedy/Macmillan administrations, and was ended by JFK's death in Dallas and the Profumo affair in Britain. In popular music the division is even more pronounced because of the arrival of The Beatles. 'Telstar', with its bitter-sweet melody, captures something of both the optimism and anxiety of the early 1960s, as well as the period's faith in science and technology.

Instrumental singles had a higher profile in the early 1960s than at any period since. This may have had something to do with the sheer novelty sound of the new popular music. The electric guitar, for example – which featured on many hits by Duane Eddy, The Shadows, Jet Harris, The Ventures, and many others – had been in production for little more than ten years. In the early 1960s it was the hippest instrument in the world – which is why it was chosen to carry the main theme for the 007 films, starting in 1962 with *Dr No*. By the end of the same year, 'Telstar' had become a huge transatlantic hit.

WRITER	**Joe Meek**
PRODUCER	**Joe Meek**
RECORDED	**Joe Meek's Studio, London**
DURATION	**3.15**
RELEASED	**(UK) Decca, August 1962;**
	(US) London, October 1962
CHART	**UK 1 US 1**

Behind this single was an important figure in the development of recording – Joe Meek. Meek had been interested in radio and electronics as a child, served as a radar technician in the RAF in the 1950s, and then worked as a sound engineer at London's IBC Studios. In 1960 he produced an album in stereo (a fledgling technology at the time), called *I Hear A New World*, which combined string sounds, effects and simple melodies. He built himself a home studio above a shop at 304 Holloway Road, north London, where he worked on many unique inventions and techniques to create his own sound; among other things he was a pioneer of close-miking (minimal space between microphone and sound source) and DI'ing (where instruments are plugged directly into the mixing desk, using no microphone at all). Known as a volatile and seemingly paranoid character, Meek became increasingly withdrawn as his chart successes dried up, and unhappy in his personal life. He killed himself in February 1967.

The Tornados formed in 1961, and served as Billy Fury's live band. The nucleus was Clem Cattini (drums), Heinz Burt (bass), Alan Caddy and George Bellamy (guitars), plus Roger La Vern on keyboards. 'Telstar' was their second single, named after the communications satellite which broadcast the first TV pictures across the Atlantic in 11 July 1962. Released within weeks, by November the single topped the UK and US charts, as both countries watched helplessly while the Cuban missile crisis brought the world to the brink of nuclear war. 'Telstar' went on to sell five million copies worldwide – the Tornados were in fact the only British group before The Beatles to get a US number 1.

CREATIVE TIPS

Never neglect your melody... Re-harmonise an individual phrase to give it a new colour.

In its day 'Telstar' had sound effects and a production that seemed futuristic. Meek finished the track off himself – adding sound effects as he bounced the recording between

two two-track machines. 'Telstar' consists of a 16-bar verse (repeated), with a 16-bar bridge taken by guitar, then another verse, half a bridge, a short link, and then a transposition up a key to D major for the last verse and coda. It has a strong lead melody – played on a clavioline, a battery-operated keyboard – with many leaps, and supported by a chord progression of majors and minors. The melody starts with the chromatic F# G G# A sequence, only establishing A major as the key with the last change of E to A.

There's also a quarter-note bassline; pattering light percussion; strummed guitar; a harp-like arpeggio; a 'stab' chord on the first beat of the bar; and the double-tracked octave melody line is doubled up by a male vocal on the last verse (symbolising the human and the technological in co-operation).

Listen for the especially poignant melody / C#m chord combination in bar 9 (at 0.35, 1.01, 1.54). The first four bars and the bridge feature the I-VI-IV-V (A F#m D E) chord sequence which was everywhere in popular music at this period (see track 6). One unexpected but effective hook is when the melody heard in bars 3-4, over D and E, is heard again in bars 5-6 over A and F#m.

LINKS

The Shadows' 'Wonderful Land' (number 1 in March 1962) has a similar era-evoking quality. Meek recorded an early, unreleased demo for The Beatles, and went on to produce hits for the likes of The Honeycombs, Mike Berry, John Leyton, Heinz and Screaming Lord Sutch; he was also approached several times by a young Marc Bolan, though he never got round to recording him. The clavioline keyboard sound was also used on Del Shannon's 'Runaway'. Four of the Tornados re-recorded 'Telstar' in 1975. For a 1970s take on the instrumental, see track 40.

TRACK 4

ISLAND OF DREAMS

THE SPRINGFIELDS 1963

"I'm a shy singer, perhaps you might say a reluctant singer, at the best of times. It takes a lot to get it out of me because of my studio nerves. So I like to hear more or less the whole thing – you know, the glamour bit – in my headphones. Somehow that brings it out: I think, 'Oh, this is what it's going to sound like, OK, I can sing now'." (DUSTY SPRINGFIELD)

Here is a record that (one bee-hive-hairdo singer aside) looks back rather than forward in popular music, and reflects the mood of a pre-Beatles 1960s that was about to pass away. After a long, severe winter, Britain in 1963 was still struggling out of the 1950s. London was definitely not Swinging. The country was still dominated by the conservatism railed against by Jimmy Porter in Osborne's *Look Back In Anger*, and described in the gloomy deprivation of social realist novels by Alan Sillitoe and John Braine (books like *Saturday Night & Sunday Morning* and *Room At The Top*). The Top 40 was dominated by anodyne pop: rock'n'roll had faded and nothing had yet taken its place. In the US, Motown was only just finding its economic feet, its classic sound still a year away. It was the era of the earliest Beach Boys hits, of guitar instrumentals, yodelling, skiffle, Cliff Richard and teen singers with improbable names like Vince Eager, Marty Wilde and Bobby Vee.

'Island Of Dreams' is cod country & western (listen to the accents). Yet for all its faults it has a yearning quality also present in 'Telstar' and 'Wonderful Land' from the previous year. It is unknowingly a swansong for a different kind of decade than the 1960s turned out to be – not necessarily better, just different. It also happens to be sung by a young woman who would be the UK's finest female pop singer of her generation: Dusty Springfield.

Lyrically, this is a love song with an escapist element. A free-time intro has a maudlin harmonica, acoustic guitar, and double bass before kicking into a gently swinging 12/8 with a clip-clop drum rhythm, a second acoustic guitar playing fills throughout, and a three-part vocal harmony. The harmonica signals not only a camp-fire ambience but also looks back to 1950s BBC light music (the Goons had Max Geldray playing harmonica on their radio show every week). Arrangement details typical of the period include the prissy string part, which is very 'BBC Light', and the high female backing voices used in English pop between 1960-63 to underscore the emotional content.

WRITER	Tom Springfield
PRODUCER	Tom Springfield
RECORDED	London
DURATION	2.35
RELEASED	Philips, January 1963
CHART	UK 5 US –

Like 'Cathy's Clown' and many early Beatles songs, 'Island Of Dreams' is structured on the verse/bridge principle, where the hook is included within the verse, not in a separate chorus, and the song is book-ended with an intro and a coda in free time. There are some interesting moments in the harmony: first, the verse contains a brief key change to the dominant (B*b* major) at the phrase "trying to forget you" – the act of trying to forget is mirrored in the modulation; but just as the forgetting doesn't work, so the music quickly subsides back into E*b*, the home key.

Towards the end of the verse there are some inversions: the bridge ("High in the sky") features the *b*VII-V-I (D*b* B*b* E*b*) change which is so wistful and expressive of new possibilities. The chord change D*b* B*b* E*b* contains a chromatic rising phrase of D*b* D E*b* in single notes – symbolically reaching the goal (E*b*, the key chord) by a difficult and unexpected transformation. (This change is also heard in 'Wonderful Land' but not often in the 1980s or 1990s.) This bridge doubles the effect by ending its first line on the words "with you" sung over D*b* B*b* (*b*VII-V). Instead of landing on chord I, the next line "far, far away" puts the B*b* under it again. So the chords have gone from *b*VII to V and then straight back to *b*VII, which has the effect of emphasising this wistful change.

Not only is the bridge the more touching part of the song because of the harmony, it also happens to be the moment when at 0.44 (and 1.31) a great pop voice is first heard in its own right as Dusty takes this bit solo (listen for the reverb on her voice as it emerges from the three-part harmony). Her "carry me" at 1.39, and the pause she puts in at 1.43, indicate Greatness In Waiting, for which 'I Only Want To Be With You' was the coronation in 1964.

CREATIVE TIPS

If you want a quintessential early 1960s chord change, try bVII-V (Bb G in C major)... On recording Dusty In Memphis in 1969, Dusty Springfield said: "I was someone who had come from thundering drums and Phil Spector, and I didn't understand sparseness. I wanted to fill every space. I didn't understand that the sparseness gave it an atmosphere."

LINKS

Brother Tom Springfield went on to write and produce many hits for Sixties middle-of-the-road-folkie pop stars The Seekers, including 'I'll Never Find Another You', 'The Carnival Is Over', and 'Georgy Girl' - and as such was a likely influence on the future members of Abba (see track 50). For more vocal harmonies, see tracks 1, 5, 7, 14, 31, 43, 50, 76, 89, 90, and 95.

"... a yearning quality also present in 'Telstar' and 'Wonderful Land'"

TRACK 5

PLEASE PLEASE ME

THE BEATLES 1963

"George Martin's contribution was quite a big one, actually. The first time he really showed he could see beyond what we were offering him was 'Please Please Me'. It was originally conceived as a Roy Orbison-type thing, you know. George Martin said, 'Well, we'll put the tempo up.' He lifted the tempo and we all thought that was much better, and that was a big hit." (PAUL McCARTNEY)

"That's more like it. That should do well." (LENNON'S AUNT MIMI)

Released almost at the same time as 'Island Of Dreams', 'Please Please Me' is a seismic indication of a revolution in the making. 'Love Me Do' had taken The Beatles to 17 in the UK chart the previous year, but 'Please Please Me' (cruelly left off the compilation *One*) is a huge leap forward. It was written by Lennon at his Aunt Mimi's house, originally as a dramatic Roy Orbison-esque ballad (Lennon particularly liked the repetition of the word "please" in the title – did he ever hear James Brown's 1956 hit 'Please Please Please'?). It was in this slow ballad form that they had first tried to record it, on 11th September 1962, with Andy White on drums; but by increasing the tempo, on George Martin's suggestion, The Beatles found the opportunity to release some of their rock energy. They did 18 takes; the harmonica was overdubbed, and Martin did the mono mix on 30th November.

WRITER	John Lennon / Paul McCartney
PRODUCER	George Martin
RECORDED	Abbey Road Studios, London
DURATION	2.00
RELEASED	(UK) Parlophone, January 1963
	(US) Vee-Jay, February 1964
CHART	UK 2 (contested) US 3 (1964)

Only two minutes long, 'Please Please Me' is simply one long hook – everything in it is absolutely earning its keep. If it were any denser in hooks it would have turned into a black hole, promptly swallowing Abbey Road and most of its environs. No wonder George Martin told them after the final take, "Congratulations, gentlemen, you've just made your first number one". It became title song of the first album.

In terms of production, this is the sound of a youthful beat quartet just off the leash. The mix contains drums, bass, acoustic guitar and Harrison's electric playing lead lines. For the verse vocal line they adapted a technique from 'Cathy's Clown' – Paul sings a static tonic E while John's voice works downwards below, creating a series of changing intervals. The verse has only two phrases then comes to a stop, and Harrison's five-note fill takes the song to the chorus. Here a call-and-answer technique builds the tension before the voices come together in three-part harmony for the hook-line. On the last chorus The Fabs manage to make this sound like four voices, with Paul swooping up for a high B.

Harmonically, the song is in E major – the most resonant key for electric guitars and bass because of the open low E-string on both instruments. The chords are mostly I-IV-V, but they insert two fleeting blues chords: the *b*III G at the end of each initial vocal line, and the *b*VI C in the last couple of bars – the Beatles were adept at using *b*III, *b*VI and *b*VII chords to toughen up their progressions and provide contrast with the straight major/minor sequences. Two minor chords, F#m and C#m, add poignancy to the chorus.

Philip Larkin famously and wittily wrote that sexual intercourse had "started in 1963", between the publication of *Lady Chatterley's Lover* in Penguin and The Beatles' first LP. It's

CREATIVE TIPS

Use blues chords (bIII, bVI, bVII) to toughen a progression... Make everything count... Use part of the melody as an instrumental phrase on an intro... Two minutes is a world of its own... Play sweaty clubs at home and abroad to sharpen your ability to record sizzling takes... Be Fab... Oh, and one last thing – it helps if you're a genius.

interesting to wonder how many record buyers realised how risqué the lyric of 'Please Please Me' was. It is indicative of the new mood of sexual openness that would be an enduring part of the 1960s revolution. And on the subject of words, what about an honorary mention for the bridge rhyme of "complaining" with "rain in"?

Listen especially for: Ringo's fill into the bridge at 1.02; George and Paul getting too close to the mike with "in my heart"; and the pop bliss of the final refrains, with extra voices appearing out of nowhere, and the harmonica further underscoring the hook.

LINKS

There's an alternate version on The Beatles' Anthology 1. *For another George Martin production, see track 8. (By the way, in 1963 George Martin supplied the UK with number 1 songs for 32 weeks out of 52.)*

TRACK 6

BE MY BABY

THE RONETTES 1963

"Our input with Phil normally took place before we went into the studio. Once in the studio, Phil had total control. We'd discuss things sometimes in the control room, but never in front of the musicians. Phil was the boss, and you were invited into one of his sessions. You didn't just go to a Spector session – you had to be asked in." (ELLIE GREENWICH)

In 1963 a number of musical talents – performers, producers and writers – were poised to transform the music business. Each in their own way had a new vision for what could be achieved on a 45rpm record. One was producer Phil Spector, who invented a production approach – the 'wall-of-sound' – that became an industry catchphrase. 'Be My Baby', along with its companion hit 'Baby I Love You', are definitive wall-of-sound productions for the time – though technology arguably helped Spector (and his arranger Jack Nitzsche) capture this sound even better on Ike & Tina Turner's 'River Deep Mountain High' and The Righteous Brothers' 'You've Lost That Loving Feeling' in 1966 (the year The Ronettes disbanded). Disappointed by the reaction to 'River Deep...', Spector quit the music business, until brought back into the fray by a persuasive John Lennon in 1969.

WRITER	Jeff Barry / Ellie Greenwich / Phil Spector
PRODUCER	Phil Spector
RECORDED	Gold Star Studios, Los Angeles
DURATION	2.36
RELEASED	(US) Philles, August 1963
	(UK) London, October 1963
CHART	US 2 UK 4

The first hit Spector wrote, 'To Know Him Is To Love Him' (apparently inspired by his father's epitaph), was a US number 1 (UK number 2) in 1958 for his own trio The Teddy Bears; but lack of control over the sessions for his first album made the still-teenage Spector vow it would never happen again. So he became a producer. For a time he worked in New York with songwriters Leiber & Stoller, doing Drifters sessions, and he co-wrote Ben E King's 'Spanish Harlem'. Then he formed his own independent label, Philles Records, and had hits with teen girl group The Crystals. His earliest wall-of-sound recording is said to be the 'Zip-A-Dee-Doo-Dah' session with Bob B Soxx & The Blue Flames in 1963.

Like Roy Orbison, Spector had a sense of the melodramatic possibilities of the pop single if the production were increased in scale. He began using a select group of musicians, known as the Wrecking Crew (including Hal Blaine on drums and Carol Kaye on bass), which helped him create the consistency of sound he desired. During recording sessions at Gold Star studios there would be little isolation between the musicians – which meant that, in a small room with a ceiling height of 14ft, the sound was going to bounce around. Spector used the natural acoustics created by the studio design itself as a major component of his productions, while building up sound-on-sound overdubs, in mono, on basic equipment (no compression, minimal tone controls).

'Be My Baby' features piano, strummed guitars, brass, percussion such as shakers and castanets, female backing vocals (apparently none of the other Ronettes, but it did feature Cher), bass, handclaps, strings and drums. Notice Ronnie Spector's voice is kept quite dry and upfront: her vocal, and those carefully rehearsed wha-ah-oh-ohs, along with the vast sound, make the record what it is.

CREATIVE TIPS

Sometimes, more is more... And if the kitchen sink is easily detached, why not bring that too?

In terms of structure and harmony, 'Be My Baby' is straightforward; it's in the key of E major, and the verse starts off with an E-F#m-B change, twice, followed by a 'wandering' G#7-C#7-F#-B7, which suggests an imminent key change without ever reaching one. The chorus uses the familiar I-VI-IV-V doo-wop chord sequence we've encountered on 'Telstar'. Spector's genius was to do something new with this progression by means of the production.

Listen for the strings that take over during the bridge, and the drum fills in the last chorus. The reverb on the drum sound is clearly audible in the two-bar gap after the third chorus.

LINKS

The famous 'link' drum pattern was re-used on Frankie Valli & The Four Seasons' 'Rag Doll' in 1964. Arranger Jack Nitzsche went on to work on some classic late 1960s Stones tracks. For another Spector production, see track 33.

TRACK 7

DON'T WORRY BABY

THE BEACH BOYS 1964

"The first time I heard 'Be My Baby', I was in the car, and the record came on the radio. I pulled over to the side of the road." (BRIAN WILSON)

"Brian used to play Spector's 'Be My Baby' to us over and over obsessively, and we're going, 'Hey Brian, we heard it already, so what?' Spector should have bowed down in front of Brian, not the other way around." (BRUCE JOHNSTON)

"In addition to being nice guys with talent, the reason the Beach Boys were so successful was that, first, we had a concept – surfing, cars, girls, all the stuff about growing up." (MIKE LOVE)

And then there was... surf. This book is founded on the fact that the history of popular music is full of connections between records. Here's a not-so-subterranean example of the principle at work: the Beach Boys' tenth US single, 'Don't Worry Baby', was directly inspired by Brian Wilson's fervent love of 'Be My Baby', which he once called "the most perfect pop record of all time". Lyricist Roger Christian gave Wilson the words – as Wilson recalls: "I met him in the parking lot at KFWB and he presented the lyrics for me. I went home and wrote the song in about an hour-and-a-half." Wilson passed word to Spector that he could use it with one of his own groups, but Spector declined.

'Don't Worry Baby' does not try to emulate Phil Spector's monophonic wall-of-sound – in fact the degree of separation on the stereo mix is quite striking. It shows more psychological depth too, because, like 'Cathy's Clown', it exposes and deals with male vulnerability, though it still harks back to a genre of car songs popularised by Chuck Berry in the 1950s, to which Wilson had already contributed numbers like 'Fun, Fun, Fun' and 'Little Deuce Coupe'. Christian's lyric is a story of teenage car racing and bragging, with fine idiomatic phrases like, "I guess I should've kept my mouth shut": on the morrow the song's anxious protagonist must walk it like he talks it – in the meantime, he has discovered that there are certain things that are more important than impressing your peer group. In this, he has made a small step towards maturity.

WRITER	**Brian Wilson / Roger Christian**
PRODUCER	**Brian Wilson**
RECORDED	**Western Studios, Los Angeles**
DURATION	**2.46**
RELEASED	**Capitol, May 1964**
CHART	**US 24** **UK 7 (B-side of 'I Get Around')**

It was recorded in two eight-hour sessions. Dennis Wilson played drums, Brian played piano, and overdubbed the bass, and Carl Wilson played guitar. The stereo mix suggests that it was recorded as a four-track. On the left of the mix we have Brian's double-tracked vocal plus the guitar fills on the intro. On the right are the block harmonies. The centre features all the supporting instruments: drums, bass, guitars, piano. The speaker's position on one side of the mix suggests his anxiety through his literal separation from the music and his peers on the far-side – he literally has to face the music after his bragging has "pushed the other guys too far".

'Don't Worry Baby' makes good use of two keys: the verse is in E major, with a progression of E A B, then opening up emotionally in the F#m B G#m C#m; the chorus is a tone higher in F# and uses a I-II-V sequence – the same that starts the verse of 'Be My Baby'. The verse key represents his own worry, while the new key at the chorus expresses the love of the girl – in fact the entire chorus is lyrically given over to her reassurance. The melody is gorgeous, with Brian's voice switching in and out of falsetto.

Things to listen out for: the song starts with the drum rhythm used in 'Be My Baby'; notice the vocal fluff at 1.16, where Wilson slightly falters on the word "she", and again at 1.22 where one voice sings "drive" and the other "cry"; and there are beautiful harmonies on the last verse.

CREATIVE TIPS

Try writing an answer song to an already existing one...

LINKS

This was still Wilson's relatively carefree period as a songwriter (domineering father notwithstanding), happy to use teen-drama lyrics for his themes. By the end of 1964 he'd retired from touring, experimented with drugs (his eventual undoing), and begun trying to convince his brothers they should be creating more meaningful and complex records. See track 14 for some developments... Also compare track 6, and (for the drum rhythm) track 56.

"'Don't Worry Baby' does not try to emulate Phil Spector's wall-of-sound"

TRACK 8

ANYONE WHO HAD A HEART

CILLA BLACK 1964

"I always tried to make songs that were like mini-movies." (BURT BACHARACH)

This song was initially a Top 10 hit in the US for Dionne Warwick – but Cilla famously stole her thunder in the UK. The problem is, anyone who has any critical sense is supposed to prefer the Warwick version. So what is it about Cilla's version that strikes such a chord? In the 1980s and 1990s British television viewers knew Cilla Black only as the host of the successful *Blind Date* series. I speak not of her, but of another Cilla: pre-nose-surgery, mop-top, Liverpudlian Girl Next Door who lives on in flickering black & white films and a handful of 1960s singles. 'What's It All About, Alfie?' might be her best technical performance, but 'Anyone Who Had A Heart' is her most touching.

At the time the Warwick camp felt Cilla's cover was far too close to Dionne's. With hindsight it is tempting, for the sake of the argument, to portray Warwick's version as clinical and high-gloss – actually, she lets the guard down a bit more than that, slurring the first syllable of each chorus line in a way that's more emotive than memory would have you believe. Warwick's trademark is to touch a melody as lightly as a feather – it was this capacity which she used so brilliantly on her two classic Bacharach numbers 'Do You Know The Way To San Jose' and 'Walk On By' (coming up soon, pop pickers). By any norm, Warwick's is the more professional, more pleasingly timbred voice. And yet... What is it about Cilla's version?

WRITER	Burt Bacharach / Hal David
PRODUCER	George Martin
RECORDED	Abbey Road Studios, London
DURATION	2.47
RELEASED	Parlophone, February 1964
CHART	UK 1 US –

The arrangement is pretty much intact across the two versions, with a sax solo in the Warwick being replaced by the higher-pitched woodwind in Cilla's cover, for a more poignant 'English' effect. Other common ingredients include the comping eighth-note piano chords, and the shards of tremolo guitar. The drummer is certainly bolder on Cilla's version, and the backing vocals shriller (sometimes sounding hysterically like Flo & Eddie from Zappa's Mothers).

On the right of the mix you'll find piano, drums, bass, female backing vocals, electric guitar; on the left, strings and cymbals. Male and female vocals double the woodwind solo, placed central in the stereo image. The production on Cilla's version is more intimate because it has less reverb; hers is also slightly quicker, at 51bpm instead of 48bpm. Dionne's starts in A minor, Cilla's a semitone lower in G#m.

The tone of Black's first verse doesn't quite prepare you for the nasal and forceful vocal when she hits the first chorus – especially when she gets to the words "too" and the highly squeezed "true". That's the moment when the contest is over. The different tone of her voice is also apparent on the coda, where there are several squeezed "toos" over a yawning chasm of a John Barry-esque chord change from G to E.

CREATIVE TIPS

Sometimes one beat is all the intro you need... And as a songwriter, never give up: "At first it was very hard. A lot of rejections. Playing a song and somebody stopping you after eight bars. I remember going in to see Connie Francis, and she lifted the needle off the demo." (BURT BACHARACH)

It's the Englishness of this record that, to this listener, has always made it more appealing. The cut has more warmth – and part of that is the sense of Liverpudlian Cilla as The Girl-Next-Door with the fab-gear accent, the Angel Of The Cavern. We all know that Girls Next Door get their hearts broken by unfeeling bounders from Stockport and Rusholme, and Cilla's vocal makes all that real. Dionne, you feel, knows what it is to have a bouquet of roses and an ice-bucket by the bed. Cilla knows only a Bakelite alarm clock and the sound of a leather football being kicked around in the alley out the back.

The harmonic progression of the song repays study. Bacharach was innovating in the context of popular music at this time: the harmonic ideas on this record are light years away from the simple I-VI-IV-V progression of 'Be My Baby'. The verse is in a modified G#m with a key change to G major on the word "so" at the end of the phrase "knowing I love you so" – an unusual key combination.

Listen for the tremolo electric guitar chords at 0.10 and 0.16; and the drum fill 1:56-2.02, and into the last chorus. And are those slightly batty "yeah, yeahs" on the coda influenced by The Beatles? (It is a George Martin production, after all). And are they sped up, to reach that frenzied pitch? We have a right to know. Listen also for the coda where Dionne's semitone phrasing on 'anyone who had a heart' (C B*b* A B*b* C), is altered by Cilla to a phrase that is all tones (B A G A B).

LINKS

This was the song that first put the name of Burt Bacharach into the mind of a youngster named Elvis Costello (see track 56). 'Anyone Who Had A Heart' was also covered by Dusty Springfield on her debut album - her version is closer to Warwick, with more reverb: she takes it in G minor and at 53bpm, and retains the sax solo; the tympani on the coda are rather misplaced, there's a dramatic cello on verse 2, and a hint of hysteria on her first "what am I to do". She doesn't take the pre-chorus as forcefully as Cilla - her "so" is very smoky - but Dusty's vocal has an intriguing combination of maturity and vulnerability, and is perhaps more sensual.

TRACK 9

WALK ON BY
DIONNE WARWICK 1964

"I still believe that you almost have to be a student of music in order to sing Bacharach melodies. He is a very unorthodox composer." (DIONNE WARWICK)

Dionne Warwick was the main interpreter of Bacharach & David's songs in the mid-1960s, after they discovered her singing backing vocals for The Drifters. They'd first used the title 'Walk On By' for a Presley-like record by Leroy Van Dyke in 1962. Dionne Warwick's voice was perfect for this second version: there is a classy reserve and a fragile delicacy about how she sings it, avoiding hysteria, suggesting the depth of the hurt. Amazingly, the song started off as a B-side, until DJ Murray The K found his listeners preferred it.

The recording has trumpet, guitar stabs, strings, and a strummed guitar on the left; on the right there's vibes, another guitar, and percussion; in the middle, piano, double bass, and vocal. The rhythm of the guitar stabs and the trumpet-fills are the epitome of Bacharach 'lounge' cool, though here they can be enjoyed without a trace of the unctuous post-modern irony that seems to grease attempts to copy these musical traits in recent years. This is a long way from Austin Powers and Mike Flowers Pops. The very best 'easy listening' was never easy.

As with 'Anyone Who Had A Heart', 'Walk On By' carries

WRITER	Burt Bacharach / Hal David
PRODUCER	Burt Bacharach
RECORDED	New York
DURATION	2.52
RELEASED	(US) Scepter
	(UK) Pye, March 1964
CHART	US 6 UK 9

Bacharach's musical fingerprints. The first note E of the piano triplet figure (E D C, heard first at 0.35) forms a major 7 against an F major chord, but then a #4 against B*b* major. This is a striking re-colouration of the note. The major 7 chord is highly romantic; the #4 dissonant and anguished. Thus, in a single chord-change, Bacharach has evoked the aching dual emotions of the singer/narrator.

The song starts with an Am-D change which implies a Dorian-inflected A minor (where the sixth note F in A natural minor's A B C D E F G is sharpened to F#). Yet there's an unexpected drop to a G minor chord (implying F major). The B*b*maj7 on "tears" at 1.16 is a typical Bacharach touch. The song is built harmonically on the juxtaposition of a Dorian A minor and F major: the former is the pain of the past, and the latter the present.

This is a song about loss, but also about trying to maintain dignity. As a vocal it is an object lesson in respecting the melody and not falsifying it by absurd, redundant ornaments (as is endemic in female chart vocalists since 1990). Hal David's lyric is a clearly visualised situation, put right before our imaginations with the opening, "If you see me walking down the street". There's a sense of violated innocence to Dionne's performance – it sounds as though it has never happened to her before, and maybe she thought it never would. Contrast it with the outbursts of passion that tear through another Bacharach/David song in Dusty's rendition of 'I Just Don't Know What To Do With Myself'.

'Walk On By' is also a fine demonstration of the fact that no written score could ever replace the *sound* of a performance and production like this. The dark heart of this record lies in its atmosphere: listen for Dionne's breath on the mike on "private" at 0.30; the shocking sound of the backing vocals at 0.40 ("don't stop") – like suddenly finding a bloodstain under a table cloth; and the way the strings ebb at 1:57 after their tumultuous instrumental break.

CREATIVE TIPS

Imagine the situation as clearly as you can in the lyric... And deep emotions don't have to be shouted.

LINKS

For other classic Bacharach compositions, see tracks 8 and 10.

> "no written score could ever replace the *sound* of a performance and production like this"

TRACK 10

MAKE IT EASY ON YOURSELF
WALKER BROTHERS 1965

"Scott, coming from LA, was aware of the Spector sound and probably had a good idea of how it was achieved, so it was him who wanted three keyboards, three guitars, three percussionists and so on. There'd also be two bass guitars making a heavy, almost monotonous noise, which all helped to get this big sound going, and then a large orchestra on top." (PETER OLLIFF)

Our trio of Bacharach/David songs is completed with the Spectoresque production of 'Make It Easy On Yourself' (a sound also heard on 'The Sun Ain't Gonna Shine Any More'). The Walker Brothers were friends Scott Engel, John Maus and Gary Leeds: for a brief period in the mid-1960s their blue-eyed soul made them teen idols (ironically more popular in the UK than their native US) until they split in 1967. Scott, taking on the surname Walker, then carved out a solo career based on a number of critically-acclaimed albums, featuring his own songs and fine interpretations of Jacques Brel.

WRITER	Burt Bacharach / Hal David
PRODUCER	Johnny Franz / Peter Olliff
RECORDED	Philips Studio, London
DURATION	3.10
RELEASED	(UK) Philips, September 1965
	(US) Smash
CHART	UK 1 US 16

The original of 'Make It Easy On Yourself' was a hit in 1962 for Jerry Butler, after Dionne Warwick had demo'd it. It's another classic 1960s break-up song. A couple of notes on the strings and a tympani bang and you just know you're in for a hard time. If you think about it, 1960s charts were full of tragic break-up songs, whereas by the 1990s these were a rarity – which may indicate that, contrary to its in-your-face aerobics'n'attitude bluster, 1990s pop is more emotionally repressed. In the 1990s the worst crime was being a loser – the typical agenda of a 1990s break-up song (cf Whitney Houston *et al*) is: "Regrets? I've had... well, none actually. You're yesterday's news, buster."

'Make It Easy' places the lead vocals in the centre of the mix. On the right are the strings, brass, and ghostly across-the-River-Styx high female vocals (yep, them again); on the left, strummed guitar, chopped electric guitar chords, piano, drums, bass, tympani, vibes and tremolo guitar (again) doing its fractured stuff on the Dmaj7 chord towards the end. It's a big production, but less unruly than Spector's wall-of-sound. Still, the studio at Philips measured only 60x20x25ft and it might be crammed with between 25 and 35 musicians, so there was bound to be a lot of spillage into different microphones, as no sound could be isolated.

The song comes in on an instrumental chorus in which only the final line is vocalised, but instantly tells you what the song is about. The chorus sequence is in A but avoids the key chord, circling round F#m C#m D and E. An unexpected B7 takes us via a key change into an E major verse. Here Bacharach has put in a couple of surprises: the first vocal line is sung over E C#m E C#m, and then C#, as if it's about to change key but doesn't. The second line is harmonised differently, with a rising E E+5 C#m E7. This simple idea – of harmonising the two lines of a verse differently – has virtually been lost to popular chart music.

'Make It Easy On Yourself' is a song of noble but tortured self-sacrifice (the kind of thing Bacharach & David knew how to write very well). If she really loves him our hero is willing to let her go – "Run to him before you start crying too", says the lyric – but if (as with 'Go Now') they're both so cut up, we ask ourselves as we pass the Kleenex round, why can't they stay together?

CREATIVE TIPS

If you have a two-line verse, harmonise the second line with different chords... Think about your ending – is it emotionally true to the rest of the song?... On songwriting, Bacharach said: "If you get away from the piano and hear the melodic contour as well as the harmonisation in your head, you're hearing a long vertical line. I like to take a long look at the song – I get a sense of balance that I wouldn't get if I was sitting at the piano. Your hands tend to go places because they've been there before."

The vocal on this record is unusual in its pitching, which is quite low. Other things to listen for: the C# major in the verse; the bridge sequence of A C#m Dmaj7 and C#m7 with an E note held under it; and the rising bassline at 2.26.

If the record has a flaw which ranks it below the previous two Bacharach tracks here, it's the ending. As with 'Bridge Over Troubled Water', there is a sense of a false consolation, a consolation neither earned nor demonstrated, but merely asserted with the pom-pom-pom-pom tympani and the rising strings and voices. You can't ride off into the sunset that easily, mister.

LINKS

For other Bacharach & David tracks, see 8 & 9.

TRACK 11

POSITIVELY FOURTH STREET

BOB DYLAN 1965

"They all had some magic to them because the technology didn't go past what the artist was doing. It was a lot easier to get excellence back in those days on record than it is now." (BOB DYLAN)

"I wasn't surprised by the reaction I got in 1965 at Newport ... Any time there's a change there's a reaction. I'm conscious of criticism. It always bothers you when you think you've been treated unfairly." (BOB DYLAN)

The vitriol of 'Positively Fourth Street' is supposed to be partly the result of being recorded four days after the *Newport Folk Festival* where Dylan had been booed for playing his songs in an electric-guitar format (after years as an acoustic folk-god). It was released as a standalone (or what critic Dave Marsh calls a 'pure') single, between the *Highway 61 Revisited* and *Blonde On Blonde* albums – it did not appear as part of an album until the *Greatest Hits* of 1967. Singles that are not pulled from albums have a magic that no-one who buys them at the time forgets – you might wait for months for the next album, but the one-off single was like getting a musical postcard from the artist: 'Hi – how are you doing? This is what I've just done. Be in touch'.

Since we're talking about Dylan I guess we should start with the words. Lyrically this is one of Mr Zimmerman's poison-pen letters, a genre he was having a lot of success with in the 1965-66 period. It's not as metaphorical as some of the others, mind; you won't find yourself encountering a Napoleon in rags and wondering, who's that? It's a lyric full of statements, building inexorably to the final twist of the knife, where Dylan wishes he could stand in the other's shoes and vice versa. Then – and we wait with bated breath for a little flicker of sympathy to break into this scenario – does he suggest this might give them a better understanding of each other's feelings? Fat chance. In his shoes, he concludes, you'd only realise, "what a drag it is to see you". Careful

WRITER	Bob Dylan
PRODUCER	Bob Johnson
RECORDED	Columbia Studios, New York
DURATION	3.52
RELEASED	CBS, October 1965
CHART	US 7 UK 8

scrutiny of the lyric, though, reveals the speaker showing a range of emotions whose instability is caused by the hurt he suffered in the first place; hence, "No, I do not feel that good / When I see the heartbreaks you embrace".

In 1978 Dylan said: "The closest I ever got to the sound I hear in my mind was on individual bands [ie tracks] in the *Blonde On Blonde* album. It's that thin, that wild mercury sound. It's metallic and bright gold, with whatever that conjures up." Typical of Dylan's desired 'mercurial' sound, the production here has drums and organ on one side, honky-tonk piano on the other, with bass, lead and rhythm guitars and voice in the middle. Occasional guitar licks cut through at 0.42, 0.58, and 2.51. Compared to the previous songs in this book, 'Fourth Street' is musically simpler: it uses a folk 'strophic' form – a long sequence of verses – with no separate choruses or bridges. The song is essentially static and circular. The lyric's tirade works to a point of insult, but the music circles around. (In a way this makes it prophetic of the drug-consciousness that was about to go centre-stage in art in the 1960s.)

One overlooked feature gives the song a musical pleasure we might not have anticipated: the guitar's bottom E is detuned to D. This means that at various moments certain chords become unusual inversions. The A chord shape (I'm ignoring the capo at fret IV) in the last two bars of the verse sometimes occurs over this low D, as does the Em, the second chord of the verse. This effect is most noticeable in the last two verses and coda.

CREATIVE TIPS

Indignation has its place... A capo and a detuned bass string open new avenues.

LINKS

For a famous Bob cover version, see track 21.

TRACK 12

THUNDERBALL

TOM JONES 1966

"The earlier Bond songs were just better: there's no analysing it, they were just better songs, with better lyrics, performed by better people." (DAVID ARNOLD, BOND COMPOSER)

"In the studio he [Tom Jones] did the whole thing in one take. But when he hit that final note, he literally blacked out and fell off the podium. We went on and did other bits of the song again, but he could never do that bit again, so that was it." (JOHN BARRY)

Few soundtracks have contributed so much to their films as John Barry's music for the 1960s Bond films. Songs like 'From Russia With Love', 'Goldfinger', 'Diamonds Are Forever', 'You Only Live Twice', and 'Thunderball' (with appropriate lyrics from the likes of Leslie Bricusse and Don Black) instantly evoke plush red curtains, flip-back seats, pop-corn, mad car-chases and beautiful women.

Tom Jones is an example of a singer gifted with a terrific voice mostly wasted on MOR material that rarely offered enough resistance to his vocal power. He was like a Ducati caught in a 10mph traffic jam. But not in this case. Rarely have a voice and a song been so suited.

There's enough testosterone in this performance to grow rugs on the chests of the male population of the northern hemisphere.

The coarse, explosive nature of the recording is probably the result of a large body of players united on a single take. The sound should be compared with the instrumental version on Barry's *Themeology* compilation, which exposes the core of the arrangement as a jazz trio of drums/upright bass/piano overlaid with orchestra and guitarist Vic Flick's strummed chords. This jazz inflection is emphasised by the heavily muted trumpet solo that snakes its way through the closing bars of the bridge. It's noticeable that all concerned get so carried away during the session that it speeds up: it starts at 90bpm, reaches 94 by the bridge and by the finish it's about 98. Who needs click tracks?

WRITER	John Barry / Don Black
PRODUCER	John Barry
RECORDED	London
DURATION	2.44
RELEASED	(UK) Decca, January 1966
	(US) Parrot
CHART	US 25 UK 35

The verse is a marvellous 16-bar construction. The initial melodic phrases are thumpingly answered by the orchestra with powerful percussion and a shrill brass motif. The third phrase is followed by the familiar 'creeping' Bond motif (Dm D+ D6 D+). What is wonderful is the change of key implied by this – so far the verse has stayed with B*b*m, E*b*m and F (chords I, IV and V) but on the word "all" we get Dm. The third note of the scale should have been D*b*, and as a chord D*b*major – instead the third has been raised to D and a D minor built on it. This weird change is prepared because the strings have an A (over the prior F chord) which is a common note with the D minor.

Harmonic tricks like this are part of the reason Barry's classic Bond songs sound as they do – he invented a musical language for the Bond films that is quite different from the prevailing harmony of 1960s pop; for instance, choosing a flat minor key (usually F minor, here B*b*m), and having chords that weren't strictly in key. The intro chords are B*b*m, E*b*m and F (I, IV and V) over which Barry scores the strident six-note motif repeated in the coda; to make this intro more discordant, Barry has the horns play C against B*b*m, D against E*b*m and D*b* against F. Dissonance in Bond music has two functions – it evokes danger, violence and evil, but also the erotic.

CREATIVE TIPS

Unrelated chords add spice and can be linked by a common note, even if that note is a 7th in one and a 6th in the next... Otherwise, get a white Persian cat to stroke during those difficult mixing sessions.

Listen out for the harp flourish at the end of the verse, and the high string part at 1.43-51. Jones' articulation of "he knows the meaning" (verse 2), "his days of asking" (verse 3), and the gravelly edge to "but he thinks that the fight" are also highlights. If you listen carefully to his final high B*b* you will hear it resolve down a semitone to A just in time for the F chord. Only a top-flight singer can do this as they black out and fall off the podium...

The sound on the left channel starts to break up on the last chord at 2.53-56. This might indicate an overload on the original master tape, or (hopefully) less serious damage to the production master used for this CD. This song certainly deserves 24-bit re-mastering.

LINKS

'Thunderball' was sung by ABC's Martin Fry on David Arnold's Bond-homage album Shaken And Stirred *(East West, 1997). For another Bond song, see track 96. Ubiquitous Sixties session guitarist Big Jim Sullivan appeared on this track, as he also did on tracks 4, 8, 10 & 23.*

"all concerned get so carried away during the session that it speeds up"

T R A C K 1 3

THE KIDS ARE ALRIGHT

THE WHO 1966

"... I still think the loss of the three-minute single is a rock'n'roll tragedy of unparallelled proportions..." (ROGER DALTREY, 1994)

Between 1964 and 1968 The Who released a string of great singles that were among the hardest rock of the time – musically powerful, colourful and lyrically adventurous, as Pete Townshend showed himself to be a courageous chronicler of teenage experience. 'The Kids Are Alright' rarely gets as much attention as 'My Generation' yet, like 'Don't Worry Baby', it exposes a vulnerability which is touching.

WRITER	Pete Townshend
PRODUCER	Shel Talmy
RECORDED	IBC Studios, London
DURATION	3.05
RELEASED	Brunswick, September 1966
CHART	UK 41 US –

It's a four-chord song – D G A and Em – the pathos coming from the Em on "But I know". The instrumentation is typical Who: 12-string electric guitar, bass, drums and vocals. Existing versions are in mono (because of a continuing disagreement with Shel Talmy who has the masters) – it's a great pity a stereo version isn't available. The single also had about 14 seconds of the second instrumental bridge cut, but the uncut version (on the Who box-set *30 Years Of Maximum R&B*) is a revelation: you have to hear the excitement when the band storm onto the A chord in unison – all the more dramatic thanks to the build-up that's gone before.

This mod anthem about the dance-hall has more depth than has been realised. First, it's about disillusionment with a romantic ideal: the protagonist finds that however much he loves the girl he still needs sometimes to "get out in the light" and to "leave her behind". Romantic love gives way under the influence of wider needs and desires. It's also touching because it is an expression of trust in the community of youth: the first line is "I don't mind other guys dancing with my girl". In the pop songs of the time that's a rare sentiment: you are much more likely to find songs about jealousy – "keep your hands off her", etc (see The Stones in this respect).

He consoles himself by saying, "That's fine – I know them all pretty well". And what a world of feeling hangs on that word "pretty". It just betrays a slight uncertainty – he knows them pretty well, but not enough to be 100 per cent confident that some young gun won't make a play for her when he's not around. The theme of the individual versus the crowd, belonging yet being yourself, is well expressed. The bridge section introduces another theme, that of conflict with parents: "I know if I go things will be a lot better for her / I had things planned but her folks wouldn't let her". This new element to the narrative is never fully explained.

Listen for Townshend's beautiful guitar picking, and the three-part backing harmonies, in particular Townshend's counter-melody up to the last chorus; and the microphones picking up Keith Moon's screams on the first bridge. The second bridge starts at 1.58; listen for the G chord by Townshend at 2:12, then at 2:15 the explosive effect as Moon settles into a pounding beat.

CREATIVE TIPS

One well-placed minor chord opens a world of doubt and sorrow.

LINKS

For a later Who song, see track 41. For another song situated in a dance hall, see track 39.

TRACK 14

GOOD VIBRATIONS

THE BEACH BOYS 1966

"People were telling me I shouldn't be doing a record like this, you know, it was too modern, too long, not commercial. But it was like I had tunnel vision, I had to keep going until I was fulfilled." (BRIAN WILSON)

"I can remember doing 25-30 vocal overdubs of the same part, and when I say part, I mean same section of a record, maybe no more than two, three, four, five seconds long..." (MIKE LOVE)

This was The Beach Boys' first million-selling single. It was also a landmark in the development of popular music, because of its unpredictable transitions and exotic instrumentation (such as the cellos and theremin). The structure of 'Good Vibrations' is also unintentionally revealing of the crisis Brian Wilson suffered as a songwriter at the zenith of his career.

I could talk about the session players who played on it, the continuing nod to Phil Spector in the drum sound and the cellos (inspired by 'Da Doo Ron Ron'). We could discuss theremins and B-movie soundtracks, discarded bass parts by Carol Kaye put through Gibson fuzz boxes, and endless vocal re-takes. But instead, let's go to the heart of a composer's dilemma.

WRITER	Brian Wilson / Mike Love
PRODUCER	Brian Wilson
RECORDED	Gold Star / Western / Sunset Sound / Columbia Studios, Los Angeles
DURATION	3.35
RELEASED	Capitol, October 1966
CHART	US 1 UK 1

In a handful of years Brian Wilson had matured from the simplicity of the early Beach Boys to the pop baroque of *Pet Sounds*. 'Good Vibrations', in both its various takes and final form, reveals the forces which overwhelmed Wilson shortly afterwards. Of course there were external pressures, like record company expectations, and trying to match whatever The Beatles were doing; but 'Good Vibrations' exposes an internal conflict. Wilson had, by his own growth as a writer, discovered two 'golden keys' to music-making: the first was the limitless arrangement possibilities offered by going beyond guitar/bass/drums instrumentation; the second was the compositional technique of *development*.

Development is rare in popular music, certainly in the early 1960s. Popular music works through what is technically known as 'statement': the presentation of a musical idea or melody. Limited to a two-to-four-minute duration, and the need to make an impression first time, popular songs are about statement and repetition. Development is where a composer takes a musical motif or melody and gets mileage out of it, not by repeating but by *changing* it. This might be done by adding or subtracting notes, altering the harmony, transposing up or down, changing key etc.

'Good Vibrations' is full of development – think of the way the hooks keep shifting pitch. No wonder Wilson called it his "pocket symphony". Early takes from the protracted sessions (available on various box-sets and compilations) show Wilson using these two golden keys of instrumentation and development on the chief melodies and chord changes. The result was a sequence of small sections, many of them successful but simply different to each other. But

creativity cannot realise its vision unless it is able to make decisions about what to keep and what not – if the critical faculty is not strong enough it will be overwhelmed by the profusion of choices available. This faculty is vulnerable to the influence of drugs.

Technology has increased a songwriter's options exponentially since 1966, but most artists are protected from this potential crisis by lack of imagination, lack of curiosity, lack of time, lack of money, lack of musical talent, and the desire to sell more records by dumbing down. In 1966 Brian Wilson was free of all of these limitations. By dint of a huge effort he managed to hammer 'Good Vibrations' into shape. Even so there is something less inevitable about its form than 'God Only Knows' – with the latter you cannot imagine it as brilliant unless it is just as we have it. But it is possible – having heard some of the rejected parts – to imagine a slightly different 'Good Vibrations' stitched together and as good as the released version.

The effort of conveying 'Good Vibrations' from his inner ear to the pressing plant exhausted Wilson. As the sessions for *Smile* proceeded, his creativity fragmented, and tragically never completely recovered.

LINKS

For another Beach Boys number, see track 7; and for a Beach Boys homage, track 95.

> "no wonder Wilson called it his pocket symphony"

CREATIVE TIPS

Get more from a strong musical phrase through development... Great music is created not only through vision but also shaped by elimination and self-criticism... Go surfing more often.

TRACK 15

THE HUNTER GETS CAPTURED BY THE GAME
THE MARVELETTES 1966

"A great awakening for me was when I began receiving letters from white kids who lived in the Detroit suburbs, places like Grosse Pointe, where blacks couldn't live at the time ... kids who would say things like, 'We love Motown. We have all your records. Our parents don't know we have them. If they knew, they'd take them away." (SMOKEY ROBINSON)

Motown's musical contribution continues to be under-appreciated. During the 'progressive' era, rock criticism passed a negative judgement that has never quite been dispelled, as is clear from the relatively few Motown songs that feature in top 100 singles polls. It said Motown music was as manufactured as the cars that rolled off the Detroit assembly lines; it said commercial was bad, and it couldn't tell the difference between artifice and artificiality. Matters aren't helped by the fact that pretty much once a year, regular as clockwork, someone has a hit by stealing the rhythm of 'You Can't

Hurry Love' or 'I Can't Help Myself'. But there's so much more to 1960s Motown than that. 'The Hunter Gets Captured By The Game' is a case in point.

The Marvelettes were the first Motown act to get a number 1, and led the way as Motown's main girl group until Holland-Dozier-Holland started bulldozing the charts with Supremes hits. Their only UK single hit was 'When You're Young And In Love' (1967) but their US successes included 'Please Mr Postman' (famously covered by The Beatles), 'Beechwood 4-5789', 'Too Many Fish In The Sea' and 'Don't Mess With Bill'.

'Hunter' is a throwback to an earlier Motown style. By late 1966 the label entered a more experimental phase, adopting some of the sonic gestures of psychedelia from the rock field, with producers like Norman Whitfield ready to make productions more funky and R&B. Although 'Hunter' doesn't have the breathless rush of a mid-period Motown classic like 'You Keep Me Hanging On' or 'Reach Out I'll Be There', it more than compensates with a slinky 12/8 rhythm. The instrumentation is quite light: James Jamerson plays a restrained bouncing arpeggio bassline; there are several guitars, with chords on beats 2 and 4 and Robert White adding little hammer-on guitar fills; there's a quiet string part later on, and at the very end a hint of backing vocals, all audible behind the plaintive harmonica solo (which sounds more like a melodica at times); listen for the drum fills too.

WRITER	**Smokey Robinson**
PRODUCER	**Smokey Robinson**
RECORDED	**Hitsville Studios, Detroit**
DURATION	**2.48**
RELEASED	**Tamla Motown, December 1966**
CHART	**US 13 UK -**

The song has an interesting episodic structure: after the intro riff we get four sections (call them A B C D), a harmonica solo, then a repeat of B, C, and D; section A leans toward D major, while the rest of the song is firmly B minor, and it never re-occurs. It has the unusual chord sequence of Dmaj7 B*b* Gm F#m Em. Listen for the four chords on the words "things just ain't the same", one per beat, breaking the expected frequency of chord change.

Lyrically this is one of Smokey's elaborate metaphors, in which the woman sets out to capture the man's affections and ends up falling into the trap she laid herself. Phrases like "You were the catch that I was after" and "What's this old world coming to?" are delivered, like roses in wet cellophane, by a husky-voiced Wanda Young – if she sang better than this on any other cut I would be amazed. Listen to the way she drags the note down a semitone on the words "change", "on", "re-arrange" and "like", all in the first section, and her sexy "ooh-ooh" at 0.51.

CREATIVE TIPS

Take a colloquial phrase like "he was quite a catch", spot the metaphor (hunting), and expand it into a lyric.

LINKS

For other Motown songs, see tracks 16, 30, 31, 35 and 36.

> "if Wanda Young sang better than this on any other cut I would be amazed"

T R A C K 1 6

SEVEN ROOMS OF GLOOM

THE FOUR TOPS 1967

"Brian [Holland] was basically the recording engineer, melody man, and producer. Eddie [Holland] wrote lyrics, and he would sing the demos for the artists. My function was melody, lyrics, I'd sing backgrounds on the demos, and I produced with Brian." (LAMONT DOZIER)

By the time 'Baby I Need Your Loving' was a hit in 1964, the Four Tops had been together for ten years. Raised in Detroit, they first sang together in 1954, formed the Four Aims in 1956, and signed with Motown in 1964. Their initial trio of singles were sophisticated, but it was on 'I Can't Help Myself' (1965) where they really started to sound like a Hitsville act.

WRITER	Brian Holland / Lamont Dozier / Eddie Holland
PRODUCER	Brian Holland / Lamont Dozier
RECORDED	Hitsville Studios, Detroit
DURATION	2.32
RELEASED	Tamla Motown, May 1967
CHART	US 14 UK 12

That was the first of a dozen or so charts 45s written for them by Holland-Dozier-Holland, who soon twigged they could get the best out of Levi Stubbs' voice by forcing him into higher keys. Essentially, Stubbs *was* the Four Tops – as a rule they tended not to go the Temptations route of passing the lead vocal around like a relay baton. Stubbs came on like the apostle of romantic desperation, and turned almost every song into an agonised outpouring. – no more so than on the nightmarish scenarios of 'Shake Me, Wake Me', 'Standing In The Shadows Of Love', 'Bernadette' and 'Seven Rooms Of Gloom'. These mid-Sixties Four Tops singles offer a terrifying spectacle, as love descends into an all-encompassing existential despair.

'Seven Rooms Of Gloom' is another reminder that Motown rhythm was far more than 'You Can't Hurry Love'. On the left you can hear backing vocals and a harpsichord-type keyboard, bass in the middle with the lead vocal; the right has two guitar parts during the intro and one extra on the verse. The track also features percussion, drums, harmonica, muted trumpet, flute, and an eerie reverb 'slap' on the right.

Holland-Dozier-Holland's later songs for Motown are increasingly adventurous in their use of chords and keys. Coupled with a quick tempo, the key contrasts here suggest the speaker is wracked by emotional storms: there's a change at 0.54 and at 1.05, and the keys are mixed. It opens with an ambiguous progression of A#m F# Fm7 G#m7 E A D F#, then there's a section D#m-F#-G#m-D#m, and a further part that goes B F# B*b*.

Lyrically this is a song of abandonment: she's gone and he's left in an empty, gloomy house. He watches a phone that never rings, the door that never opens, lost "in the silence surrounding me". He sings "I'll keep waiting, waiting" like a threat – a kind of infantile passive aggression. At times Stubbs handles the melody like a man clinging with one hand onto a rope thrown across an abyss.

Listen for the entry of drums at 0.32, and explosive fills on side drum at 0.48, 1.25, 1.36, and 1.47. The violent key changes almost seem not to exist for bassist James Jamerson, whose locomotive line simply powers across any change H-D-H's chord-sheet has for him (for instance the figures at 0.47 and 0.54).

CREATIVE TIPS

Violent emotions sometimes need violent chord or key changes.

LINKS

For other Motown songs, see tracks 15, 30, 31, 35 and 36.

TRACK 17

SEE EMILY PLAY

PINK FLOYD 1967

"I remember I really started to get worried when I went along to the sessions for 'See Emily Play'... Syd was still functioning OK but he definitely wasn't the person I knew. He looked through you. He wasn't quite there." (DAVE GILMOUR)

"I only know that the thing of playing, of being a musician, was very exciting. Obviously, one was better off with a silver guitar with mirrors and things all over it than people who ended up on the floor or anywhere else in London." (SYD BARRETT, SIC)

Personally, I wouldn't swap this (and 'Arnold Layne') for any amount of post-*Dark Side Of The Moon* gatefold gloom. With these singles the Syd-era Floyd created two of the finest English psychedelic songs of the 'Summer of Love'. 'See Emily Play' was originally called 'Games For May' and written as a theme song for a May 1967 concert at Queen Elizabeth Hall in London. There was a real-life Emily, too – Emily Kennett, described as one of the 'psychedelic debutantes' who precociously threw themselves into the underground music scene at clubs like UFO and Middle Earth.

Pink Floyd formed in 1966, naming themselves after two American bluesmen, Floyd Council and Pink Anderson. They were actually rather put out by their singles chart successes, and refused to play them live – as Roger Waters said, "We considered the three-minute form irrelevant to the idea of live performance." But this single rises to the challenge of evoking the psychedelic experience in song; sound was now to be cut-up and used in more of a montage fashion, rather than in the controlled arrangements of a Brian Wilson.

WRITER	Syd Barrett
PRODUCER	Norman Smith
RECORDED	Abbey Road Studios, London
DURATION	2.52
RELEASED	(UK) Columbia, July 1967 (US) on US album Piper At The Gates Of Dawn, Tower Records
CHART	UK 6 US –

The track starts with a glissando, Doors-like organ, and an octave bass figure (soon to be deployed to sinister effect in 'Careful With That Axe Eugene'), then a heavily accented A G chord change, reinforced by an overdub, ushers in the verse. The lead vocal, right up at the front of the mix, is double-tracked, and there's a drone guitar that appears mid-solo, plus a fuzz guitar, and echoed slide for high pitch effects.

Keyboardist Rick Wright explained: "That 'Hawaiian' bit at the end of each verse was just Syd using a bottleneck through echo. The part that sounds speeded-up, was speeded up: John Woods, the engineer, just upped the whole thing about an octave." The churchy connotations of the organ here take on an ironic quality, as if the LSD experience were religious yet subverting conventional religion at the same time. The most striking discontinuity is the mad interruption at 0.50 (perhaps an unconscious influence on R.E.M's 'Get Up' with its 12 music boxes).

The psychedelic experience also leaves its fingerprints on the harmony: the song begins in A minor, the verse eventually finds its way to G major, but the chorus seems to be in a mixolydian E (the *b*VII chord D) before an E7 lands on A7 and then G. The flattened 7th/mixolydian harmony is typical of acid-rock. Bar lengths are also uneven throughout; and the coda lands on a D major and fades out, unresolved.

CREATIVE TIPS

Sometimes a song needs to be seriously interrupted – like a model train that is thrown off the tracks and then put back on.

Lyrically, 'See Emily Play' manages to gently admonish the young woman to whom it's addressed (for jumping on a bandwagon she doesn't understand) and at the same be erotically inspired by her (hence the *double entendre* of "let's try it another way"). Simple statements are loaded with meaning, so the direction to "put on a gown that touches the ground" seems ritualistic. English psychedelia is noticeably more pre-occupied with childhood than its American counterpart, often a historical childhood symbolised by Victorian/ Edwardian stories such as the Alice books ("float on a river forever and ever") and Peter Pan. The third verse is full of a sense of passive surrender of the ego – a fate its composer would succumb to all too soon.

LINKS

Barrett was The Floyd's creative soul in their early years. Gilmour was an old school friend, who began helping out as Syd gradually became less capable. For more classic Sixties psychedelia, try Jefferson Airplane's 'White Rabbit'. For a live Floyd freak-out, see track 26.

TRACK 18s

A WHITER SHADE OF PALE

PROCOL HARUM 1967

"Keith [Reid] was very well-read... by the time he was 14 he'd read everything... We wrote a song for Dusty Springfield and one for the Beach Boys, without any luck, so it was a bit disheartening. In the end Keith suggested that if nobody else was going to sing our songs, I'd have to. We sat down and thought about the type of band we needed. It was kind of like the stuff we had been listening to... American gospel and R&B using two keyboards. We wanted a more sophisticated sound with Hammond organ and piano... I always thought that with two keyboards and a guitar you could have plenty of solos and still give them a powerful backing." (GARY BROOKER)

Yes, it's magic. But why...? The fastest-selling single in the history of Decca went to number 1 in June 1967, and has sold in excess of ten million copies. 'A Whiter Shade Of Pale' is one of those rare records that doesn't build an atmosphere, it simply presents one – like they've been playing since the Cretaceous period and you just happened to tune in, and they'll still be playing it in some smoky club where the clock always stands at quarter to three (am) when our sun finally expands into a red giant. Procol Harum were a sign of the increasing ambition of pop, and a willingness to combine any number of styles – as here, a bit of classical melody with an R&B combo. 'A Whiter Shade Of Pale' has unfortunately eclipsed their two other great cuts, 'A Salty Dog' and 'Homburg'. So... why?

WRITER	Gary Brooker (via Bach) / Keith Reid
PRODUCER	Denny Cordell
RECORDED	Olympic Studios, London
DURATION	4.00
RELEASED	Deram, May 1967
CHART	UK 1 (13 in 1972) US 5

For a start, the Bach angle is a red herring – a classical borrowing doth not necessarily a great record make...

The production is a mono mix with organ, piano, bass, drums, vocals and, somewhere buried in it all, guitar (you can catch a couple of Steve Cropper-type fills at 3.23-28). It was recorded live in the studio – Brooker has been quoted as saying the sound on that day was pretty much a happy accident, unlikely to be repeated.

Harmonically the song consists of a plunging, descending chord sequence that seems to go on forever; periodically it pitches itself up again and then commences another descent – as though the lovelorn and homesick were looking for the stairs up and only finding a variety of stairs down. The song benefits from two melodies – the vocal line, and also the organ, which provides a counter-pointed melody of its own, and is just as much of a hook.

As for the lyrics... There's the story about a queue of the recently deceased standing before the throne of the Almighty: "What did you do with the life I gave you?" asks God of the first. "I was a brain surgeon", comes the reply. "Excellent," says God, and turns to the next: "And what did you do with the life I gave you?". "I worked as a dancer and dance teacher", answers the second. "Excellent... And you, what did you do with the life I gave you?". "I was a rock critic, specialising in lyrics". "Ah," says God, "well I've got this theory about 'A Whiter Shade Of Pale'..."

It's a lyric all about suggestion and imagery – much in the same vein as the lyrics Pete Brown was supplying for Cream around the same time.

But the magic isn't the words – it isn't the miller or the 16 vestal virgins heading for the coast. And it isn't the Bach. It isn't even the smoky R&B Percy Sledge organ. You see, it's all in the drums... that wonderful draggy beat, like Ringo on Mogadon, the fills echoing in that fuzzy reverb. Take a bow, Bill Eyden.

LINKS

In 1977 'A Whiter Shade Of Pale' was voted joint Best British Pop Single of the last 25 years (with Queen's 'Bohemian Rhapsody'). Bill Eyden went on to a varied career as a jazz drummer; Brooker's own profile was revived in the late 1990s.

CREATIVE TIPS

Nothing succeeds more than a descending bassline – except maybe two descending basslines.

"like they've been playing since the Cretaceous period and you just happened to tune in"

FROM THE UNDERWORLD

THE HERD 1967

"When we recorded it, the studio was jammed with session musicians and the band was surrounded by Phil Spector-inspired noises." (ANDY BOWN, THE HERD)

The Herd are one of those 1960s English also-rans, cult favourites who never quite matched the success of The Kinks, The Yardbirds or The Searchers. They had just three UK hit singles and one minor-hit album, *Paradise Lost* (1968). But they did have Peter Frampton on guitar – dubbed "the face of 1968" and later to see solo chart action in the mid-1970s after a stint with Humble Pie. 'From The Underworld', penned by producer/writer/management team Howard & Blaikley, was the Herd's second single and their first hit. It is a minor classic of the English side of the summer of love, gloomy and other-worldly.

In 1967 rock and pop were in the full throes of musical ambition. It's the *sound* of this record that automatically hits you: the tolling bell and the descending piano, doubled an octave above with an organ, leading to a blast of heavily fuzzed guitar, drums, bass and tympani. Male voices sing a simple melody with prominent reverb – listen for the cello doubling them in verse 2. A trumpet counterpoint breaks out in the more upbeat bridge. The bass has that typical trebly guitar tone – an early example of the style that came to be known as 'click bass' (see also Cat Stevens' 'Matthew & Son'). The lead vocal is double-tracked left and right, with most of the instruments in mono in the middle. You can spot the doubled vocals because they sing harmonies at some points, and at about 2:27 there's a vocal ad lib on one side only.

WRITER	Ken Howard / Alan Blaikley
PRODUCER	Ken Howard / Alan Blaikley
RECORDED	poss RG Jones Studios, London
DURATION	3.14
RELEASED	Fontana, September 1967
CHART	UK 6 US –

In keeping with its lyric, the song has a static structure – each verse is made up of variations on the same melody over an alternating I-IV-V or I-II-V sequence; the song is essentially as trapped and circling as the protagonist.

The Spectoresque production is complemented by the grand allusion of the lyric – a tale of paradise lost at the last minute. It features unusually long lines – the first of which is, "Out of the land of shadows and darkness / We were returning towards the morning light". It starts as a love song but turns out to be a pop version of one of the oldest Greek myths – the story of Orpheus descending into the Underworld to rescue Eurydice. The couple are guaranteed a safe return to the surface as long as Orpheus does not look back during the ascent – but he does, and he loses her forever. If the modern lovers parallel the Greek characters, we are left to ponder on the modern equivalent of that backward glance. The speaker can find no answer to the question, "What was the stubborn will to destroy the love and joy I nearly held?", as he lays the blame at his own feet.

Like Cream's 'Tales Of Brave Ulysses', 'From The Underworld' pulls off the astounding trick of looking back to the myths at the root of Western civilisation, and managing to put one of them into the Top 20.

CREATIVE TIPS

If you're stuck for words, why not reach for Robert Graves' The Greek Myths?

LINKS

Writer/producers Howard & Blaikley's other claims-to-fame were managing The Honeycombs and discovering Dave Dee, Dozy, Beaky, Mick & Tich. The Herd later opted to sack the pair in favour of Stones mentor, Andrew Loog Oldham – with even less success.

TRACK 20

A HOUSE IS NOT A MOTEL

LOVE 1967

"… when I did that album, I thought I was going to die at that particular time, so those were my last words." (ARTHUR LEE)

At the time of its release, Love's album *Forever Changes* failed to make much of an impact (it reached number 24 in the UK, though only 152 in the US). But slowly over the years it has gradually won something of the audience it deserves. It was the band's third album, and their last in their 1960s incarnation with the line-up of Arthur Lee (guitar/vocal), John Echols (guitar), Bryan MacLean (guitar/vocal), Ken Forssi (bass) and Michael Stuart (percussion).

Forever Changes is both of its time and timeless – it captures the dark and the light of the 'summer of love'. The songs are acoustic-based, with brass and strings enriching the bright 12-string guitars, and occasional outbreaks of electric violence, as in 'A House Is Not A Motel'. The gentle beauty of much of the music belies the troubled, disconcerting imagery in the lyrics – this tension is partly where the album's greatness comes from. It is musically innovative – the songs have unpredictable chord sequences and juxtapositions of rhythm, and unconventional melodies where phrases stop and start where you'd least expect it. The album also has a few delightful moments of sonic trickery – such as the needle-skipping end of 'The Good Humor Man', the super-imposition of the words "yellow" and "white" in 'Old Man', and the original end of 'A House Is Not A Motel', of which more in a moment.

Lyrically, 'A House…' is a disturbing song with some stirring lines, such as: "You are just a thought that someone somewhere somehow feels you should be here"; and the prophetic, "The news today will be the movies of tomorrow" – which certainly turned out to be true of the Vietnam war.

The track starts with 12-string guitar on the right – a churning low riff in E minor. Drums and bass are compressed into the left channel, and the vocal is centre. It is one of the sparser tracks on the album, but shows how much tension can be created with just three instruments and a voice. After verse 2, an electric guitar appears on the left, with two phrases that use the top E-string as a drone while fingering notes on the second string. (Listen for the tape hiss when the drums stop at the end of this bridge.) After verse 3, a drum break (with reverb audible off to the right) leads to a twin-guitar coda (with strange vocal noises in the middle). This twin-guitar part is the highpoint of the track – after eight bars together the two guitars solo independently, as if raging at one another. Rarely has the electric guitar been employed to such fine effect – it's a milestone, because these guitars are not being played simply as amplified acoustics, but as instruments in their own right. There is a direct link here to Hendrix's approach. (Arthur Lee and Hendrix went on to record together in 1970.)

WRITER	Arthur Lee
PRODUCER	Arthur Lee / Bruce Botnick
RECORDED	Sunset Sound Recorders, Los Angeles
DURATION	3.25
RELEASED	(album, Forever Changes) Electra, November 1967
CHART	not a single

The puzzle is this: on both the original CD and the 2001 remastered version, the track is faded out. This is an appalling act of vandalism. The original vinyl version of the song ends with a spectacular and expressive sudden stop, right as the guitars are fighting each other, plunging the listener into a shocking silence before the gentle opening chords of 'Andmoreagain'. This transition is the spirit of *Forever Changes* in a nutshell. The fact that it's been changed is simply outrageous. Write to your congressman or MP immediately. And while you're at it (here comes tragedy number 2) you could just mention that the original multi-track tapes of this wonderful album are currently missing...

LINKS

Love's first single was a Bacharach & David song. Troubled genius Arthur Lee seemed to suffer a chemical-induced derailment in the 1970s (cf Barrett and Wilson), though rallied enough in the early 1990s to play a legendary gig in Liverpool backed by local band and devout Love fans Shack (themselves known to cover 'A House Is Not A Motel' on-stage).

CREATIVE TIPS

Acoustic-based songs can be dynamic... Electric guitars have a potential for musical expression all their own, which comes from them being electric, not just guitars.

> "these electric guitars are not being played simply as amplified acoustics, but as instruments in their own right"

TRACK 21

ALL ALONG THE WATCHTOWER
THE JIMI HENDRIX EXPERIENCE 1968

"I'm like Bob Dylan. Neither of us sings in the accepted sense. We just 'be ourselves'. Sometimes I do a Dylan song and it seems to fit me so right that I figure maybe I wrote it. I felt like 'Watchtower' was something I'd written but could never get together." (JIMI HENDRIX)

"Strange though how when I sing it I always feel like it's a tribute to him in some kind of way." (BOB DYLAN)

To parody Wallace Stevens' poem 'Man With The Blue Guitar': "Things as they are / Are changed upon the white guitar". This was Hendrix's biggest hit single in the US – his only hit song there, as opposed to his nine in the UK. It's perhaps the ultimate demonstration of a rock 'cover': compared to the original it's like going from 8mm film to widescreen Technicolour. Hendrix revered Dylan – he played 'Like A Rolling Stone' at Monterey in 1967 – and when he heard 'Watchtower' on the *John Wesley Harding* album in January 1968, he allegedly exclaimed, "We gotta record that – I gotta do that" (though Kathy Etchingham also claims she talked him into it). Initially he wanted to

WRITER	Bob Dylan
PRODUCER	Chas Chandler
RECORDED	Olympic Studios, London / Record Plant, New York
DURATION	4.01
RELEASED	Polydor, September 1968
CHART	UK 5 US 20

do 'I Dreamed I Saw St Augustine', but decided it was too personal. He started recording 'Watchtower' a couple of days after hearing it, as a four-track recording, with Traffic's Dave Mason on 12-string and bass. Something like 24 takes were recorded of the initial band track; an initial mix was done on January 26, but Hendrix added more overdubs between June and August in the US, which included playing a new bass part.

In terms of instrumentation, the song features stereo drums (you can hear the snare coming from two seemingly different places in the mix), heavily reverbed 12-string guitar, bass and tambourine. The lead vocal is accompanied throughout by wonderful guitar fills.

The song has no separate chorus or bridge – it proceeds via a series of verses, which alternate with guitar breaks, to an extended instrumental in the middle that comprises three distinct guitar sounds: first slide, then wah-wah, then trebly chording on the top three strings. (listen for the side-to-side panning of the guitar parts during the solos). In these three breaks Hendrix is adapting blues, rock and R&B styles respectively. His lead playing throughout is an emotional language, not a series of licks.

The popularity of Hendrix's version has made 'Watchtower' a much-abused song in the hands of others – primarily because bands play it as though it only has three chords (cf U2's rendition in *Rattle & Hum*). Hendrix's version actually implies *five* chords: the main C#m B A sequence is augmented with an implied F#m at "relief" (0.34), "worth" (0.51) and "joke" (1.24), when the lead guitar sounds an F#; and also on "late" (1.40) and "too" (3.05). At 3.28 in the coda there is what sounds like a G# chord inserted between C#m and A.

A number of songs on *Electric Ladyland* reflect the incendiary atmosphere of 1968. The apocalyptic imagery of 'Watchtower' fits the spirit of the year – a line like, "Businessmen they drink my wine" came across more powerfully to the anti-capitalist counter-culture of the day than it does now. It's a lyric that presents us with a sequence of memorable images, suggesting big events without ever letting us know where these events are headed. It ends with two riders approaching, and the wind beginning to howl. We are left to imagine what happens next.

CREATIVE TIPS

One of the factors that made the greatest rock music of the 1966-73 years excel was the influence of Motown, specifically, and soul generally, on the rhythm sections.

Hendrix was always critical of his own singing ability. He needn't have worried. Listen for the Dylanesque drawl on "so let us not talk falsely now", his tender "oh babe" (3.47), and his splendidly authoritative singing of the title at 3.53. Another highlight is Hendrix's manic bass-playing – a kind of tribute to James Jamerson's Motown work. The Motown influence is also apparent in Mitchell's use of the snare in verse 3. Above all, listen for the timing hiatus 9-15 seconds in, where the drums are clearly off the beat for several seconds, and only then finally on it. If you don't believe me, try clapping in time throughout the intro.

LINKS

As well as the many live recordings Hendrix made of this song, there's an alternate mix on the album* South Saturn Delta*. For an original Dylan recording, see track 11.

"compared to the original, it's like going from 8mm film to widescreen Technicolour"

TRACK 22

STREET FIGHTING MAN

THE ROLLING STONES 1968

"They told me 'Street Fighting Man' was subversive.... It's stupid to think you can start a revolution with a record. I wish you could" (MICK JAGGER)

"The first time I realised the value of acoustic instruments was on 'Street Fighting Man'." (KEITH RICHARDS)

In 1968 The Stones were on the point of re-inventing themselves to take account of the changes that had happened in rock music. Brian Jones was still with the band at this point too, but edging out of the picture. This song started out as 'Primo Grande', and was then re-titled 'Pay Your Dues'; then Mick Jagger saw the Grosvenor Square riot of March 1968 at first hand and wrote some new lyrics. The single has an odd release history, though: put out in the US amid the agitations of 1968 it made sense; its 1971 release in the UK (in a money-spinning move by their former label Decca) made it seem a record out of time.

In production terms, there is a narrow stereo image. Jagger's vocal is initially double-tracked, but triple-tracked for the last verse; and you can hear a rudimentary harmony on the last chorus. The instrumentation includes sitar, piano, bass, drums (hi-hat to the left), and a number of guitars, said to be all acoustic. Richards: "The only electric instrument on there is the bass, which I overdubbed afterwards." There's also various touches of additional percussion. All this works together to sound a dramatic opening call-to-arms.

WRITER	Mick Jagger / Keith Richards
PRODUCER	Jimmy Miller
RECORDED	Olympic Studios, London
DURATION	3.16
RELEASED	(US) London, September 1968; (UK) Decca, June 1971
CHART	US 48 UK 21 (1971)

Keith Richards had found his open G tuning and was putting it to good effect. The main riff is a B chord and then a Bsus of some kind, with E F# and C# as the other chords. The C# constitutes a new key just before the drop back at the hook. The first 24 seconds are suspended over a tonic pedal: Richards changes chord, but the bass, first heard at 0.9, stays on the key note until 0.24.

'Street Fighting Man' is a revolutionary song written *pour encourager les autres*, as is clear from the chorus line: "What can a poor boy do / But sing for a rock'n'roll band?". That's the classic cop-out, where rock'n'rollers realise that they want to be on a stage rather than in a party committee room. That's the trouble with democracy – it's not glamourous enough. Was London really so 'sleepy' in 1968...? 'Street Fighting Man' is one of a number of Stones songs in which Jagger was drawn to act out the image of the devil in the collective – here he sings, "My name is called Disturbance". Fortunately, the Stones come up with a suitably inspiring sound.

Sonic highlights include: the bass fill at 0.49; the pick-up in the drum pattern at 0.58; the cry of "get down" at 1.47; and at 2.24 the three voices finishing at different times. At 2.32 a horn note starts up like something out of ancient Egypt, coming in on a *b*7 and then pitching the root note; on the fade you'll catch an ascending figure at 2.28 on the left, and a piano arpeggio at 2.50.

CREATIVE TIPS

To add tension and drama to a progression, keep a fixed bass note... During this period the Stones also used the trick of recording some basic parts on a cassette and then transferring that to an eight-track, which would add a certain grainy character to the finished recording.

LINKS

Producer Jimmy Miller – who was originally a drummer (that's him on cowbell on 'Honky Tonk Women') – worked on five of the Stones classic albums in the late Sixties/early Seventies, including Beggars Banquet *and* Sticky Fingers.

TRACK 23

JESAMINE

THE CASUALS 1968

"David Pardo played the Bystanders version to us in Milan, and we thought, 'Shit, that's good – but let's swish it up a bit'. Their version was very simple – just a four-piece group and a flute. We used an 80-piece orchestra." (JOHN TEBB)

Not everything was revolutionary in 1968. The Casuals remain essentially a one-hit band (despite a brief period as the top British act in Italy). In the UK they came to fame by winning TV talent show *Opportunity Knocks* three weeks running. 'Jesamine' was recorded first by The Bystanders (who went on to become Man), and was written, under the Manston/Gellar pseudonyms, by Marty Wilde (father of Kim and the UK's top pre-Cliff teen idol) and Ronnie Scott (not the jazzman). It is the perfect English pop song – the 'There She Goes' of the 1960s – and not the least of its charms is its innocence. And at one point in October 1968 it out-sold no less a single than 'Hey Jude' to get to number 2 – a feat The Casuals never matched, though 'Toy' reached number 30 later that year.

WRITER	F Manston / J Gellar
PRODUCER	David Pardo
RECORDED	Chappell Studios, London / and Milan
DURATION	3.38
RELEASED	Decca, September 1968
CHART	UK 2 US –

'Jesamine' is best appreciated if you can get the stereo mix rather than the more common mono one found on compilations. On the left are drums, bass, vibes, acoustic guitar, and an electric guitar chord in time with the snare; in the centre is the double-tracked lead vocal with vocal harmony; on the right are strings, woodwind and the vocal counter-melody.

It begins immediately with a question – "What am I supposed to do / With a girl like Jesamine?" – over a chromatic descending line. This leads to a chorus, and then a change of rhythm for the verse at 0.47 (a Bacharach-type syncopation). The main chords are D Em G Gm A. A triplet quarter-note floats on top of the rhythm on the word "Jesamine" just before the chorus – compare it with the similar triplet feel in the Miracles' 'Tracks Of My Tears', at the "my smile is my make up" section before the last chorus.

'Jesamine' is blessed with a beautiful melody that rises and falls across an octave. The woman of the title is the ideal muse of English pop, the "butterfly child" who cannot be tamed and is all-desirable. Perhaps she is half-sister of The Floyd's Emily; the phrase "beautiful days lost in her eyes" carries an echo of the summer of love.

Listen for the unexpected vocal harmony (a *b*7) on "makes my" at 1.04; the brass fills at 1.18 and 2.02; the pizzicato strings and woodwind at 1.34; the vocal slip at 2.04 where "so" is sung against "she"; and the clarinet melody at 2.19. Listen too for the drum fills at 2.43 and 2.52; and at 3.21-25 there are accented pushes where bass and drums come together. The coda is based on the chorus but dispenses with the voices for a while – as if words can't express the feeling adequately.

Above all, the unsung hero here is Alan Taylor on bass. This is one of the greatest basslines ever played on a British Sixties pop single. It's in the 'click bass' style – an attempt to imitate a Motown bassline's eighth and 16th-note syncopation with a pick and a trebly tone. You can hear a very Jamerson-like fill at 1.35.

CREATIVE TIPS

"Being musical is not a crime." (Elvis Costello)... Vocal counter-melodies make amazing hooks.

LINKS

For more click bass, try 'Je T'Aime', 'Diamonds Are Forever', The Casual's own 'Never My Love', and Manfred Mann's 'Fox On The Run'. Singer John Tebb now plies his trade in the clubs of southern France, while a band of non-originals called The Casuals still tours the UK.

TRACK 24

HARLEM SHUFFLE

BOB & EARL 1969

"The original version by Bob & Earl had horns on it, straight-ahead soul-disco style. It was probably the first disco record. It was still the early Sixties when they did it, but the sound and beat were very connectable to that early disco stuff." (KEITH RICHARDS)

This has to be the creepiest dance record ever made. Like 'Whiter Shade Of Pale', it's a performance whose atmosphere hits you right in the gut every time – one of those magic moments that sometimes happens with popular music when the tape rolls in the studio. Apparently a simple two-chord change and a lyric about dancing, it is much greater than the sum of its parts. It also sounds like it was recorded underwater, which is part of its murky power – though personally I could live with this version *and* a nice, cleaned up one too.

Bob & Earl are often confused with that other soul duo Sam & Dave, who had more hits. But that's not the only confusion in their history: Bobby Day (also known as Bobby Byrd, but not James Brown's sidekick Bobby Byrd) and Earl Nelson (also known as Jackie Lee) met in 1957 when Nelson joined Byrd's group The Flames (but not the James Brown/Bobby Byrd Flames – still following this?). Together they released a number of records as Bob & Earl from 1957-59. Day was then replaced by Bobby Relf (also known as Bobby Garrett), and the new Bob & Earl's first hit was 'Harlem Shuffle'.

WRITER	Bobby Relf / Earl Nelson
PRODUCER	Fred Smith / Gene Page (assisted by Barry White?)
RECORDED	Los Angeles, 1963
DURATION	2.48
RELEASED	Island, 1969 (originally Marc, 1963)
CHART	UK 7 US –

Legend has it that this track was produced by a young Barry White, but it's more likely to have been either Fred Smith or Gene Page (White's own arranger in the Seventies), while White himself may have played a minor role in the studio (he may actually have contributed some piano, or even percussion – he certainly went on to drum for Earl on tour in the late 1960s). On its initial release in 1963 'Harlem Shuffle' only just made the lower reaches of the US Top 50, but it was reissued in 1969 and became a UK Top 10 hit.

It starts with a now-famous free-time brass intro whose two chords, C and F, do nothing to prepare you for the shock of the entry into A minor, with a tympani roll on the first beat, a flourish of piano, and handclaps on beat two. A chopped guitar chord comes in on the third off-beat. There's a three-note piano motif, and relentless drumming (listen for the hi-hat ticking like an unexploded bomb) that sends a thunderous fill sweeping across the mix every time it goes back to the key chord from F7.

The melody itself is a two-voice vocal harmony through much of the song, with female backing vocalists who come in from time to time, drawling "yeah, yeah, yeah, do the Harlem shuffle" like they know something mortals aren't supposed to know and are feeling mighty pleased about it.

Harmonically, 'Harlem Shuffle' is in A minor and moves only to an F7 (instead of the Fmaj7 which might be expected) where the piano is more noticeable, giving a tougher sound than the Fmaj7 would have had. At 1.49 there's a semitone key change to B*b*m, for "hitch, hitch-hike baby", which is also faintly disturbing – A minor and B*b* minor may be only a semi-tone apart, but they're distant keys.

There is a long tradition in popular music of writing songs that give instructions on how

CREATIVE TIPS

Toughen a chord progression by turning chord IV into a dominant rather than a major 7 (Natalie Imbruglia's 'Torn' does this, as does the bridge of 'Ticket To Ride').

to do the latest dance craze. These lyrics are often metaphors for a certain other popular activity between consenting adults. Need I mention the pony and tailfeather reference, the "real" with a blank after it, and double entendres such as "how low can you go"? No, I thought not. Bob & Earl clearly know what they have in mind, as the vocal at 1.28 and the whoops in the coda testify. Awwwll-riiight...

LINKS
Watch out for compilation versions that fade too early. The Rolling Stones covered 'Harlem Shuffle' in 1986, taking it to number 13 in the UK and 5 in the US.

> "apparently a simple two-chord change and a lyric about dancing, it is much greater than the sum of its parts"

T R A C K 2 5

MAN OF THE WORLD

FLEETWOOD MAC 1969

"It's in the same vein as 'Albatross', but it's a song. It's a sad song, so it's a blues, but people will say it's not, because it hasn't got a 12-bar format. It's got a really great melody, and I've got some good ideas to make it more complete. It's very sad – it was the way I felt at the time. It's me at my saddest." (PETER GREEN)

Long before they became a mid-Seventies AOR hit machine, Fleetwood Mac enjoyed an earlier incarnation as a British blues outfit, ploughing a similar furrow to John Mayall. Their line-up had one of the steadiest rock rhythm sections, in John McVie and Mick Fleetwood; it also had, in Peter Green, a guitarist to rank with Clapton, Beck and Page. The first Mac played the blues with less bombast than some of their peers and were inventive in their rhythms, but their best music is in the rock format of hits like 'Oh Well', 'Albatross', 'Green Manalishi', 'Black Magic Woman', and the *Then Play On* album.

WRITER	Peter Green
PRODUCER	Mike Vernon
RECORDED	New York / Kingsway, London
DURATION	2.46
RELEASED	Immediate, April 1969
CHART	UK 20 US –

Structurally, 'Man Of The World' has all the compression of a sonnet: two verses, a solo, a bridge, a third verse and a coda. It's in D major, with D A6 Gm D D A6 G6 Bm as the main sequence. The rock use of a minor version of chord IV (Gm instead of G) anticipates Radiohead, who made this change a trademark. The sixths give exotic flavour (obvious at 2.01). The bridge is F#m Em F#m A6.

On the left of the mix you can hear a lead guitar melody and a second lead figure; centre has bass, nylon guitar (just before verse 2), and drums which come in on verse 2; on the right is strummed electric guitar.

Green's genius was really only fully released outside of straight blues – good though he is at that. But this single shows a far greater potential. His tragedy was not to realise this – just as it was Lennon's artistic tragedy not to realise that the objective craft of a song like 'Being For The Benefit Of Mr Kite' is worth just as much as the confessional angst of the *Imagine* album.

Listen for Green's alarming exclamation, "but I just wish that I had never been born", erupting out of the understated way he sings the verse. "Flown over every tide" is also an evocative phase. Green once told me how he heard the first line of this song as a Jewish idiom: "Let me tell you about my life..."

Other things to listen out for: the blues lick on verse 1, on the left (0.43, 1.31); twin slide guitars at 1.32; the drum entry at 1.41; and superb guitar phrases on the left at 1.43, 1.50, and 1.54. Listen for the reverb on the vocal at 2.29 on "love".

LINKS

For more tortured geniuses in their prime, see tracks 3, 6, 14, 17, 20, 36, 78.

CREATIVE TIPS

'Man Of The World' is an object lesson in the whole use of structural compression, poetic lead, dynamics and silence.

TRACK 26

ASTRONOMY DOMINE

PINK FLOYD 1969

"It doesn't really have a meaning or a story. It's a very typical Syd Barrett song." (ROGER WATERS)

"My leaving sort of evened things out within the group." (SYD BARRETT, 1970)

Ummagumma was an ambitious and self-indulgent double album, half studio and half live. The four live songs are far superior to any of the studio tracks, capturing Floyd's extended trippy performances in which they turned songs like 'Astronomy Domine' into epics. This opening track of *Piper At The Gates Of Dawn* was a staple of their live set long before it was recorded – the original Floyd line-up performed it on a BBC2 programme as early as May 1967. But by the time *Ummagumma* was released, Syd Barrett had been edged out of the band.

This is a good live recording, with echoed guitar on the left, keyboard on the right, and drums, bass and vocals in the middle (along with reverb from the keyboard). The vocal doubles the synth as it descends at the end of the verse. The drum style is in the free-flowing mould of Mitch Mitchell or Ginger Baker. Listen for the double bass drum around 6.00.

Despite its length the track's structure is relatively simple. It starts with a keyboard intro, with bass coming in at 0.26, and the first guitar E-chord at 0.52. Verse 1 ends with a descending "ooh"; verse 2 ends at 2.53, and a wah-wah'd guitar solo follows until around 4.06. Here the sound thins out, and by 4.50 the keyboard is solo – drums, cymbals and guitars have dropped out. At 5.32 the bass comes in with a 5th figure. The last verse starts at 7.10, and the coda at 7.40 with a new chord change.

WRITER	**Syd Barrett**
PRODUCER	**Pink Floyd**
RECORDED	**Mothers, Brimingham / Manchester College of Commerce**
DURATION	**8.14**
RELEASED	**(album, Ummagumma) Harvest, October 1969**
CHART	**not a single**

The tripped-out psychedelic quality of the music results from a fair number of chromatic chord changes, such as Hendrix used in '1983', and as makes up the coda of 'I Am The Walrus'. The keyboard intro implies G# but the bass enters on E; the first chord change is the accented E-E*b* – the whole verse sequence is E E*b* G A E Fmaj7*b*5 E E*b* G G A*b* A, culminating in a descent through every major chord between A and D, finishing D D# E; the guitar break uses an E E*b* G A extracted from the verse; the coda has an unexpected D Dm7/ F change which causes the song to finish on D major.

Barrett's evocative lyrics offer us a Coleridgean vision with plenty of internal rhyme in "Floating down, the sound resounds / Around the icy waters underground", with the 12/8 time making the rhymes bounce. It then provides a list of planets and their moons: Jupiter, Saturn, Oberon, Miranda and Titania, Neptune, Titan. They were rubbing shoulders with Dan Dare. ('Domine' in the title, by the way, would appear to be an archaic form of 'domain'.)

Listen for: the dramatic first chord change at 0.52; the wonderful off-key vocal harmony in verse 2; the downward bass runs in the first bit of the solo; and the E chord's return at 6.37.

CREATIVE TIPS

Chromatic chord changes by semi-tones create a feeling of dislocation of ordinary consciousness – which might imply an erotic, painful or spiritual experience.

LINKS

There is a studio version of this on* Piper At The Gates Of Dawn. *For a Barrett-inspired track with astronomical connections, listen to 'Far Out' on Blur's* Parklife. *And see track 17.

T R A C K   2 7

WICHITA LINEMAN

GLEN CAMPBELL 1969

"It's not strictly a country song, although a lot of people think of it as such. But its chord progression is different... it's certainly not a country progression." (GLEN CAMPBELL)

"I'm a song-title man. Give me a title and I'll give you a song." (JIMMY WEBB)

WRITER	**Jimmy Webb**
PRODUCER	**Al De Lory**
RECORDED	**Gold Star Studios, Los Angeles**
DURATION	**3.03**
RELEASED	**(US) Capitol, November 1968; (UK) Ember, January 1969**
CHART	**US 3 (1968) UK 7 (1969)**

This was Campbell's first UK hit, though in the US he'd already had a few minor successes in the pop and country charts. Campbell was a mainstream C&W singer who managed to cross over into the MOR market with 'Wichita Lineman'. Writer Jimmy Webb once explained that the song came about as a follow-up to 'By The Time I Get To Phoenix' – it's one of those songs that trades on the geographical size of America, the romance of the frontier, a sense that if things are bad here you can always move out and start another life (often in stunning scenery) someplace else. Would anyone have ever written a song about a man who climbs telegraph poles in Essex...? So what is it about this record that has touched so many people?

It starts inauspiciously with a standard MOR intro, until Campbell's crisply-sung first line opens up a new dimension. The instrumentation itself holds few clues to the power of the record: the baritone guitar break, reprising the verse melody, recalls Duane Eddy; the string parts are more expressive than they might have been, their high sustained notes and 'telegraph' rhythm evoking a sense of the great wide open. But to get closer to the source of the mystery we need to look at harmony and lyric.

'Wichita Lineman' makes significant symbolic use of key: there is a direct link between the harmony and the emotional effect. It starts off in F major, but the verse begins on B*b*maj7 (IV), where he sings, "I am a lineman...". The B*b* chord signifies the narrator. The verse proceeds to Am7 C Dm Am7 – so far, we are still in F major. But an unexpected G major (instead of G minor) takes it to the key of D major by a gentle IV-I cadence – you can hear this change at 0.26. The chorus works down a sequence of inversions, C9- G/B- Gm/B*b*-D/A- A7sus4 A7, then instead of the expected D we go up a semitone to B*b* and then C. This implies F major, but the 'home' chord is never heard after the first few seconds of the song. F major symbolises the past, the world from which the lineman is exiled; D major is the key of the present, the future and the great outdoors.

The C chord at the start of the chorus could be V in F – it turns away from D major, whose leading note is C#. Thus the chorus enacts his turning away from D major (the outdoors). From C the sequence starts to work downwards slowly, as if heading for F, but the A bass is harmonised not with F/A or Am7 but a second inversion D, then goes to A (D's chord V) only for the anticipated perfect cadence into D to be changed to a B*b* (*his* chord) and then C.

To put himself into the new life requires a new outlook: this is symbolised by the *b*VI-*b*VII-I progression (B*b*-C-D), which would establish D major, except it never gets completed.

CREATIVE TIPS

A key or a chord may have a symbolic value, not just an alteration of pitch – either can represent a person, a place, an emotion, a desire, an event: think of key-changing as musical topography... Jimmy Webb – who also penned 'Galveston' and 'MacArthur Park' – on writing a hit song: "First you need a catchy tune. Second of all, you need kind of an infectious rhythm, even for a slow song. Third, a memorable lyric, something with a natural rhythm that sticks in the mind so that the person is able to sing along... There's a subtext to classic hit songs, and that subtext is the common experience."

The song ends with the Bb-C change, harmonically either IV-V in F major or bVI-bVII in D major, never resolving – as we leave the lineman suspended between two lives, just as he is suspended between the earth and sky.

Webb's first-person lyric starts with the neatest of introductions: "I am a lineman for the county / And I drive the main road". From that point on his Wichita lineman becomes a romantic, everyman figure, that we picture poised between the land and sky in all weathers. His isolation is both a pleasure and a curse – the solitude of being human. He is an existential symbol, yet so concretely realised that you never consciously think of this even as you are moved by it. Somewhere at the back of his dilemma is a great love: "And I need you more than want you / And I want you for all time." But we don't know what will happen, or what needs to happen. So we remain fascinated.

LINKS

Compare Andy Williams' version, recorded a tone higher in G/E with brass replacing the guitar solo. Glen Campbell joined The Beach Boys for a while in 1965 as a touring stand-in for already-ailing Brian Wilson.

TRACK 28

LITTLE GIRL BLUE

JANIS JOPLIN 1969

"'Janis called herself a candle, burning on both ends,' Linda Gottfried said. Janis would ask, 'When am I going to burn out?'. Linda felt Janis knew she was going to die young, because she said it so often." (LAURA JOPLIN – *LOVE, JANIS*)

"I don't stand for any movement, man. I'm just myself. But I'll tell you what I believe in. I believe you should treat yourself good. Get stoned, get laid. Unless it kills you, do it. Every minute is your own. You should be happy." (JANIS JOPLIN)

The musical legacy of Janis Joplin has had mixed fortunes since her untimely death in 1970. Her star has shone less brightly than that of Hendrix or Morrison, the other members of the trio whose deaths helped mark the end of the 1960s. This is partly because her music was not as stylistically ground-breaking as Hendrix or The Doors; it is also because wider cultural shifts have in turn changed how female singers portray themselves. Joplin often positions herself as a victim in her music, pleading for her man – or any man – to come and Make Things Right. This neediness is her key as a singer, eliciting sympathy but perhaps condescension too. In recent decades women in popular music have increasingly defined themselves by their strength and their independence from men. The female audience's taste has been re-shaped by such artists as Siouxsie Sioux, Deborah Harry, Patti Smith, Cyndi Lauper, Madonna, PJ Harvey, Tori Amos, Bjork and Alanis Morissette.

The other problem with Joplin as a singer has to do with delivery – her tendency to 'over-soul'. The remarkable timbre of that sandpaper voice was a constant temptation. In concert it didn't matter so much, but in the studio it meant sometimes she over-did the blues shouting

and inflections in frantic pursuit of (an illusory guarantee of) emotional authenticity. She was the foremost white female beneficiary of the rock audience's unfounded belief that there is anything *intrinsically* 'soul-full' about the mannerisms of blues-influenced singing. That said, her improvisations always seem genuinely hers and never have the cold, machine-precision of 1990s 'soul' divas.

Though not as well-known as 'Me & Bobby McGee' or 'Mercedes Benz', 'Little Girl Blue' is surely Joplin's greatest studio vocal. It is ironic that a Bacchanalian 1960s rock singer should find her perfect vehicle in a much-covered tune composed by Rodgers & Hart for the Broadway musical *Jumbo*.

In the mix, the drums are pushed slightly to one side, with the organ; the bass is central, as are the strings, and a clean electric guitar plays a counterpoint melodic line on the opposite side. It's quite subdued, but builds in the later verses. Joplin sings the song in F major; its harmony has no unexpected or unusual twists, but it's in the re-shaping of the melody and lyric that we find the secret of why this is such a moving performance.

CREATIVE TIPS

Look for buried 'text' inside a well-known song from another genre or time.

As Nina Simone had done before her, Joplin dropped the first verse of the original – in that, the middle-aged heroine sings of how, when she was young, she was dazzled by the circus. The full lyric also contains the possibility that someone will come to her rescue. Joplin makes the song bleaker. The speaker is talking to a woman in depression. Life, says the speaker, is like that – the rain and yourself are all you've got to count on. Joplin infuses the vocal with a sympathy which is genuine because it's rooted in her own palpable vulnerability. She might also be singing to an image of herself – underneath the hard-drinkin, cacklin', boogie-mama persona, she is the little girl blue.

WRITER	Richard Rodgers / Lorenz Hart
PRODUCER	Gabriel Mekler
RECORDED	Columbia Studios, New York
DURATION	3.49
RELEASED	(album, I Got Dem Ol' Kozmic Blues Again Mama!) CBS, September 1969
CHART	not a single

Joplin doesn't over-do the singing – she has one blues-inflected phrase at the end of verse 1, and at the close of verse 2 ("all around you"). But there is an emotional generosity about her interpretation that marks a moment of self-transcendence; instead of being trapped in self-pity at her own agonies, she discovers a bridge of empathy to the subject. The marvellous nature of the vocal means it's as if we are catching her at the very moment of discovery. This is partly to do with the tentative way she sings it, laying down short phrases like stepping stones That's why, for all the heart-pulling sorrow, there is, somewhere at the bottom, a note of joy – however moated by trouble – because her loneliness has been relieved by empathy. She sings, "All you can ever have to lean on is gonna feel just like those raindrops" – yet the song at least partially disproves itself by this act of identity. If there is anything to lean on, it's that.

As for her phrasing, catch the searing, "Ooh I know you're unhappy" after verse 2; the cumulative force that leads to "you must be through"; and the heartbreaking last phrase, "I know, honey I know just how you feel". Difficult as it is to tear your attention away from Joplin, listen also for the guitar counterpoint

LINKS

She performed this song on the This Is Tom Jones ***TV show in September 1969. On the live version in Joplin's*** Box Of Pearls ***set (Columbia, 1999), recorded in July 1970, Joplin actually name-checks the Nina Simone version on the intro.***

TRACK 29

SOMETHING IN THE AIR

THUNDERCLAP NEWMAN 1969

"On 'Can't Explain' we had been fully manipulated in the studio – the like of which hasn't been seen since. Aside from my dastardly treatment of Thunderclap Newman..." (PETE TOWNSHEND)

Here's a song about revolution in the air (its original title was in fact 'Revolution'), just as the 1960s ended, in the year of Woodstock and the moon landing. The times were changing again, and so for many people 'Something In The Air' has a certain pathos – like a hymn for a God whose existence has just been disproved. The idealism of the 1960s may not have achieved all it thought it could – it had not counted on either how powerful the reactionary forces were that resisted it, and the contradictions within the counter-culture that broke it up – but the irony of this record is that there had been a revolution, the world was changed, and more for the better than worse.

The 1960s was not, as is so often absurdly stated, defeated by either a few thugs at Altamont, the untimely deaths of three musical luminaries, or by one homicidal maniac named Manson. It planted the seeds for social change that sprouted to the end of the century and beyond. 'Something In The Air' is too close to events to see the big picture – hence the pathos. But under that is a feeling of celebration at something achieved. The idiomatic lyric says, "We've got to get together sooner or later" – but actually the decade had 'got it together' already; not permanently, but enough to build a foundation for the good to come.

WRITER	John 'Speedy' Keene
PRODUCER	Pete Townshend
RECORDED	London
DURATION	3.54
RELEASED	Track Records, May 1969
CHART	UK 1 US 37

As a recording and song, 'Something In The Air' is splendidly eccentric and unpredictable. For a start it has a tempo that varies, from 86bpm to a bridge at 93 and then 90 for the last section. Here's that clicky bass again (played by Townshend, under the pseudonym Bijou Drains), and with no audible kick drum the bass is free to move around.

The track also features double-tracked vocals and clear jangly guitars, augmented by strings for verse 2, with brass, hints of woodwind, a honky-tonk piano, duelling handclaps, and an out-of-tune tuba – an instrument associated with military brass band music and old public school Colonel Blimps, so its appearance in the bridge adds a satirical flavour of the Bonzo Dog Doo-Dah Band.

CREATIVE TIPS

Take out the beat for part of the song... Transpose verses into a different key.

The underlying celebratory feel is enacted by the song's harmonic freedom: 'Something...' starts in E major, and at 1.05 goes up to F# major; the piano at 1.58 goes through the sequence F#7 E7 F7 G7 C F7 four times, these seven chords preventing any stable sense of key. When the song reaches verse 3 at 2.56 it is in Ab major, with the effect of bursting into sunlight. Key changing becomes a metaphor for revolution. It is also content to drop the regular beat for the middle section.

Listen for the psychedelic two-note string phrase at 1.36, which goes up an octave at 1.41, and occurs again at 3.27-37 where the brass also plays a motif from the *Marseillaise* (recalling 'All You Need Is Love'). Also note the use of the lead guitar to play fills throughout; and the rollicking outburst of triplet rhythm on the piano at 2.48.

LINKS

Thunderclap Newman was a band helped into existence by Pete Townshend, and named after bulky keyboardist Andy Newman. Guitarist and singer John 'Speedy' Keene was a former John Mayall roadie and early Who collaborator, who later went on to produce Johnny Thunders & The Heartbreakers; the band also included teenage guitar prodigy Jimmy McCulloch, who joined Wings in the 1970s. 'Something In The Air' featured in the film The Magic Christian, *to which Badfinger and some of the Beatles also contributed.*

"like a hymn for a God whose existence has just been disproved"

1970s

30	The Supremes	*Stoned Love*
31	The Four Tops	*Still Water (Love)*
32	James Brown	*Get Up I Feel Like Being A Sex Machine*
33	George Harrison	*What Is Life*
34	Mountain	*Pride And Passion*
35	Rod Stewart	*I Know I'm Losing You*
36	Marvin Gaye	*What's Going On*
37	Isaac Hayes	*Theme From Shaft*
38	T.Rex	*Telegram Sam*
39	David Bowie	*John I'm Only Dancing*
40	Focus	*Focus II*
41	The Who	*Relay*
42	Roxy Music	*Pyjamarama*
43	Bruce Springsteen	*Incident On 57th Street*
44	Queen	*Now I'm Here*
45	Led Zeppelin	*Kashmir*
46	Alan Stivell	*Spered Hollvedel / Delivrance*
47	Boston	*More Than A Feeling*
48	Television	*Marquee Moon*
49	The Sex Pistols	*God Save The Queen*
50	Abba	*Knowing Me Knowing You*
51	Kate Bush	*Wuthering Heights*
52	Van Halen	*Ain't Talking 'Bout Love*
53	The Jam	*When You're Young*
54	The Clash	*London Calling*

TRACK 30

STONED LOVE

THE SUPREMES 1970

"I never resented Diana's position ... I just felt I was doing less than I was capable of ... and by Florence and I becoming '& The Supremes' it demeaned us. It was one of those things that ate away at us inside, and ate away at the fabric of the group ... People always ask me how it felt being in the background, and I say, 'What do you mean, in the background?'." (MARY WILSON)

As the musical decade that Motown had dominated came to a close, the label's musicians and writers overhauled the Sound Of Young America one last time, and created music of greater maturity than before, most famously on Marvin Gaye's *What's Going On* (which we'll come to in a moment). 'Stoned Love' was the second chart hit for the post-Diana Ross Supremes, following 'Up The Ladder To The Roof'. In a complex arrangement of a musically simple song, ideas come thick and fast, so there's plenty to listen for. Jean Terrell, Ross's replacement, brought a noticeably warmer vocal to The Supremes when she joined Mary Wilson and Cindy Birdsong (who'd herself replaced Florence Ballard in 1967). The honeyed tones of Terrell's singing bring a sensuous immediacy to the religious lyric – there's no dichotomy between spirit and flesh here. Please form an orderly queue for the Church of the Revelation of St Jean (Detroit Chapter)...

WRITER	**Frank Wilson / Yennik Samoht**
PRODUCER	**Frank Wilson, arranged by David Van De Pitte**
RECORDED	**Hitsville, Detroit / Los Angeles**
DURATION	**4.06 (edited version 2.56)**
RELEASED	**Motown, October 1970**
CHART	**US 7 (1970) UK 3 (1971)**

CREATIVE TIPS

Hold back one of the three primary minor chords (II, III or VI) until the bridge.

The effect of the mono and stereo versions (either full or edited) is noticeably different. The opening of the single is delightfully inelegant, as it comes in with a crude tape splice right across a mixture of ambient noise. (There's a fair amount of audible tape hiss too.)

The song is initially carried by a pounding 4/4 beat with a prominent 'loose' hi-hat, reinforced by occasional handclaps and a foot-stamping effect, which was a Supremes trademark from 'Where Did Our Love Go' onward. Once you've adjusted to the melody and rhythm, try listening to the intersecting guitars: a fuzzy guitar on the left is answered by one on the right. This interplay is complicated by interjections from brass and backing vocals – the latter lyrically unclear, apart from the title, though still managing to sound like the wisdom of Solomon. Notice where the backing vocals diverge into a harmony, and the strings go hard left.

'Stoned Love' exists in three versions: the longest starts with a glitzy gospel intro of 47 seconds, with overwrought piano and cod-angelic harp – listen for the piano crossing the stereo image toward the end of this. As Terrell sings the title for the first time we are into the single version, with the drums entering at 0.53. (The 47-second intro was deemed not radio-friendly.) Other cuts are made elsewhere on four occasions (though not on the 40th anniversary box-set version): there's an edit of a title at the start, a sax break at around 2:52, and another extra section after the bridge which repeated the hook. Just before the coda there's a delightful rhythm break where many of the harmony instruments drop out.

Verses and chorus consist of a single three-chord four-bar phrase, D Bm Em D (chords I VI II and back to I), over which either verse or chorus can be sung. The middle-eight moves onto F#m (chord III), D and then Em, twice.

In November 1970 CBS axed a performance of this song from *The Merv Griffin Show*, fearing it might have drug connotations. 'Stoned Love' is actually a religious song, though you might not guess that initially from the feel. The reference to the "man on whose shoulders the world must depend" is the clincher, as well as the "pray" and "amen" at the end of verse 2. The war between "our nations" could be taken as either internal race relations or Vietnam.

Other highlights to listen for include the bass arpeggio in bar 2 of the bridge (on "nations"); the ascending string flourish under Terrell's urgent and sexy vocal (3.51); and the flourish of congas on the fade. The bassline is unusually simple for a Motown track of this period, being mostly eighths (count it 1&2&3&4& etc) so it might not have been resident bass genius James Jamerson (there is some dispute over who played on which Motown sessions).

LINKS

For the effect of edits, see songs 13, 47 and 92. Members of The Supremes re-recorded 'Stoned Love' for the Motorcity label in 1990.

> "the foot-stamping effect was a Supremes trademark from 'Where Did Our Love Go' onward"

TRACK 31

STILL WATER (LOVE)

FOUR TOPS 1970

"We had a lot of hits, and we managed to keep our heads above water. By the time the calm came – like Billy Eckstine says, 'All of a sudden it gets calm' – we accepted it and went with the flow." (LEVI STUBBS)

WRITER	Smokey Robinson / Frank Wilson
PRODUCER	Frank Wilson
RECORDED	Hitsville Studios, Detroit
DURATION	3.09
RELEASED	Motown, August 1970
CHART	US 11 UK 10

In the manner of the descriptive marginalia to Bunyan's *The Pilgrim's Progress*, 'Still Water' should be sub-captioned, 'Virtue Rewarded: or how after many trials and tribulations Pilgrim Stubbs came upon a mighty but calm river, and the love thereof...'

The Tops were probably the act most affected by Motown's loss of songwriting team Holland-Dozier-Holland, who had supplied most of their big hits. As we saw earlier, most of those hits revolved around the scenario of Levi's tormented persona lurching from one romantic disaster to another, and this makes 'Still Water' all the more moving. The combined talents of Frank Wilson and Smokey Robinson granted the tortured soul of 'Seven Rooms Of Gloom' some release and serenity in this hypnotic, under-rated hit.

This track desperately needs some expert remastering (listen for the strange buzzing on the right side). The watery effect is caused by the echo on Levi's voice. But it's the arrangement (by Jerry Long and James Roach) that carries the song – a delicate interplay of instruments and vocals. On the left we have female voices, organ, tambourine, brass, harp glissando and lead guitar (echo fed to the right); in the middle we have lead vocal, bass, drums, percussion and Tops; on the right, flute or piccolo, woodwind and a clavinet-type keyboard. Jamerson takes the simple three-chord change and weaves his usual miracles on bass underneath, adding chromatic notes to the progression but never obtruding.

CREATIVE TIPS

If you use a single four-bar phrase for a song, make the arrangement as varied as you can.

Like 'Stoned Love' this track reflects the increasing simplicity of the Wilson/Whitfield Detroit sunset (the baroque complexities of H-D-H songs were carried on by Ashford & Simpson – compare this with 'Ain't Nothing Like The Real Thing' or 'Ain't No Mountain High Enough'.) The basis of the music amounts to a mere four bars and the sequence E*b* Cm B*b* (I VI V). It has a long intro, the verse starts at 1.04, then there's a chorus and a coda. It's a triptych – a mosaic of melodic fragments.

The many highlights of this mosaic include: at 0.13 the melody high on the right; 0.23 the entrance of the Tops in harmony; 0.43 a harp glissando; female voices singing the title, answered by the Tops and echoed back; 1.11, the faint woodwind line on the right; 1.25, the first snare hit; 1.35, the five-note arpeggio down on the brass; 1.38, a telegraph-sound brass figure on the left; 2.03, drum fills into the coda, followed by a more insistent kick drum pattern; 2.25, Levi's high phrase; 2.30, return of the telegraph figure; and the dovetailing of voices.

Much of the song is wordless, but the lyric starts enigmatically with the idea of a love too great to speak of to others, before working up to the proverbial title. This song calls forth a different type of vocal from Stubbs, other than his usual impassioned holler: the speaker seems assured in his masculinity, less embattled than on the early records, where to cry might be a sign of weakness.

LINKS

The B-side was a slowed-down version of the same song called 'Still Water (Peace)' (2:42), with more reverb, more strings, a few ripples of wah-wah guitar, and Levi spelling out what each letter of "peace" stands for. The vocal may be kitsch but the music on either of these arrangements is the equal of anything on* What's Going On. *For another Four Tops number, see track 16. For a song in a different style, but also based on a four-chord sequence, see tracks 42 and 97.

"This song calls forth a different type of vocal from Stubbs, other than his usual impassioned holler"

TRACK 32

GET UP I FEEL LIKE BEING A SEX MACHINE JAMES BROWN 1970

"We were playing a gig in Nashville, Tennessee, and I wrote 'Sex Machine' because we were saying, 'Get up, get on up' in a jam and I saw people respond to that – so I came back[stage] and I wrote a song on the back of a poster. We finished playing, packed up real quick and went to the studio, and we cut 'Sex Machine' the same night. 'Cause that's really the time to record."

(JAMES BROWN)

Both 'Stoned Love' and 'Still Water' are harmonically simple songs, but James Brown was taking the process of intensifying the rhythmic element of music even further. Brown had his first hit in 1956, and averaged several chart singles a year thereafter. His 1963 *Live At The Apollo* album was a huge critical and commercial success – the biggest-selling R&B record of its day (not to mention a breakthrough in the art of location recording). But his 'vintage' years started in 1965 with the transatlantic hit 'Papa's Got A Brand New Bag', followed by the likes of 'I Got You (I Feel Good)', and 1968's cultural milestone, 'Say It Loud, I'm Black And I'm Proud'.

WRITER	James Brown / Bobby Byrd / Ron Lenhoff
PRODUCER	James Brown
RECORDED	Starday-King Studios, Nashville
DURATION	5.09
RELEASED	(US) King. July 1970 (UK) Polydor, September 1970
CHART	US 15 UK 32

This was a new, harder, more primal soul sound than almost anyone else having hits; Brown almost single-handedly created funk, essentially by shifting emphasis heavily onto the first beat of the bar, down-playing melody, and generally stripping the music back to rhythm and riffs – backed by tight big-band arrangements – creating tracks inspired by drum parts or basslines rather than traditional 'tunes'.

This is what made him a major influence on most later dance music – a mixed blessing, in my view. By taking Brown's rhythmic obsession (often literally, by sampling his records) and having machines execute it, the result all too often displays a stifling loss of groove and nuance. (The dance music genre, as it's not, strictly speaking, song-based, is largely outside the scope of this particular book.)

In 1970 Brown lost most of his band (he's a notoriously severe bandleader), including guitarist Jimmy 'Chank' Nolen, but he soon recruited fresh young blood – among them William 'Bootsy' and his brother Phelps 'Catfish' Collins. 'Sex Machine' was their first record, based on a previous hit 'Give It Up Or Turnit A Loose', and Bootsy Collins' bassline in particular is a central element in the track's urgency.

The spoken intro and other bits of talk (like Bobby Byrd's backing vocal answers, and the band's affirmations) suggest the sense of community often felt in black music (think of the intros of 'What's Going On' and 'I Wish It Would Rain'). Brown's self-referential injunctions about taking it "to the bridge" were almost revolutionary in themselves, seeming like a secret language to non-musicians.

'Get Up' is typical of Brown in the way it locks onto a single-chord groove for minutes at a stretch, allowing for plenty of vocal improvisation. The harmony itself is static until, at 2.11, the bridge goes to an A*b*, but the essence of the arrangement lies in the interlocking of the many separate rhythmic phrases to make one over-arching groove, with drums and

CREATIVE TIPS

Try a dominant 9 chord for funk... Put together an arrangement and think about the rhythmic quality of everything you include... Try recording straight after a gig...

piano (Brown takes the piano solo himself) towards the left, vocal in the centre with the bass, and guitar on the right.

LINKS

Brown also had some more traditional 'song-based' hits, such as 'It's A Man's Man's Man's World'. Overall, his influence on modern soul, funk and various strands of dance music is almost immeasurable – as is his importance as a cultural icon. See track 70 for one of the more obvious fans. For another track that uses static harmony to a completely different effect, see 66.

> "a new, harder, more primal sound than almost anyone else having hits"

TRACK 33

WHAT IS LIFE

GEORGE HARRISON 1970

"Some of the sessions were very long in the preparation of the sound, and the arrangements had at times various percussion players, sometimes two or three; two drummers, four or five acoustic guitars, two pianos and even two basses on one of the tracks. The songs were played over and over again until the arrangements were sorted out so that the engineer in the control room could get the sound with Phil Spector. Many of the tracks were virtually live."

(GEORGE HARRISON)

CREATIVE TIPS

Try using part of a scale as a hook – Bowie's 'Man Who Sold The World' is another good example... Try writing a part where bass and guitar move together.

It had always been a bone of contention for Harrison that he was unable to find an outlet for his songs in The Beatles, owing to the songwriting presence of... erm... those other two geezers (the names'll come back to me in a minute). After the split, Harrison relieved this artistic log-jam with a triple album. Like most doubles (let alone triples) it would have made a fine single disc, containing as it did 'My Sweet Lord', 'What Is Life', 'Awaiting On You All' and 'If Not For You', but at the time there's no doubt the release of a triple album (*All Things Must Pass*) was a bold statement on many levels.

As Beatles chronicler Ian MacDonald has noted, Harrison's muse can be a bit gloomy. 'What Is Life', on the other hand, is a thoroughly upbeat number, and one of the last flowerings of the Spector wall-of-sound. In the sleeve-notes to the remastered album (2001), Harrison says he would have liked, "to liberate some of the songs from the big production", which he now thinks is, "a bit over the top" Thank goodness he didn't – that sound is part-and-parcel of the glory of 'What Is Life' and how it conveys its sentiment.

The song starts with a two-bar guitar riff based on the scale of E major, recorded in stereo. It's doubled by bass, then a strummed acoustic comes in on the left, then the band enter with big brass chords, acoustic guitar on the right, drums and percussion. During the verse guitar and bass play a counter-melody to the double-tracked vocal. At the first chorus the brass re-enters and there are backing vocals on both sides of the mix, including a swooning high three-note phrase. Verse 2 adds a low level organ sound; a brass fill at 1.26; then, halfway through, the strings enter on the left, and a brass fill takes us into chorus 2. The second chorus has strings on the left, using the notes of the guitar riff in a slightly altered rhythm. Listen for the tambourine too. At the end of the second chorus the song stops dead, and it all builds up once more from the guitar. Verse 3 has a double-tracked slide guitar fill (Harrison's trademark) at 2.52, with a fine brass fill at 2.58 and strings at 3.02.

WRITER	**George Harrison**
PRODUCER	**George Harrison / Phil Spector**
RECORDED	**Abbey Road / Trident studios, London**
DURATION	**4.22**
RELEASED	**(US) Apple, December 1970; (UK) B-side of 'My Sweet Lord', December 1970**
CHART	**US 10 UK 1 (as B-side)**

'What Is Life' has a straightforward love lyric which you could imagine The Four Tops doing. There's a verse and chorus but no middle-eight. It's firmly in E major, the chorus using a strong I-V-IV sequence and the verse moving through E B C# F#m D B.

Oh for a time machine to take a demo of this song back to Abbey Road in the spring of 1964 – imagine George Martin at the helm and a Ringo swishing backbeat, two guitars and a vocal harmony...

LINKS

'What Is Life' was written for that most feted of rock wives, Patti Boyd (or Harrison, as she was then) - for whom Clapton was to write 'Layla'. There is an instrumental mix of it on the remastered All Things Must Pass. *For another Spector production, see track 6.*

TRACK 34

PRIDE AND PASSION

MOUNTAIN 1971

"The most important thing is being a songwriting team. Me and my old lady fight, but never about that, that's always straight ahead." (FELIX PAPPALARDI)

Rock critics have never been kind to Mountain, dismissing them at the time as a mega-watt Cream clone. Yes, they riffed. Yes, they had the poetic lyrics, tempered singing, live improvisation, and high volume. Yes, they could be self-indulgent (witness the sprawling live double album *Twin Peaks*). Bassist Felix Pappalardi actually produced Cream's *Disraeli Gears* (1967); and when Pappalardi quit Mountain in 1972, guitarist Leslie West even linked up for a time with Jack Bruce... But the Cream comparison obscured some genuine strong points.

Formed in 1969, and named after West's bulky proportions, Mountain's use of keyboards gave them a big harmonic advantage over Cream (the archetypal guitar power trio) – no more

big holes in the sound when the guitarist takes a solo. They played live throughout 1969, including at *Woodstock*; the first album, *Mountain Climbing* (1970), made the US Top 20 and contained the fine 'Theme For An Imaginary Western' and the bludgeoning 'Mississippi Queen' (their only hit single). It was followed by a change of drummer and further albums, *Nantucket Sleighride* and the half-live/half-studio *Flowers Of Evil*.

'Pride And Passion' is a hard rock song with a number of stimulating ingredients, and innovative in its combination of structure and harmony. It starts with an instrumental section, featuring slide guitar played through echo and reverb but using violin tone effect. At 1.15 you can hear sustained backward piano notes which culminate in a quarter-note melody at 1.32. The piano link is unusual in that there is a different chord on each of eight beats, starting at 1.40. Drums kick in at 1.46. The first progression is Bm A G D Em Bm, three times, resolving onto an A at 1.59, where there is a drop into half-time.

WRITER	Felix Pappalardi / Gail Collins
PRODUCER	Felix Pappalardi
RECORDED	Record Plant, New York
DURATION	7.09
RELEASED	(album, Flowers Of Evil) Island, October 1971
CHART	not a single

West plays his first solo over a descending D C# C B Bb bassline, and then over a D A/C# Bm A progression. The fact that the sequences are quite rich in terms of major and minor chords means West's mostly pentatonic major notes sound so much more expressive than they would over a straight blues progression. As he demonstrates here, West is a lead player with the ability to play evocative, lyrical breaks.

The verse starts at 2:22, with a solo link at 2.48. A second verse ends with a variation in the chords, then at 3.27 the chorus ("sons are breathing discontent") works down through a lovely sequence of first inversions: E/G# Bm G Em B/D# Bm/D A/C# Am/C Bm Bm/A Bm/G# G – it is unusual to hear a chord sequence like this in a hard rock song. At 5.11 the track reaches a reprise of the intro, this time condensed and with backward piano 5ths. At 6.23 we get the four-bar piano link, a fragment of a last verse, and at 6.41 the drop into half-time, before the song concludes with a few bars of solo piano.

Note that the vocal delivery is not the high-pitched wailing of most hard rock singers, but more understated, which plays off against the power of the instruments – a trick Cream pioneered. The lyrics seem to be linked to the Vietnam war, with some memorable individual lines, such as, "And a million nameless candles flicker out just one last time".

CREATIVE TIPS

A tip for guitarists: the musical effect of your scales depends on the chords over which you're playing... And remember, you're never alone with an inversion.

LINKS

Like many of Mountain's songs, 'Pride And Passion' was penned by husband & wife writing duo Felix and Gail Pappalardi (nee Collins), who also co-wrote Cream's 'Strange Brew'. After a volatile relationship - hinted at by the quote above - Gail shot and killed Felix in 1981 (she claimed it was an accident, but she still got four years in jail, and effectively disappeared from the music scene).

"note that the vocal delivery is not the high-pitched wailing of most hard rock singers"

TRACK 35

I KNOW I'M LOSING YOU

ROD STEWART 1971

"Al Jolson was a strong influence on me... Then I got into folk music, listening to Woody Guthrie, Jack Elliott, Leadbelly. Then into black music – Sam Cooke, Otis Redding... David Ruffin was another influence... another that's kicked the bucket. I was really good friends with Ruffin. Woody [Ron Wood] has got a wonderful picture of me looking down David's throat because we couldn't work out why he didn't lose his voice and I did. So I'm looking down to see what he's got that I haven't." (ROD STEWART)

Once upon a time there was a young man with a pineapple haircut and a fondness for towing mike stands around stages. He sang in a raspy voice a touch higher than Joe Cocker, redolent of drink and rough living, disappointment and destitution. He made great records. This, believe it or not, was Rod Stewart. If all Stewart means to you is the vulgar pink-satin-buttocked grind of 'Do Ya Think I'm Sexy', chances are you won't believe your ears if you listen to what he did prior to 1973.

WRITER	Norman Whitfield / Eddie Holland / Cornelius Grant
PRODUCER	Rod Stewart
RECORDED	Morgan Sound Studios, London
DURATION	5.22
RELEASED	(album, Every Picture Tells A Story) Mercury, July 1971
CHART	not a single

Every Picture Tells A Story was the album that lifted him to major league status. His first two – *An Old Raincoat Won't Let You Down* (1969) and *Gasoline Alley* (1970) – were fine efforts, but the essential ingredients of his folk-rock gelled on the third, a platter that oozes a rough-diamond charm. Everyone of course knows 'Maggie May', which went to number 1 on both sides of the Atlantic (as did the album), but with Dylan's 'Seems Like A Long Time' and Tim Hardin's 'Reason To Believe' he proved himself an excellent interpreter of songs. The same applies to 'I Know I'm Losing You', where he is supported by The Faces doing their usual had-me-a-real-good-time vibe. Who else but Stewart could have taken on this Temptations number and held his own with David Ruffin?

Rock and Motown had an uncomfortable relationship at the end of the 1960s. Rock critics particularly loathed Motown's showbiz pretensions – gigs at the Talk Of The Town, *The Supremes Sing Rodgers & Hart* etc – without grasping that from an African-American perspective such aspirations had different cultural ramifications than, say, Engelbert Humperdink heading for Las Vegas. As for rock bands, doing Motown covers became a blood-sport (eg Vanilla Fudge's 'You Keep Me Hanging On'). Coming from the opposite angle, Motown tried to get their own rock label, Rare Earth, off the ground, with little success.

Generally speaking, your average pub band will happily knock off any number of Stax/Atlantic classics like 'Knock On Wood' and 'In The Midnight Hour', but you rarely hear such bands doing Motown covers. Why? Because they're much harder to do than they seem...

Harmonically, the basis of the track is three chords suspended over the key note. It starts with solo Ron Wood guitar, then Ronnie Lane's bass enters on the right (listen for a background "hey" at the 0.30 mark), then piano and vocals, and finally drums at 0.49, just before a rollicking piano phrase by Ian McLagan. At 1.49 there's a wonderful roar by Stewart. The arrangement thins out into humming at 2:03 before the instruments return: an urgent bass and a cymbal roll at 2.31 lead to battering snare rolls at 2.39 and 2.47; after a few guitar licks at

CREATIVE TIPS

Never under-estimate the effect of a rallentando – put that click track away.

3.18-3.24 the drums are alone at 3:41. Listen for the increase in the reverb here. The guitar returns at 4.11 and the tempo pulls up at 5.04, and pulls right back for the last vocal.

LINKS

The Temptations' original (produced by Norman Whitfield in 1966) has a change from minor chords on the hook-line to a major chord for the first verse. There's a clear division between verse and chorus which the Stewart/Faces version doesn't have. But the four-note chromatic line is preserved at the intro. For other cover versions, see songs 8, 21, 28, and 85.

> "who else but Stewart could have held his own with David Ruffin"

TRACK 36

WHAT'S GOING ON

MARVIN GAYE 1971

"[Motown] didn't like it, didn't understand it, and didn't trust it. Management said the songs were too long, too formless, and would get lost on a public looking for easy three-minute stories. For months they wouldn't release it. My attitude had to be firm. Basically I said, 'Put it out or I'll never record for you again'." (MARVIN GAYE)

"I said, 'Marvin, we learn from everything. That's what life's all about. I don't think you're right, but if you really want to do it, do it. And if it doesn't work you'll learn something – and if it does, I'll learn something'. I learned something." (MOTOWN BOSS BERRY GORDY)

Another star shining in the golden sunset of Motown's Detroit era, *What's Going On* was the most significant album the label ever released. It gave Marvin Gaye a road back from the wilderness into which he had gone following the death of singing partner Tammi Terrell. In it he took his own music forward into new areas, satisfying on the one hand his long-held ambition to sing more sophisticated material, and on the other his impulse to respond to the plight of his brother Frankie serving in Vietnam (along with the thousands like him), and to the social upheaval that was taking place in America at the close of the 1960s. *What's Going On* is a creative balance between personal and public concerns. At Motown it opened the door for labelmate Stevie Wonder to pursue his musical ambitions in a sequence of ground-breaking albums. The label that had been associated with the hit single had belatedly discovered the album as an artistic entity in its own right.

In strictly musical terms it is also an unusually cohesive album; partly because of the segueing of tracks into one another, but also in the vocal phrasing, and the re-using of certain chord progressions – for example the bridge of 'What's Going On' becomes the intro of 'What's Happening Brother', and its main progression is deployed in 'Mercy Mercy Me'.

In 2001 Motown issued an exemplary 'Deluxe' edition of the record which provides a wonderful opportunity for active listening. It contains two live and four studio takes of the title track. I want to focus on the studio versions: the primary album version (call it A), the Detroit mix (B), the mono single (C) and the 'strings & rhythm' mix (D). Comparison of the four provides not only an insight into the track itself but the artistic implications of the mixing stage.

WRITER	**Marvin Gaye**
PRODUCER	**Marvin Gaye / arranged by David Van De Pitte**
RECORDED	**Motown Studios, Detroit / possibly United Sound**
DURATION	**3.53 (album version)**
RELEASED	**(single) Tamla Motown, January 1971**
CHART	**US 2 UK -**

Version A opens with the multiple voices of a party – symbolic of something more than just atmosphere: the community of voices represents not only the ideal the album articulates (brotherhood) but the fact that it is a collaborative effort. Talented as Gaye was he could not have realised this music without the help of a number of gifted musicians, including the Funk Brothers and David Van De Pitte, who did the string parts. To his credit Gaye listed these people on the original sleeve – including, as he says, the "incomparable James Jamerson" – breaking with Motown's tradition of keeping sessioneers un-named.

Version A's mix has the rhythm section and two lead vocals in the centre (the second voice makes itself felt at 0.48), with sax and one or two guitars to the left, guitar and vibes to the right. The strings are heard in stereo. One of the percussive 'signatures' of *What's Going On* is the congas, which have an unusual amount of reverb on them; listen for the echoing 'slap'. The vocal approach is innovative – not only Gaye's venture into 'scat' singing, which was a departure for him, but the dual lead vocal, which violates a production rule: most record producers feel you must not confuse the listener by having competing parts vying for attention. So, for example, a record shouldn't have a lead guitar solo going on at the same time as a lead vocal. (This arguably underestimates how much people can follow.) At 1.15 the strings enter, and the bridge part (on an Am chord) features some great bass from James Jamerson when the chord shifts to B at 1.57.

Version B – the Detroit mix – is a fascinating contrast. Its drier texture (there's much less reverb) looks back more to the Motown of yesteryear. It starts without the party voices, and the various instruments are re-positioned in the stereo image. Most striking of all is the dividing of the lead vocals into hard left and right, the second lead vocal making a dramatic entry on the right at 0.40. This division makes Gaye's spoken parts on the bridge very clear.

Version C – the mono mix for the single – demonstrates that 'What's Going On' was made for stereo. In mono, with all the parts crammed together, much more of the detail is lost. This mix puts a lot of reverb on the congas and the strings are further back. Some of the vocal phrases are thinned out. Listen for the "got to find a way" at 0.31, which is less apparent than on versions A or B.

Version D is a new mix which, unlike the above, was done from the 16-track original with the purpose of revealing more of the musical parts. What a treat this is – not only because of the pristine quality, but being able to hear the parts one at a time. It is structured so you hear in turn the entry of sax and bass, piano at 0.09, two guitars left and right with vibes at 0.38, strings and handclaps at 1.07, congas, and lower strings at 1.30, and drums in at 1.59. Listen for the higher notes on Jamerson's bass dying fast because of his use of a foam mute on the bass; and the string parts at 2.42.

CREATIVE TIPS

For Gaye this album marked the discovery of a new way of singing: "I felt like I'd finally learned how to sing. I'd been studying the microphone for a dozen years, and suddenly I saw what I'd been doing wrong. I'd been singing too loud, especially on those Whitfield songs. It was all so easy. One night I was listening to a record by Lester Young, the horn player, and it came to me. Relax, just relax."

LINKS

For other Motown tracks, see 15, 16, 30 and 31.

TRACK 37

THEME FROM SHAFT

ISAAC HAYES 1971

"When you're a sharecropper and you're poor and have no shoes, you think of that pair of shoes you want to wear. When you have no clothes, you think of the wardrobe you want. When you have no roof over your head, you think of the fine home you want to live in. Somewhere in the back of my mind I knew I would not spend the rest of my life as a sharecropper." (ISAAC HAYES)

This theme song from the film 'Shaft' was a surprise hit in 1971 but deserved its success. In the small scale of a three-minute piece it moves through an unpredictable structure that makes for a compelling ride. The most famous production facet of 'Theme From Shaft' is the wah-wah pedal guitar. For those who don't know, wah-wah is a foot-operated effects unit, used in some Motown recordings and by players like Clapton and Hendrix in the rock field from about 1967 onwards; by opening and closing the pedal, frequencies are boosted or cut, resulting in the distinctive 'modulated' sound. Wah-wah guitar became ubiquitous on TV and film detective shows for the next few years – probably the most high-profile guitar sound since Vic Flick did a Duane Eddy on the original 'James Bond Theme' back in 1962.

Harmonically, the song uses three chords – Em, Fmaj7 and G – and the key is G major (with a slight mixolydian flavour because of the F). Structurally, it falls into a first section, using the F Em change, a second on G starting 1.12, a third with vocal at 1.49, and a coda at 2.45.

WRITER	Isaac Hayes
PRODUCER	Isaac Hayes
RECORDED	Stax Studios, Memphis
DURATION	3.16
RELEASED	(US) Enterprise, September 1971 (UK) Stax, November 1971
CHART	US 1 UK 4

It's a textured arrangement, with more going on than first appears: after the hi-hat intro, listen for the wah-wah threading all the way through – the guitarist on this session is damping quite a few of the strings and playing 16ths on an octave G, consistently for the length of the track. And note the first piano chord which comes in on an unexpected F. The ear takes the first note it hears – the wah-wah G – as the key note, but the piano F at 0.10 unsettles that, creating a sense of ominous drama. There's a second wah-wah guitar on the opposite side of the mix that just plays chords. Brass, strings and woodwind all have separate motifs over a Fmaj7-Em change.

The song hits the key chord at about 1:12 and stays there until 1.49. Notice the strings from 1.30 playing a blues flat third against the G major harmony. The churning bass riff under the vocal section is in the 'I Can't Help Myself' Motown mode, with bass and piano together. Excitement is increased by the punchy staccato rhythms at 2.52, 3.00 and from there onwards. The wah-wah is panned across the mix during these last few seconds before the music settles on an unresolved romantic Fmaj7.

CREATIVE TIPS

Write a song that starts out as if it were an instrumental... Try getting lead and backing vocals to talk to each other.

The whole shape of the song is altered by the fact that the vocals don't come in until over half-way – for the first part you think you are listening to an instrumental (a common feature of Hayes' production style).

When they arrive, the lyrics are kept to a minimum and are full of hip Seventies black speak: Hayes raps with the backing chorus about this "dick" who is a "sex machine" with all the "chicks". There's a touch a humour when he's about to say "mother******" and the women tell him to shut his mouth. It may sound tame by today's standards, but this was all pretty daring stuff on a record in 1971.

LINKS

Hayes re-recorded this track for the Shaft *sequel in 2000. The soul legend's biggest UK hit was, bizarrely, as the Southpark chef on 'Chocolate Salty Balls'... For another song where a single musical element is sustained through its entire length, see track 68.*

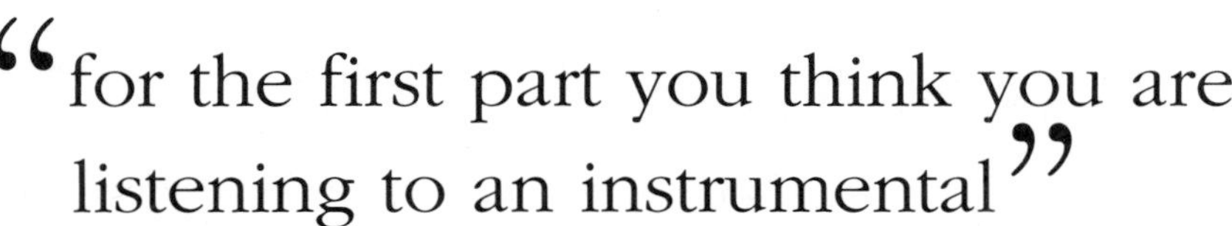

"for the first part you think you are listening to an instrumental"

TRACK 38

TELEGRAM SAM

T.REX 1972

"The music grew through three albums to what it is now, and people did all that bullshit about instant overnight electricity, which was ludicrous because it had taken two-and-a-half years. From *Unicorn* upwards, it's very obvious."

(MARC BOLAN)

On 8th December 1971 a couple of hundred people saw T.Rex mime to an as-yet unreleased song in a small London TV studio for a series called *Music In The Round* (the performance has been available on video). Bolan was conservatively dressed... *ahem*... in Anello & Davide women's shoes, mustard yellow patterned trousers, an electric blue velvet smock with turquoise trim, and an unruly mop of corkscrew hair. Stroking his orange-amber re-finished Les Paul and singing over the backing track, he looked every inch a man-child whose aura mirrored the adoration of hundreds of thousands of people. I was fortunate enough to have been in the Cockpit Theatre for that TV show, young and thoroughly impressionable, and would like the court to take this into consideration, Your Honour, with regard to the charge that I have over-praised this record. On the other hand...

WRITER	Marc Bolan
PRODUCER	Tony Visconti
RECORDED	Rosenburg Studios, Copenhagen
DURATION	3.43
RELEASED	T.Rex Wax Co / EMI January 1971
CHART	UK 1 US –

'Telegram Sam' was fifth in the march of T.Rex's chart hits (since they trimmed the Tyrannosaurus in 1970), following 'Ride A White Swan', 'Hot Love', 'Get It On' and 'Jeepster'. At the time of its release T.Rex were the biggest singles band in the UK and their concerts featured scenes reminiscent of Beatlemania. But unlike the boy-bands of the 1990s, Bolan was a rock'n'roller with a head full of visions and imaginative lyrics in which figures like Alan Freed, John Lennon, and Pasolini could be set in a landscape of Cadillacs, English woods and Tolkein. 'Telegram Sam'

was the first release on his own label, set up under the aegis of EMI, with advance orders bigger than anyone since The Beatles. It was dismissed by many DJs as sounding the same as his others – a remark which applies to pretty much all of Chuck Berry's output and 90 per cent of the blues.

'Telegram Sam' is classic glam-rock, the delightful groove generated by the interaction between Bill Legend's straight-ahead drums, Bolan's syncopated rhythmic boogie and Steve Currie's frequently syncopated bass. The arrangement is essentially carried by the guitars, bass and drums – Mickey Finn's congas are largely inaudible. Bolan's guitar work features probably two acoustics, one each side – it's not so much the chords you can hear but the percussive 'click' of the strumming. There are probably three electrics: two rhythms, left and right, and a third playing the higher A6 riff. This riff interacts with the sax, which 'burps' a two-note motif on the last beat of a bar and the first of the next. Visconti is very restrained with the strings on this, chiefly adding a strong cello part to the chorus, which is doubled by guitar and bass. This three-note motif is a favourite of Bolan's, but here he harmonises it less conventionally with a second inversion chord. On some of the later verses, listen for low pizzicato string notes which double the bass.

CREATIVE TIPS

Try working with six and three-bar phrases... Honour your Ma and Pa... and Chuck Berry.

Verses consist of three six-bar phrases, with Bolan singing over four bars and the riff taking up two. The chorus is a three-bar phrase repeated to make six (this six/three pattern is unusual – I am not aware of any parallel in Chuck Berry – but is a Bolan trademark). The song is in A major with a I-IV change on the verse; the chorus changes key to A minor with a VI-VII-I sequence – this contrast of a major key verse with a minor key chorus is an important feature of the song.

Bolan structures his lyric around various characters, reflecting the high-speed communication and wheeler-dealing of his new-found stardom: "main man" was street-talk of the period (and also the name of David Bowie's management company); Bolan's manager at the time, Tony Secunda, claimed that he was the "Telegram Sam" of the title, and that his assistant was "Jake"; Bolan also name-checked Dylan as "a natural born poet" who is "outasite".

Listen for: Bolan's elfin imitation of Howlin' Wolf's famous "whoo-ooh" on the coda; Legend's drum fills on the break; and Bolan's guitar chord after the word "Sam" in each chorus. Bolan also gets in a charming reference to his "corkscrew hair".

LINKS

There's an acoustic demo on Rabbit Fighter/The Alternate Slider *(Edsel 1994), and a raunchy backing track on* Bump'n'Grind *(Thunderwing Productions/Imperial Records 2000). The* BBC Sessions 1970-76 *includes a version with a double-tracked vocal. The* T.Rex Live In Concert *LP and the* Born To Boogie *film featured live versions.*

"Bolan was a rock'n'roller with a head full of visions and imaginative lyrics"

TRACK 39

JOHN I'M ONLY DANCING

DAVID BOWIE 1972

"What I do and the way I dress is me pandering to my own eccentricities and imagination... Nowadays there is really no difference between my personal life and anything I do on stage. I'm very rarely David Jones any more. I think I've forgotten who David Jones is." (BOWIE, AT THE TIME)

"I thought I might as well take Ziggy out to interviews... Looking back it was completely absurd... I can't deny that experience affected me... I think I put myself very dangerously near the line. Not in a physical sense, but definitely in a mental sense." (BOWIE, WITH HINDSIGHT)

Like 'Positively Fourth Street', 'John I'm Only Dancing' is a single that was never on an album in its day. It's one of the great glam singles, and captures Bowie midway between Ziggy and Aladdin Sane. What's also intriguing about it is the two versions which crop up on Bowie compilations (Bowie re-recorded the song in 1975, and the two versions were actually released together on a single in 1979). I'll call the two versions A and B.

Version B has acoustic guitar to the right, then one on the left. Listen for the electric glissando at 0.06. On this version the electric guitar doubles the bass in single notes, and Mick Ronson's verse guitar lick is mixed down. At the end of the chorus there's a harmony on the lead phrase (0.47), double tracked on the right.

Version A has acoustic guitar on both sides from the start, plus saxophone, and a boomy reverb. Ronson's verse guitar riff is on the left. There are strong guitars going into the chorus, with the unison lead lick left and right, but no harmony on it. Sax appears on choruses 2 and 3, left and right.

WRITER	David Bowie
PRODUCER	David Bowie / Ken Scott
RECORDED	Trident Studios, London
DURATION	2.46
RELEASED	RCA, October 1972
CHART	UK 12 US –

The semitone verse riff, F#-G, is 50 per cent Bolan and 50 per cent Eddie Cochran (the same riff loomed large in the punk revolution of 1976-77, courtesy of The Sex Pistols). It's typical of the functional minimalism of Ronson's approach. The chorus is harmonically more ambiguous as it rises from Em to F and then Em E F G A. The song ends with a coda on A which doesn't connect back to G, it just subsides onto it.

Lyrically, 'John I'm Only Dancing' is sort of 'Excerpts From A Teenage Spaceage Opera' or 'The Kids Are Alright' post-Mars invasion – the kids are still alright but that one's not sure whether he's a boy or a girl... and *that* one has three heads and a raygun. Hhmmm. Bowie sings it like an alien who's just discovered this rilly interesting human activity. The title apology could be taken two ways – a bisexual to his male lover, or two straights about to start a fight .

There are many points of comparison between the two versions: listen for the scream at 2:20 on the B version, and the clear echo on the left. Version A has a vocal "uh-huh" (like Elvis) at 1:10, and far more blatt guitar noise with Ronson's toggle-switch feedback. Notice the handclaps on the chorus, and Ronson's wide vibrato on the coda scale phrase. The cry "touch

CREATIVE TIPS

For toggle-switch feedback on a Les Paul, turn the volume off on one pickup and then flick the switch from the 'on' pickup to the centre... Try writing a song about the dance-hall from an unusual angle...

me" leaps out at 2:14, as does Bowie's next-stop-asteroid-belt "won't someone dance with me" at 2:05 (to which the answer is: not if you're a silicon-based lifeform from the wrong side of Neptune who'll leave a trail of green slime on my collar).

LINKS

Putting aside the name-check in 'All The Young Dudes' and 'Lady Stardust', this is Bowie's best, if inadvertent, tribute to T.Rex – compare the verse G-C-Am changes of 'Hot Love'. (If you're a fan of Ziggy-era Bowie, you probably already know Mike Harvey's painstakingly detailed website, www.5years.com.) For a 1990s take on Bowie, see song 81.

"the kids are still alright, but this one's not sure whether he's a boy or a girl"

TRACK 40

FOCUS II

FOCUS 1972

"I stopped looking at other guitarists around about 18 or 19. I knew what was going on in the world with the Beatles and things like that. Suddenly I said to myself, 'Shut up – I don't want to listen to anything except good music. Just practise my own thing'." (JAN AKKERMAN)

CREATIVE TIPS

Develop a musical phrase by moving it up or down in pitch.

The prosecution case against Progressive Rock... The charges are: 1, That it did knowingly create long musical compositions that were intended to be art (not disposable pop) – a possible dereliction of duty; 2, That it attempted to do this by simply bolting together shorter bits of music while claiming said compositions were on a par with a symphony or concerto; 3, That it did knowingly harass and abuse perfectly honest riffs by forcing them into 5/8, 7/4 or any number of ungainly time signatures; 4, That it encouraged a worship of instrumental virtuosity for its own sake, and committed grievous bodily harm via drum solos, dry ice, mirror balls, and the stabbing of innocent Hammond organs; 5, That it led to the public exposure of sixth-form-level poetry on gatefold sleeves, posing as gems of philosophical insight on a level with the collected works of Marx, Jesus and Kant; 6, That it encouraged the wearing of satin capes in built-up areas and the staging of ice-skating spectaculars... The case seems overwhelming.

Pretention in popular music usually stems from two musical areas (we'll leave lyrics aside). First, by trying to make large-form musical structures without the necessary knowledge of the techniques of development – popular music is essentially about statement and repetition, not development: it finds great short ideas, states them and repeats them; it doesn't need to develop them because it operates on a short time-scale. Secondly, pretension arises when the simplest of ideas are dosed in strings and tons of reverb (see 'new age' mood music, for example).

But Focus were guilty of none of this. Half the band were classically trained at the Amsterdam Conservatoire, and therefore schooled in classical composition. They combined this know-how with a healthy love of improvising in a jazz-rock vein. They could take a short medieval-sounding motif like the one in 'Anonymous' and run with it for five minutes, or a good 26 They also managed to fluke two instrumental hit singles: the yodelling-infested 'Hocus Pocus', a send-up of hard rock with blistering lead guitar by Jan Akkerman, and the delicate 'Sylvia' – the 'Apache' of the 1970s.

WRITER	**Thijs Van Leer**
PRODUCER	**Mike Vernon**
RECORDED	**Sound Techniques Studios, London**
DURATION	**4.03**
RELEASED	**(album, Moving Waves) Polydor, 1972**
CHART	**not a single**

'Focus II' is a 'pocket symphony' – an instrumental that rewards careful listening. It owes little to the American rock-blues tradition, often regarded as the only source of musical integrity and 'soul' – Focus were European in their musical roots.

The mix lays out organ on the left; piano, drums, and bass in the middle; guitar on the right. Akkerman's initial guitar tone is created by manipulation of the volume control on the guitar (as heard on track 34). A mellotron appears at the back of section C and continues thereafter with a lot of reverb on it to give depth.

Here's a chance to practise following the way musical phrases are developed using sequential repetition. 'Focus II' starts with four statements of a four-bar melody, each in a different key: the first has organ and piano in F major; the second with violin tone guitar in Cmajor; the third in G major; and the fourth with distorted high lead in D major. None of the phrases resolve onto its key chord.

The piece proceeds with section B – eight bars in double tempo with a jazzy feel; section C – slightly slower in 7/4; then section D, a one-bar phrase repeated with various modifications. We then get section A (last two phrases only), section B, section D in G with octave phrase, section E with a half-time swing in G mixolydian, and section F – a coda with a James Bond-type guitar line rising from an Emadd9 chord to C/Bb base.

Listen for: the rising mellotron string line in section F at 2:25, going up B C C# D D# E F# as the bass goes from E to Bb; the two stereo drum fills; the piano fill at 2:49, rising up at 3:03; the strings in-between the guitar harmonics 3:04-20 (a four-note answering phrase). At 3:22 the four-chord turnaround is repeated then altered, although the melody stays the same, and finds its way back to the home key of Bb – the average rock band would simply have taken the turnaround and repeated it four times without change.

LINKS

For a writer-producer influenced by the sound of Focus, see track 47. For an instrumental from an earlier era, see track 3.

"it owes little to the American rock-blues tradition"

TRACK 41

RELAY

THE WHO 1973

"We were a weird mixture. I believe Pete and I aimed for the same thing, only from different angles. Pete was either the angry young man or the seeker of truth. I think I was more down to earth. John Entwistle was always the quiet one. He never said much, but he added a lot of humour. And Moon was our comedy, and also very creative in the studio. He would come up with the whackiest ideas, and somehow they came off." (ROGER DALTREY)

"Forget that tired old myth that rock'n'roll is just making records, pulling birds, gettin' pissed and having a good time. That's not what it's all about." (PETE TOWNSHEND)

Between 1969 and 1973 The Who were at their peak, live and in the studio. The concept album *Tommy* had moved them on from their initial phase as a chart singles band; it had given Townshend added courage in pursuing his musical visions. Then came the over-ambitious *Lifehouse* concept, parts of which were salvaged as their best album, *Who's Next*. Townshend was so creative during this period that The Who were also releasing singles that never made it onto albums: 'Let's See Action' (1971), 'Join Together' (recorded four days before 'Relay') and 'Relay' itself. They were on a roll, and the next stop was *Quadrophenia* – in musical terms far superior to *Tommy*. At the time, though, Townshend doubted 'Relay': was he being defensive or facetious when he said, "We're The Who – we can put out crap singles if we want to"? Yet the song turned up in the band's winter 2000 concerts.

WRITER	Pete Townshend
PRODUCER	The Who / Glyn Johns
RECORDED	Olympic Studios, London
DURATION	3.34 single (4.00 box-set)
RELEASED	Track Records, December 1972
CHART	UK 21 US 39

'Relay' has an arresting intro: the dramatic sound of an acoustic guitar spitting blood'n'funk as it emerges from a frequency modulator. The band enter with strummed acoustic guitar on the right, plus bass and drums. As the song develops an electric guitar comes in, again towards the right, providing Pete's trademark power-chords, and in verse 2 playing a single-note riff with the bass. This electric guitar also occasionally breaks into lead phrases, and takes a solo in the instrumental bridge.

The broken-up drumming is unusual for a rock record, as it doesn't supply a regular beat. How did Moon arrive at this rhythm? Did he first try his usual 'continuous fill' drumming and find it didn't work? Instead he plays clumps of drums, in verse 2 almost following the rhythm of the guitar and bass. Entwistle's bass, meanwhile, is typically fluid, with plenty of scale runs.

Harmonically, 'Relay' is archetypal hard rock, with no minor chords: the main sequence is E D A – Townshend's favourite sequence of I *b*VII and IV (as on 'Won't Get Fooled Again'); the pre-chorus uses B E D and A; the chorus is F# to E.

'Relay' has a counter-culture-era lyric in which the key word is revolution and the general themes are democracy, communication, people passing information among themselves. But Townshend usually balances such exhortations with a sense that revolutions are easily corrupted ("hand me down a solution") and that the real, necessary revolution is one in consciousness, for "The only quiet place is inside your soul" (see track 57). The lyric is sung with conviction by Daltrey, who was just perfect barking out this stuff. No-one else among his peers could have done it. Consider the contenders: Robert Plant – too narcissistic/sexual; Paul Rodgers – too introverted and down-key; Steve Winwood – not muscular enough; Joe Cocker – too ravaged; Rod Stewart – too devil-may-care. Fine singers all, but they couldn't have done it. Not even Jagger – the Stones feel was nihilistic and lacked selflessness. Of all the great rock singers, Daltrey alone was capable of expressing the struggle for self-surrender to a greater ideal that made him the perfect voice for many of Townshend's songs.

Listen for: the 'spitting' intro; the bass runs at 1.40; the first bit of lead at 0.39; the piano glissando at 2.42; Daltrey's "yeah" at 1.07, immediately answered by the guitar, and his high vocal at 3.07 and 3.18

CREATIVE TIPS

Write a song where the drums do not supply a steady beat.

LINKS

The version on the box set lasts 25 seconds longer (the single fades out). For an earlier Who track, see 13. For examples of their influence, see tracks 53 and 89

> "the dramatic sound of an acoustic guitar spitting blood'n'funk..."

TRACK 42

PYJAMARAMA

ROXY MUSIC 1973

"The thing that really annoyed people was that we said we were 'inspired amateurs'. We just thought, it's not about the dots or about how technically brilliant you are. Five years later, of course, this was the basis for punk."

(PHIL MANZANERA)

WRITER	**Bryan Ferry**
PRODUCER	**John Anthony**
RECORDED	**London**
DURATION	**2.52**
RELEASED	**Island, March 1973**
CHART	**UK 10 US –**

Along with Bowie, Roxy Music were the intelligent art-rock end of glam, drawing on a host of references which had hitherto been regarded as hopelessly establishment and *infradig*. Ferry's donning of a tuxedo, for one thing, was a shock in rock circles. Rock criticism believed that music started from year zero of 1956 – crooners like Sinatra *et al* and the songwriters on which they drew were out, as was anyone who dressed up (except Peter Gabriel). Roxy also combined synths with traditional rock instrumentation. Still, the male rock fan could forgive seeing Eno all tarted up because they had drummer Paul Thompson, who looked like an average bloke.

'Pyjamarama' is not as weird a single as 'Virginia Plain' – it's more cohesive, and romantic, with typical eye-fluttering, slinky vocals by Ferry. It's a pity Smokey Robinson never did a cover of it – underneath the glam-rock is a song that could easily be a Miracles cut. On the intro Roxy come on all Wagnerian with some Townshend-like power-chords from bug-eyed Phil Manzanera (who once told me that the song used an altered tuning so the progression required only one finger, allowing Ferry to play it live).

'Pyjamarama' has a very simple musical structure: a verse equals a four-bar phrase four times – single four-chord sequence, I I-maj7 I-7 I-6, played in a wiry guitar arpeggio. Verse 1 is followed by a sax break, with two guitars left and right in the background stealing in like howling cats. Verse 2 is followed by a guitar solo at 2:00, with guitars left and right but not playing in unison. The instrumental break uses a Bo Diddley rhythm with maracas.

The title is a witty and sexy lead into to a romantic apology song which Ferry conducts with arch references like "couldn't sleep a wink last night", "bill and coo", and "boogaloo a rhapsody divine" – not the kind of phrases your average sweaty denim-clad rock band used. The lyric builds up to the delightful art-deco pay-off: "Diamonds may be your best friend / But like laughter after tears I'll follow you to the end". Ferry's sly phrasing of "apologise" (1.41) is a quintessential moment in glam rock.

Listen for: the ring of acoustic guitar left and right underneath the electric; Thompson's meaty drum fills with the entry of the bass at 0.16; the bass coming up from a low pitch at the end of each vocal line; the lead guitars' first note overlapping the vocal at 2:00, just before "the end", and deviating from each other in the solo at 2:17 and 2:20-24. The bleeping on the intro is a variation of the famous Motown 'telegraph' sound (0.36), and can also be heard in the verse – it gives a sense of urgency to the communication.

CREATIVE TIPS

If you have a guitar solo, do a second pass without listening to the first and use both panned left and right... Bryan Ferry on songwriting: "Those little notepads you get at hotels, I usually have one of those by the bedside. If anything flashes into my mind then I'll write it down, and hopefully it will find its way into my pocket or suitcase... when it comes to lyric writing time I'll get all these pads out and see if anything there is appropriate for a song."

LINKS

A similar guitar effect to the one in this solo can be heard on track 81. Brian Eno left Roxy shortly after this hit, becoming a cult solo artist and a fine producer (or "enabler" as he might term it) in his own right, successfully "enabling" the likes of Bowie, David Byrne & Talking Heads, Ultravox, Devo, John Cale, U2 and James.

"it's a pity Smokey Robinson never did a cover of it – underneath the glam-rock is a song that could easily be a Miracles cut"

INCIDENT ON 57TH STREET
BRUCE SPRINGSTEEN 1973

"The songs I write don't have particular beginnings and they don't have endings. The camera focuses in and then out." (BRUCE SPRINGSTEEN)

Recently Damon Gough (Badly Drawn Boy) extolled the virtues of side two of Springsteen's second album, suggesting it was one of the greatest ever recorded. He was right on the money. *The Wild, The Innocent And The E Street Shuffle* (from which 'Incident' comes) is a festival of delight. Every song teems with local colour, characters, places – almost like little novellas. At that time Springsteen was playing a kind of funk-rock, and the soul influence warms up the music. He would never be as light-footed as this again. This music is as sensual an experience as being out on the street in early morning sunshine with the smell of coffee and the traces of last night's perfume.

There is a whole audience that didn't pick up on Springsteen until *The River* (1980), and then another crowd who got on board for *Born In The USA* (1984) and promptly got off again. The latter album fixed Springsteen in the mind of millions as a flag-waving pit-bull rocker capable only of a crass air-punching racket. Would they could hear either of the albums Springsteen made before his breakthrough with *Born To Run* (1975): both have the lack of self-consciousness that early recordings tend to possess, and which once lost cannot be recovered.

WRITER	Bruce Springsteen
PRODUCER	Mike Appel / Jim Cretecos
RECORDED	914 Sound Studio, New York
DURATION	7.44
RELEASED	CBS, November 1973
CHART	US 59 (1975) UK 33 (1985)

In 1973 critics dismissed Springsteen as a mix of Dylan and Van Morrison – his own personality and virtues were obscured. For a start, Springsteen has always been much less stylised as a melody writer than Van Morrison, who, like Morrissey, has certain favourite intervals he returns to again and again, regardless of the chord progression.

'Incident On 57th Street' is a love song with a subtle dynamic and the cinematic colour typical of the album. The song has two piano parts, one by David Sancious (whose playing lights up 'New York City Serenade') and the other by Danny Federici. An organ helps fill out the sound. When the drums come in there's a brief and very typical Springsteen guitar solo, on the left, using that wiry Fender sound, lots of pronounced bends and pick attack on the strings; it sounds as though the level is brought up on the last note to make it sustain, because there's an increase in ambient noise on the left at the end of the solo. Listen for the echoed guitar phrases on the right at 0.14. Notice the boxy drum sound – not much reverb and quite bright. Listen for the vocal reverb (on the right) at 4.49 on the word "fight".

The harmony of the song is driven by I, IV, V with IV, often voiced as an expressive major 7. 'Incident' has the extended song structure Springsteen deployed at this time: a verse with three parts to it, a chorus, an edited second verse, and then, just when you are expecting a second chorus, the music is stripped back to a vocal and bass guitar on a variant of the verse at 4.00. The last chorus is only finally reached after a delightful suspended organ chord at 5.02. The song ends with four choruses, each one of which slowly builds in intensity. Chorus 2 is sung with delicacy, and at 5.18 beautiful backing vocals appear. Chorus 3 picks up a bit in intensity, and in chorus 4 distorted electric fills out the middle of the picture. On this chorus Springsteen really tugs at the melody and ends with a sustained note, which is picked up in chorus 5 by a guitar solo. The faders are pulled back on most of the instruments except the ethereal backing vocals and the piano. The E Street Band roars into the distance,

followed by the voices, leaving only the chiming piano arpeggios and a segue straight into the guitar-driven live favourite 'Rosalita'.

The strong, unconcluded narrative focuses on the love affair of Spanish Johnny and Jane. It is full of street incident (as are many of his early songs) and a far cry from the lyrical generalities which mar parts of *The River*. It mentions Romeo & Juliet, and may have influenced some of Dire Straits' material (they employed a later Springsteen pianist, Roy Bittan, on *Love Over Gold*). The chorus phrase "We may find it out on the street tonight" gathers together a host of longings. The lyric's detail is especially good in the 'fire escape" section with lines like "Jane sleeps in sheets damp with sweat / Johnny sits up alone and watches her dream on, dream on". Years before *The Ghost Of Tom Joad*, Springsteen was writing fine narrative songs, as seen here, and in the likes of 'Meeting Across The River' on *Born To Run*.

CREATIVE TIPS

Find two people and write a song about where they're going – if anywhere... On the coda of a song pull back some of the instruments but leave others in place.

LINKS

For a later Springsteen song, see track 80

> "as sensual an experience as being out on the street in the early morning sunshine with the smell of coffee and the traces of last night's perfume"

TRACK 44

NOW I'M HERE

QUEEN 1974

"That song's about experiences on the American tour, which really blew me away. I was bowled over by the amazing aura which surrounds rock music in America." (BRIAN MAY)

This was Queen's third hit single (following 'Seven Seas Of Rhye' and 'Killer Queen') and the second from their third album, *Sheer Heart Attack*. Much resented by critics and seen as something of a manufactured glam band, Queen had a mouthy, camp front man and enough PhDs to start a science faculty. They pitched their initial musical vision midway between Led Zep-style hard rock, prog-rock and glam, with a Spectoresque ambition for layering their music – either through harmonised guitar choirs or multi-tracked vocals. (1974 was a quiet year for Led Zep, so for starved fans this slice of

CREATIVE TIPS

If a thing is worth doing it's worth doing excessively – . sometimes

riffing did nicely as a substitute). Later overshadowed by its follow-up single ('Bohemian Rhapsody'), 'Now I'm Here' is something of a neglected gem – even though at the time it was an *NME* single of the week.

Roy Thomas Baker's approach is typically dense, so there's lot to follow: 'Now I'm Here' starts with damped 5ths from May (possibly three guitars – left, centre and right) and then a descending sequence from D to C to B, similar to that in 'Badge' by Cream. After Mercury's echoed vocal phrases, it erupts on a Who-like Asus4 A Bsus4 B roar ("just a new man") and then crashes into a 'Black-Dog'-type convoluted four-bar riff (which is cleverly edited when it re-appears in the coda).

The arrangement is carried by guitar, bass, drums and vocals until the solo, where you can here piano, and after that a subtle organ part. The general air of carnival extravagance is assisted by the colourful imagery in the lyric – "Your matches still light up the sky" – and a namecheck for "Hoople" (Ian of Mott...?).

For a hard rock song, 'Now I'm Here' has plenty of musical ideas to match its big arrangement. The song makes much use of transposition – taking phrases and moving them up in pitch. The verse daisy-chains a sequence of V-I cadences: G C A D B E C# F#, for example, on the "whatever came of you and me" bit; and the verses in general don't always finish on the same chord. The coda rocks out with some Chuck Berry double-stops.

WRITER	**Brian May**
PRODUCER	**Roy Thomas Baker**
RECORDED	**Trident / Wessex / Rockfield / AIR Studios, UK**
DURATION	**4.14**
RELEASED	**EMI, December 1974**
CHART	**UK 11 US –**

LINKS

It's clearly a tribute to Chuck Berry, with its "Go, go little Queenie" reference - three years after Bolan had alluded to the same song in 'Get It On' by singing "and meanwhile I'm still thinking". May went on to do a fine, full-blown 1950s pastiche on 'Crazy Little Thing Called Love' (1980). The D-C- G/B progression is also found in songs 47 and 85.

"they pitched their initial musical vision midway between Led Zep-style hard rock, prog rock and glam, with a Spector-esque ambition for layering their music"

TRACK 45

KASHMIR

LED ZEPPELIN 1975

"We went to Bombay in 1972 and recorded 'Friends' and 'Four Sticks' with Indian musicians there. We did that while people were still trying to figure out how I played 'Whole Lotta Love'... The nature of how good we were is in the riffs. We had all these multi-faceted diamonds. There should never have been any boundaries. And we made sure there weren't." (JIMMY PAGE)

So much for the pretenders to the crown... but what about the champs? Although not as widely known as 'Whole Lotta Love', 'Rock And Roll', 'Black Dog' or 'Stairway To Heaven', 'Kashmir' is one of Led Zep's finest moments. Even people who cannot stand the vast proportion of what they did have a grudging respect for its epic power – even if only to compliment Bonham's drumming. In 1979 when Paul Morley reviewed their Knebworth gig (the scathing "Ghosts of Progressive Rock Past" *NME* piece) he singled out 'Kashmir' as one of the few moments when Zep lived up to what he considered their over-inflated reputation.

Physical Graffiti was Led Zep's sixth album and their first double. After nearly five years of hectic touring and recording, the band took a holiday in the late summer of 1973 – which turned into an 18-month spell away from the limelight (during which Plant had an operation on his ravaged vocal chords). Back in the studio, they continued and extended the experimentation that had marked *Houses Of The Holy* (1973) – the length of the new material, plus the fact that they had songs in the vaults, made them decide *Physical Graffiti* would be a double album. It was released to rave reviews (and reaching number 1 in the US and UK), in an expensive sleeve with cut-out windows through which a variety of photos could be lined up.

WRITER	**Jimmy Page / Robert Plant / John Bonham**
PRODUCER	**Jimmy Page / Andy Johns**
RECORDED	**Headley Grange / Olympic Studios, London**
DURATION	**8.31**
RELEASED	**(album, Physical Graffiti) Swansong, February 1975**
CHART	**not a single**

Unlike their later imitators, Zep were eager to try their hand at different styles while retaining their own intensity: on *Graffiti* they proved they had no contestants when it came to Ye Noble Arte Of Banging Heads, but there was also acoustic stuff, blues-based numbers, and cross-bred rock-funk. They showed a softer side with 'Ten Years Gone', one of their best ballads and a showcase for Page's guitar arranging skills. And if that wasn't enough, they gave you two slices of the mystic East with 'In The Light' and 'Kashmir'.

'Kashmir' is built on a powerful but steady drum beat, a bass which moves in octave Ds, and a four-note riff. At various points mellotron orchestra effects are overdubbed by John Paul Jones in a descending sequence. The guitar, in DADGAD tuning, is not particularly prominent. In terms of construction, it has the intro riff, two verses, a bridge section on A ("Baby I've been flying"), a chorus that moves restlessly from G to A ("All I see"), two more verses, the chorus, and the coda, where an ascending scale of G A B*b* C D E F G A B C# appears, replete with little Middle Eastern trumpet flourishes (session musicians were brought in to build up the horns etc).

CREATIVE TIPS

Sometimes parts in an arrangement can deliberately obscure one-another for dramatic effect.

The clever main chord riff is D5-D+5 D6 D7 – it's like a sonic equivalent of an Escher optical illusion: every time you get to the end of the riff it sounds as though it is a bit higher – but isn't. This is even more pronounced when the descending sequence is laid over the top –

sing and tap out the main riff when it disappears behind the descending sequence and you'll be amazed how it emerges...

Lyrically, this is one of Plant's spiritual quest pieces, which usually, and rather handily, combine spiritual attainment with consummation of a more carnal variety... "Let me take you there" he howls over the fading coda, like a hormonally-challenged wolf in a sunset. *Not aarff*, as Alan 'Fluff' Freeman would say. The Kashmir of the title has in the end little to do with the actual place, but is about the trials and tribulations of an inner journey. Unlike The Who, Led Zep were always the most apolitical of bands – one of their quintessentially 1970s qualities. Border conflicts between Pakistan and India? Terrorism, religious extremists, the legacies of colonialism...? Our Percy's just not interested. Led Zep's 'Kashmir' exists in the imagination. It's safer.

Musically, this track is largely a showcase for the power of Bonham's drumming – including some sizzling snare-rolls on the fade.

LINKS

In concert the band slowed it down a little, every kick drum beat sounding like a depth-charge going off (1975 is probably the vintage to seek out). Page & Plant revisited it in the 1990s for the No Quarter *project and produced a fine alternate version. 'Kashmir's hypnotic drum beat not only served for the soundtrack of* Godzilla, *courtesy of Puff Daddy, but inspired countless bands – including The Mission (see track 73), Kingdom Come, Deep Purple, The Cult, and Rage Against The Machine – to attempt to write their own 'Kashmir'-type epic.*

> "a sonic equivalent of an Escher optical illusion"

TRACK 46

SPERED HOLLVEDEL / DELIVRANCE
ALAN STIVELL 1975

"I'm being pulled in two directions... deep in myself my aim is to do today's music, and do new music every day, even if it's based on my Celtic roots, but at the same time I always want to show that I have authentic roots." (ALAN STIVELL)

In popular music some musicians are notable as instrumentalists, some for fusing styles, and some for the political/spiritual vision they espouse. Alan Stivell is all three. Born in Brittany in 1944, he plays the Celtic harp, and has successfully wedded the ancient purity of its sound with electric guitars, bass and drums, and through his music has championed Breton/Celtic culture. Better-known in mainland Europe, he nevertheless has a small but passionate audience in the UK.

The best of his early solo recordings is the award-winning *Renaissance Of The Celtic Harp*

(1971). Steeped in the folk music of Brittany, Scotland, Wales and Ireland, Stivell took the melodies and rhythms of Celtic music and turned them into electric folk. *From Celtic Roots* (1973) is a fine representation of what he could do in the studio. Both the live albums – *A L'Olympia* and *A Dublin* (1975) – show his band to good advantage

A Dublin has the usual exhilarating jigs and reels and odd-time rhythms, but it opens with something of a political manifesto and a chunk of Celtic idealism: 'Spered Hollvedel' ('Universal Spirit') begins with a typically Celtic tune on organ, taken up in turn by bagpipes and guitar. Dan Ar Bras gives one of the best demonstrations I know of how to use feedback in a musical way, his sustained notes melting into the higher overtones (at 2.23, 2.43-45). This flows into Stivell's 'Delivrance' (OK, I've cheated, there are two tracks here, but they run seamlessly together – one preludes the other), a kind of Breton rap over a lush chord sequence that sounds like The Smiths rehearsing in a megalithic tomb. If you're not hooked by these two tracks you're probably immune to Stivell's spell. If you're an incurable romantic you won't be able to resist, and the modern world will never look the same again.

WRITER	**Traditional, arr Stivell / Stivell**
PRODUCER	**Alan Stivell / Peter Rice**
RECORDED	**By Frank Owen on the Island Mobile, Dublin National Stadium**
DURATION	**3.57 / 2.00**
RELEASED	**(album A Dublin/E Dulenn) Fontana, 1975**
CHART	**not a single**

The solo organ starts on the left, but other notes enter on the right, with bass guitar in the centre playing mostly roots. The bombard (a double-reeded wind instrument) enters on the right to play the melody the second time. Notice that the last bar of each section has a chord on each beat. The guitar enters at 2:11 along with the string sound. On the fourth melody, at 3:07, bagpipes and drums enter with the guitar playing a counter melody. Listen for the change of register on the guitar as it goes up higher at 3.32. The second track has strummed acoustic, and lots of 'flams' – where the snare is hit with both sticks. The bass lets loose with plenty of syncopated phrases.

The music is in the Celtic key of C minor (the key used for harp tuning). There are plenty of suspended 4ths, which give much emotional force (at 0.46). Notice how the fourth phrase resolves via a suspended 4th onto an unexpected major chord (1.42).

As with Le Mystere Des Voix Bulgares and the Cocteau Twins, there is a special pleasure in listening to lyrics you can't necessarily understand. The original album sleeve provided a literal translation, which described how the Breton spirit seeks to maintain friendship with France yet seeks to relate to "our closest brothers" in Wales, Scotland and Ireland. Stivell mentions the suppression of Breton identity and language and then promises that they will help with an ecological revival, bring about political justice for the oppressed from Brittany and Spain, from Mali to Chile, Indo-China to Palestine. Brittany will be the "centre of the inhabited world", a refuge, eventually looking to the frontiers of the earth and sea "to the limits of this world and the next". Stivell's impassioned delivery, taking full benefit of the oratorical poetry of the French accent, sounds like a man demanding entry to paradise, and who won't take no for an answer.

CREATIVE TIPS

Liven a chord sequence by inserting bars where chords change on each beat... Purchase more Alan Stivell records – this man is a long way behind Paul McCartney in the musician billionaire stakes.

LINKS

Kate Bush invited Stivell to play harp on her album The Sensual World ***(1989)***

"there is a special pleasure in listening to lyrics you can't necessarily understand"

TRACK 47

MORE THAN A FEELING

BOSTON 1976

"I first became fascinated with a wide stereo spectrum when I heard the song 'Hocus Pocus' by Focus. That had a lot to do with the kind of production I went for in Boston." (TOM SCHOLZ)

Along with Fleetwood Mac, US rock band Boston defined Adult Oriented Rock in the mid-1970s. They were led by Tom Scholz, who learned piano as a child and had a Masters in mechanical engineering from the Massachusetts Institute of Technology. He recorded much of the first album in the basement studio of his apartment, using a Les Paul guitar and an enthusiasm for multi-tracking guitar parts.

The arrangement of 'More Than A Feeling' is chockfull of guitars – acoustic left and right, 12-string, electric rhythm and lead. The stereo drums use a wood-block in the gentler verse and bring in the snare (along with the handclaps) on the chorus. The main vocal is double-tracked, with backing vocals on the chorus. At 3:39 the highest vocal note (G) appears to have a guitar note above it (B) to generate a harmony.

WRITER	Tom Scholz
PRODUCER	Tom Scholz / John Boylan
RECORDED	Home studio, Boston / Capitol Studios, Los Angeles
DURATION	(album) 4.20, (single) 3.25
RELEASED	Epic, October 1976
CHART	US 5 UK 22 (in 1977)

The album version is longer than the single. It runs: intro, verse 1, chorus, verse 2, chorus, solo, verse 3, chorus, with an extra link to the last chorus. The single version is far better because it builds dramatically straight after the first chorus, editing out some of the intro D C G riff (a sequence also used in Cream's 'Badge'), and going from verse 1 and a chorus straight to the bridge and solo. (The single edit is from 1.08-2.16 of the album version.)

The chorus hook is a I IV VI V turnaround – G C Em D. Compare and contrast 'Smells Like Teen Spirit' (see track 78). It's the kind of turnaround which sorts out those hard rock bands who have something of a 'pop' sensibility lurking beneath the surface (in the same way that some dinosaurs had two brains) from those who don't. You wouldn't find such a major/minor turnaround on a Metallica or Deep Purple song, but you would find it on a track by Rainbow (think of 'Since You've Been Gone). Scholz puts in a nice touch with the chromatic move from C to Eb at the end of the chorus, and then Em7 just before "I see my Marianne". The guitar solo is something of a 1960s throwback – it's a melody rather than a bunch of licks and, distortion aside, its contours are reminiscent of Hank Marvin and 'Wonderful Land'. Its radio-friendly lyric is about the power music possesses to bring back the past; it's about love and memory.

Listen for: guitar harmonies at 2.58; the guitar glissando at 0.40; the great jangly Em7-A7sus4 change at 1.07-1.11 and 2.16-20; the crunch section at 3.17; the feedback note G at 3.47-56 which ties the last pre-chorus to the chorus; and the drums at 4.11-12.

CREATIVE TIPS

Try writing a song that follows the structure of the edited 'More Than A Feeling' – go straight from chorus 1 to a bridge that builds the excitement up to the last verse.

LINKS

Scholz denied being into Brian May, but his recording could be seen as a development of what May was doing with Queen in 1974-75. Scholz's other claim-to-fame was as developer of a power-soak for guitarists (to get distortion at low volumes), and the Rockman headphone guitar amp.

TRACK 48

MARQUEE MOON

TELEVISION 1977

"I came out of playing piano when I was a kid, not really remembering much except the melodic sense and the idea of two hands playing independent parts. Then I went to saxophone, which had to do with making a note do something... There really isn't a chorus in that song. What would you call it? A violent contraction. An answer to a verse. Which didn't ask a question." (TOM VERLAINE)

Television was a short-lived group consisting of Tom Verlaine (lead vocal/guitar), Richard Lloyd (guitar/vocal), Fred Smith (bass/vocal), and Billy Ficca (drums). They made two albums in the late 1970s, and a third in the early 1990s. Their first album, *Marquee Moon*, was a gem, removed from the excesses of AOR yet more sophisticated than punk/new wave: here were guitars used in a new way, and solos that owed nothing to the blues.

The title track is a rough diamond and, like most rough diamonds, all the more moving in its unexpected grandeur – like the Carpenters releasing some ace slice of heavy metal, it's the kind of track that has you scratching your head and asking, how did they come up with this? It has a mysterious power too, emotionally expressive in a way neither the vocal nor the lyric can account for. It is also a song whose effect depends on its length. I know it's treason to say this, but something like Led Zep's 'In My Time Of Dying' would be no less powerful if it were seven minutes instead of 11; but you could not cut 'Marquee Moon' without crippling it.

WRITER	Tom Verlaine
PRODUCER	Andy Johns / Tom Verlaine
RECORDED	A & R Studios, New York
DURATION	10.35
RELEASED	Elektra / Asylum, March 1977
CHART	UK 30 US –

There is a lovely story connected with the making of the album. Rock producer Andy Johns flew to New York to engineer the first album, and spent his first hours setting up the drums. Tom Verlaine came into the studio for the first day's recording to find, to his horror, that Johns had happily provided him with John Bonham's huge drum sound. He then had to insist on a much drier production.

'Marquee Moon' starts with the guitar on the right playing 4ths, while the one on the left plays a D D6 change, and bass and drums are in the middle. During the chorus at 1.05-21 a piano plays high on the right and a third guitar enters in the middle. Richard Lloyd takes the first guitar solo at 2.58 after the major 7 chord at 2.54. The middle instrumental starts at 4.27 with a reprise of the intro.

CREATIVE TIPS

Like 'Start Me Up', 'Marquee Moon' is a song that fools with the listener's sense of where the beat is at the start: the initial guitar chords might be taken as being on beats 1 and 3, but when the drums enter it is clear they are in fact on beats 2 and 4. So try disguising your beat.

At 4.51 Verlaine's guitar solo starts tentatively on a root note, then at 5.07 starts to move up, with a chordal guitar appearing on the left at 5.40, and the piano thickening the sound. At 7.09 the lead guitar starts a long climb over an open D-string on a D mixolydian scale (the C natural can be heard at 7.45). Then after some thirds and a staccato hammered figure at 8.13, the song reaches a climax of unexpected beauty from 8.42-9.18, as the lead guitar chirrups over a stereo guitar triplet arpeggio. This triplet of B D F# keeps going even though the chords change. The song is completed by another intro riff and verse, and ends with the single note guitar scale phrase.

The lyrics of 'Marquee Moon' are obscure, and though some lines like "I remember how the darkness doubled" catch the ear, you are not likely to worry about it while you listen to those guitar lines.

LINKS

Television were central to the New York new wave scene thriving at the club CBGBs, which also spawned bands like Talking Heads and Blondie (whom bassist Smith also played with). Their early demos were produced by Brian Eno. Original bassist Richard Hell went on to punk legends like The Heartbreakers and the Voidoids.

> "guitars used in a new way, and solos that owed nothing to the blues"

TRACK 48

GOD SAVE THE QUEEN

SEX PISTOLS 1977

"The reason we all got on was basically because we all were into the Faces. In fact the first thing I played at a sort of audition... was a song called "Three Button Hand Me Down" from the Faces' first album." (GLEN MATLOCK)

"He [Matlock] would write these songs and play them to us on guitar and they sounded diabolical. And he wanted me to play the same as him.... the chords were jazz almost – all minors and 7ths, wanky Beatles chords... If he'd done what he wanted with those songs they wouldn't have sold shit." (STEVE JONES)

An incendiary rock single that connected with the times, released in the year of the Queen's silver jubilee, and taken from a seminal 1970s rock album, *Never Mind The Bollocks*, which, for all its punk despair, is riotous fun. It was the Pistols' second single, recorded for A&M then withdrawn, then re-issued by Virgin, and it cemented their reputation as public enemy number 1.

WRITER	Steve Jones / Glen Matlock / Johnny (Lydon) Rotten / Paul Cook
PRODUCER	Chris Thomas
RECORDED	Wessex / AIR Studios, London
DURATION	3.16
RELEASED	Virgin, May 1977
CHART	UK 2 US –

Johnny Rotten's vocal style is one of the most recognisable in rock history. Like Dylan, his refusal to pitch conventionally expresses rebellion. The off-key sneering power can be traced to several features (to analyse it musically, in a very un-punk manner), such as his vibrato-less use of *b*3 and *b*5 notes (there's a *b*5 at 1.22 on "seems" and a *b*3 at 0.36 on "being"), and his use of a quarter-

tone between the $b3$ and the normal 3rd, as at 1.28 on "parade". The era-defining "we mean it, maann" (1.53 and 2.21) uses a 4th, a hard D against an A chord. The lyrics – a bilious and cynical tirade – are given further force by sarcastic touches like the rolled "r" in "moron" and the pseudo-exultant exclamation of "money".

As is often the case, the band's music was hardly revolutionary. The semitone shifts for the main riff, A*b*-A, D*b*-D are pinched from 1950s rock'n'roll like Eddie Cochran, and Steve Jones' guitar breaks recycled Chuck Berry with overdrive on a Les Paul through a Vox AC30 (with only one speaker working). It was the second time in the 1970s that rock had gone back to its roots to revive itself: the lead is not far removed from Brian May's on 'Now I'm Here' (track 44) – the intent, however, was entirely different. It was a long time since the UK music scene had heard a band play with such ferocity and an attitude that gave what was left of the 1960s musical legacy a good kicking. Here was a band that wasn't interested in peace and love.

CREATIVE TIPS

Sometimes not hitting the dots is more important than hitting them.

The verse is in two sections, the second part going up to an E-B change. During the guitar solo the main change is transposed to F#– B. The "no future" coda hung its disdain on a queasy D C# B A chord progression, with all four as majors (in A major you would expect D C#m Bm A, as used by The Jam in 'When You're Young').

The production uses a narrow stereo image: you can hear the drums panned out left and right, but the guitars seem to be pretty central with the vocal. Listen for: the typical Pistols' 'galloping tom' fill at the end of verse 1; the busy kick-drum part; and the octave G in the gap before verse 2 – an artful touch on a record whose sheer power might lead you to think it had just crawled out of the sludge at the bottom of the Thames.

LINKS

Producer Chris Thomas has enjoyed a colourful career, from co-producing (and even playing) on the Beatles White Album, *to punk-production legend on* Bollocks, *via Pink Floyd's* Dark Side Of The Moon.

> "it was a long time since the UK music scene had heard a band play with such ferocity"

TRACK 50

KNOWING ME, KNOWING YOU

ABBA 1977

"I was just working from images. I saw a man walking through an empty house for the last time as a symbol of divorce. I just described what I saw. I hadn't been through that myself then." (BJORN ULVAEUS)

The best of Abba's music has transcended the Euro disco scene with which they were associated. This was their ninth hit in the UK (fifth number 1) and marked a break away from the lightweight subject matter of the singles cast in the mould of their Eurovision hit 'Waterloo'. 'Knowing Me, Knowing You' was the first of Abba's mini-epics of domestic angst: the chorus is sodden with fatalism as the title repeats, on the way to which we go on a tour of lonely rooms where children used to play, etc.

This is classic pop songwriting, where hooks come thick and fast. Abba songs are like a rich dessert in which any one of the layers would have been fine on its own, but as you go on eating you find one delight after another. 'Dancing Queen' is the obvious example: there's plenty of fun to be had following the rhythm section (especially the hi-hat work and bassline), and the classic high piano octaves which punctuate it (also to be found on 'Oliver's Army', 'Walk Away Renee', and 'I Close My Eyes And Count To Ten').

WRITER	**Benny Andersson / Bjorn Ulvaeus / Stig Anderson**
PRODUCER	**Benny Andersson / Bjorn Ulvaeus / engineered by Michael Tretow**
RECORDED	**Metronome Studios, Stockholm, Sweden**
DURATION	**4.00**
RELEASED	**(UK) Epic (US) Atlantic, February 1977**
CHART	**UK 1 US 14**

In terms of production, Abba records sound 'fizzy' because of the synths, the abundance of high frequencies, and the way the female vocals are treated. It may be they approached the mix in a similar manner to Motown in the 1960s, shaping the sound so the records would cut through on car-radios and small domestic speakers.

'Knowing Me, Knowing You' is ushered in with an eighth-note stereo electric piano figure that sounds like it fell off a Supertramp record. This is supported by vibes and an acoustic guitar, while an acoustic piano comes in on the second half of the verse. The latter part of the verse ("walking through...") deploys a suspended 4th chord on "eyes" to create drama, and you can hear a hint of a guitar power-chord. The song also uses a twin-lead guitar part as a link after the chorus, where the solidity of the I-III-IV-V progression is reassuring after the inventive chord movement under lines like "breaking up is never easy I know". The chorus keeps moving away from the key chord of D, displacing it, whereas on the guitar link D sits squarely at the front of the phrase.

Listen for: the spoken vocal echo on the second phrase, and the hook "uh-huh"; on the chorus there is a high woodwind sound which sketches the melody an octave or so higher; and there's an impressive piece of vocal arrangement – not only parallel harmonies, but three different lines, one low down, and the higher one splits to the left on "this time".

LINKS

At the time regarded as something of an embarrassment by hipper music fans and critics, especially in the post-punk era, Abba have since enjoyed a re-appraisal and their classic songwriting abilities (and pervasive influence on popular culture) acknowledged, and celebrated in both music and film.

CREATIVE TIPS

To make a simple chord sequence more interesting, displace chord I from the start or end of the phrase into the middle.

TRACK 51

WUTHERING HEIGHTS

KATE BUSH 1978

"I wrote it in my flat, sitting at the upright piano one night in March, at about midnight. There was a full moon and the curtains were open, and every time I looked up for ideas, I looked at the moon. Actually it came quite easily. I couldn't seem to get out of the chorus – it had a really circular feel to it ... I had originally written something more complicated, but I couldn't link it up, so I kept the first bit and repeated it. I was really pleased, because it was the first song I had written for a while." (KATE BUSH)

Kate Bush is one of the UK's most undervalued musical talents – her achievement yet to be fully appreciated. Her own disdain for live appearances and the promotional games of the music industry, coupled with an increasing gap between albums (eight years at time of writing...) are part of the reason. The other is this song – a milestone that became a millstone. Few debut singles in pop have had the impact of 'Wuthering Heights' (and, ironically, it was the debut she insisted on, as EMI had scheduled 'James And The Cold Gun'). The story of two of the most famous lovers in world literature, delivered by a stratospheric voice over an orchestral arrangement, captured the public imagination to such a degree that, ever since, it seems loathe to accept much else from Bush – she's still widely associated with this one song, despite her excellent work over 20-odd years.

WRITER	Kate Bush
PRODUCER	Andrew Powell
RECORDED	AIR Studios, London
DURATION	4.40
RELEASED	EMI, January 1978
CHART	UK 1 US –

To condense the essence of Emily Bronte's novel into a short song was a remarkable feat: Bush homed in on the relationship between Heathcliff and the first Cathy, singing the song from Cathy's point-of-view. In February 1978 she said: "I loved writing it ... It was a real challenge to precis the whole mood of a book ... Also, when I was a child I was always called Cathy, not Kate, and I just found myself able to relate to her as a character. It's so important to put yourself in the role of the person in a song. There's no half-measures. When I sing that song, I am Cathy."

It begins with a twice-repeated high piano motif; then the verse dramatises Cathy's passion and the other-worldly atmosphere of the book with a progression of four major chords – A F E and C# – where both the F and the C# are unexpected. C# major is in fact the true key, not the A major on which the song begins. The verse also has a pre-chorus built around Fm. The chorus uses a four-chord turnaround involving chords I, II, IV and V, but puts them in such an order that the sequence never stays long on the key chord of C# – this is the part she found she could not get out of when she was composing it. There's a fine middle eight too, perhaps the creepiest section, where Kate sings in a more anguished way.

CREATIVE TIPS

For a lyric idea, try to capture the atmosphere or themes of a famous book

LINKS

It's always fascinating to see an artist re-visit a recording and try to re-do it, as Bush did with 'Wuthering Heights' for the 1986 compilation The Whole Story. *She told* Q *magazine in 1991: "It sounded very dated to me: my voice sounded so young, the production*

sounded so Seventies. I like the idea of taking the song I'm most associated with, and making it me now as opposed to a very young girl, as I was in 1977". But going back and re-recording the vocal was only going to be at best a triumph of technique and self-consciousness over fortuitous innocence. What resulted from this revisionist impulse was an assault on her youthful self and her most famous song, which seemed almost (if understandably) resentful. The updating consists of adding more reverb and a new, lower-pitched vocal, which is more up-front in the mix, less integrated with the instruments. She can't quite get the high note at the end of the middle-eight, and her scat-singing of the guitar solo is about as endearing as watching Hello Mum being spray-canned over an Old Master. Ironically, from the perspective of a new century, the 1986 version sounds no more contemporary than the original.

> "there's a fine middle-eight too, perhaps the creepiest section"

TRACK 52

AIN'T TALKING 'BOUT LOVE

VAN HALEN 1978

"We went in and did our first album the way we play live. I asked Ted Templeman and [engineer] Donn Landee, 'Can I just play the way I play live?' and they're going, 'Sure – do whatever you want'." (EDWARD VAN HALEN)

While the UK reverberated to the noisy clatter of the punk/new-wave bands, over in the States another rock group found a new way forward. If you're feeling depressed put away that Smiths album (yes, I know they're very good, *but*...) – stick Van Halen's exuberant debut on instead. Much of its inspiration and energy derives from a certain guitar virtuoso: Van Halen was the first guitarist since Hendrix to shake up rock guitar technique and open a door of sonic possibilities – though he had less to say emotionally than Hendrix.

WRITER	Eddie Van Halen / Alex Van Halen / Michael Anthony / David Lee Roth
PRODUCER	Ted Templeman
RECORDED	Sunset Sound Recorders, Los Angeles
DURATION	3.47
RELEASED	(album, Van Halen), Warner Brothers, February 1978
CHART	not a single

He didn't *invent* 'tapping' (any day now someone will discover that the previously unheard-of Sunny Jim Crowbar, friend of Robert Johnson, actually used to 'tap' on his back porch of a hot summer evening back in 1941, but he just refused to do it on record for blues chronicler Harry Smith...); but Eddie certainly popularised this

guitar-hammering technique – which a host of less-talented rock guitarists persistently abused throughout the 1980s, until grunge rose up out of Seattle and cried, "Enough already with the widdling".

Tapping is a guitar technique where fast clusters of notes are obtained by using both hands on the neck, forcefully fretting the string by striking the picking hand's fingers on the fretboard. Overdrive and amplification make these otherwise not-so-loud notes perfectly usable. Van Halen's showpiece instrumental 'Eruption' became a rite-of-passage for aspiring guitarists, just as Clapton's 'Hideaway' had been for a previous generation and Stevie Ray Vaughan's 'Rude Mood' would become in the 1980s. In other hands Van Halen's techniques became mere pyrotechnics. In Van Halen's playing they usually feel like an extension of his fundamental musical personality: mercurial, witty, impatient, devil-may-care (a wider audience heard this character through Eddie's playing on Michael Jackson's 'Beat It').

The guitarist found a perfect complement in David Lee Roth's vocals. Never mind Plant and the squeezing of lemons, Roth's feral howl has the pheromone content of a sweaty football dressing room. He sings 'Ain't Talkin' 'Bout Love', and the rest of the album, with the gum-chewing insouciance of a man who spends those little gaps between songs bungee-jumping into the Grand Canyon, returning seconds later with a grin and a rose between his teeth. Listen for the relish with which Roth sings, "My love is rotten to the core" at 1.12 and at 2.22. As for the bridge, where he sings, "I've been to the edge / And I stood and looked down" – is this a terrifying glimpse into the heart of an existential darkness? Of despair, doubt, fear?... Nah. It's another opportunity for a bungee-jump. Wa-a-a-a-yyyyy to go-o-o-o....

CREATIVE TIPS

Try writing a guitar riff around arpeggiated chords instead of single notes

Some of the record's power comes from the production – essentially a recording of a hot rock band playing live, with only a couple of overdubs, such as the backing vocals on the hookline. The famous arpeggio riff (based on Am, G and C) cranks in on the left, and you can hear the notes racketing about in the reverb on the right. Drums are central, with the bass slightly to the right. Van Halen's legendary 'brown sound' guitar tone is a mixture of echo/distortion and phasing on a customised Strat with a fat Gibson humbucking pickup at the bridge, played through a Marshall Super Lead 100-watt amp – few bands or producers would have resisted doubling the guitar riff on the right, but it sounds amazingly full as it is. The guitar solo is doubled on the right, though, on an electric sitar guitar – try moving the balance from side to side and see what you hear.

Like Mark Knopfler's lead on 'Sultans Of Swing' (though a different sound), Van Halen's guitar provides the track almost with a second 'voice'. Among the guitar highlights on 'Ain't Talkin...' are the first guitar glissando in the first chorus, the phased harmonics at 2.05-18, and the tremolo 'dive-bombing' at 3.33 and 3.42.

LINKS

Living Colour's album **Vivid** ***offers a similar spectacle of a hard rock band recorded with minimal overdubs – see track 74.***

> "Van Halen was the first guitarist since Hendrix to shake up rock guitar technique"

TRACK 53

WHEN YOU'RE YOUNG

THE JAM 1979

"Some people have described this song as defeatist and pessimistic... well, I don't think so at all..." (PAUL WELLER, ONSTAGE AT THE RAINBOW, 1979)

"I think bands have a tendency to give themselves all the credit for what goes onto a successful record. I know we did. It's only now that I realise we'd have been thrashing about in the wilderness if Vic hadn't been there". (PAUL WELLER, 1992)

WRITER	Paul Weller
PRODUCER	Vic Coppersmith-Heaven
RECORDED	Townhouse Studios, London
DURATION	3.10
RELEASED	Polydor, August 1979
CHART	UK 17 US –

During the late 1970s The Jam were one of the biggest-selling rock acts in the UK, with 19 chart singles between 1977 and 1982. Although initially branded a punk band, their affiliation was actually to the 1960s mod scene and bands like The Who, the Small Faces and soul music – these influences bore fruit on their third album *All Mod Cons* (1979) and the singles that followed, 'Strange Town' and 'When You're Young', neither of which were on an album at the time. The Jam ploughed a narrow emotional furrow – the angst of youth, as idealism encountered the real world and soured into pessimism. They were a trio driven by Rick Buckler's robotic drumming, Bruce Foxton's running basslines, and the 'ard-as-nails barrow-boy vocals of Paul Weller. But their brutal live sound gave no hint of the poetry of songs like 'Life From A Window', 'Tonight At Noon' or 'Fly' – songs beyond the reach of any of the other new wave groups.

'When You're Young' is typical Jam: bright, cracking drums, clanky Rickenbacker bass (apparently recorded in stereo to provide two tones – one trebly, one not), and guitars left and right. Weller took a Rickenbacker guitar and dirtied it up by pushing it through a Marshall stack – an unconventional guitar/amp paring. The resulting guitar sound was once described as being able to strip paint off a wall at 100 yards. Weller sings a vocal harmony with bassist Foxton, who also sings the odd lead line (not uncommon in the band's arrangements). A fast eighth-note guitar figure comes in on the right in the second section of the verse. The dub section, 1.56-2.09, mimics reggae (similar touches adorn 'Eton Rifles' and 'Going Underground'), and has an answering guitar figure that goes right, left, right. Listen also for the snare roll at 2.14. There's no separate chorus – the title hook is incorporated into the verse. One clever arrangement detail is that, at the start of the verse, the guitar stays on an A chord while the bass moves from A to F# and E, implying the chords A F#m and E. 'When You're Young' is in A mixolydian, with G as chord *b*VII.

Weller was one of the better lyricists of the new wave/punk scene. 'When You're Young' is a pessimistic portrayal (despite Weller's claims) of a world in which the ideals of youth are bound to be defeated. It has many witty phrases, like "the world is your oyster but your future's a clam" – a line Morrissey could have penned, though not sung with the hectoring force Weller brings to it. The forces reigned against youth are pictured in a dice/board/king/pawn metaphor. Anyone who cares anything about rock has the opening three lines etched on their hearts: "Love is timeless, days are long when you're young / Used

CREATIVE TIPS

We don't hear enough of the magic art of harmonised feedback – there's a fine example in this song's D C#m Bm A coda. At 1.01 a high guitar plays a five-note phrase which ends in feedback on "time" until 1.12 (same thing happens at 1.39-1.51). In the coda the first guitar note is an F#, which feeds back at a high C#, and the second note is an A, which feeds back an octave up. On 'Strange Town' Weller gets three guitars going like this – it's a way of doing harmonised guitar which avoids the bluster of May or Scholz's more baroque confections.

to fall in love with everyone / Any guitar and any bass drum". The coda's final image of lights "going out in thousands of homes and millions of flats" is unexpected and touching – a humane gesture such as rock rarely attempts. It would be pleasing to imagine that The Smiths' 'There Is A Light That Never Goes Out' is an answer to this bleak vision.

LINKS

You can enjoy more of Weller's barbed guitar playing on 'And Through The Wire', a song on Peter Gabriel's third album. For another example of an implied chord sequence, see U2's 'With Or Without You' (track 72).

> "their brutal live sound gave no hint of the poetry in their songs"

TRACK 54

LONDON CALLING

THE CLASH 1979

"People always used to ask us if they listened to the lyrics in America. I think it's rash to presume they didn't. I think they knew damn well what was going on. Anyway, maybe the message wasn't in the lyrics. Maybe it was in the energy, the vigour, the drive." (JOE STRUMMER)

In the class of '77, The Clash were the Stones to the Sex Pistols' Beatles, with The Jam as The Who. There's much to be said against The Clash: all that cheap revolutionary posturing, the bullet belts, army fatigues – it's the dumb association that says my argument is right because I've got a big stick; the macho association of authority with violence. Actually, if The Clash made a subversive record it was 'Rock The Casbah' – at least there they specified a worthy target. But 'London Calling' is a timely prophecy of doom about the 1980s: its lyric states, "now war is declared..." and within a couple of years there was bloodshed in the Falklands.

WRITER	Joe Strummer / Mick Jones
PRODUCER	Guy Stevens
RECORDED	Wessex Studios, London
DURATION	3.20
RELEASED	CBS, December 1979
CHART	UK 11 US –

'London Calling' has a grandeur rarely heard on punk records. The production is hard and atmospheric, with layered guitars and backing vocals that double the title left and right. The guitar chords on beats 2 and 4 at the start of the verse give a slight reggae influence, much beloved of the band and many other post-punks.

Harmonically, this is a simple song in E minor. The initial chord change is Em to C, with a chopped high guitar chord that stays the same while the bass note changes. The chorus is Em to G, and ends on a D, with a fine sinister walking bass underneath it.

'London Calling' was a potent title, stirring associations with the Blitz and the spirit of British resistance. The lyric, in Strummer's excellent phlegmy vocal, offers an apocalyptic vision phrased as a rallying call, though it raises more questions than it answers. "'War is declared": what war? Against whom? Who are the "zombies of death"? There's a great line about "phoney Beatlemania has bitten the dust". The chorus invokes the Ice age, the sun's destructive force, ecological failure, a nuclear error (this was around the time of Three Mile Island). Puzzlingly, the singer has no fear, even though London is drowning and he lives "by the river"...

Listen for: the increasing high frequencies on the crescendo that leads from the intro to the verse; the toggle-switch morse-code feedback; the double howling backward guitars during the break; the feedback at the start of verse 2; the echo regeneration around the 2.00 mark; and the vocal howls before the last verse.

LINKS

For static chords and changing bass notes, see track 53.

"it has a grandeur rarely heard on punk records"

CREATIVE TIPS

Use chords as a rhythm feature rather than just as a harmonic wash.

1980s

55	The Cure	*A Forest*
56	Elvis Costello	*Clubland*
57	The Police	*Spirits In The Material World*
58	Madness	*House Of Fun*
59	David Sylvian & Ryuichi Sakamoto	*Forbidden Colours*
60	Simple Minds	*Waterfront*
61	The Smiths	*This Charming Man*
62	R.E.M	*Perfect Circle*
63	Frankie Goes To Hollywood	*Relax*
64	Siouxsie & The Banshees	*Overground*
65	The Smiths	*How Soon Is Now?*
66	Roy Harper	*Frozen Moment*
67	Tears For Fears	*Everybody Wants To Rule The World*
68	Kate Bush	*Running Up That Hill*
69	Paul Hardcastle	*19*
70	Prince	*Kiss*
71	T'Pau	*China In Your Hand*
72	U2	*With Or Without You*
73	The Mission	*Tower Of Strength*
74	Living Colour	*Desperate People*
75	The Stone Roses	*I Wanna Be Adored*

TRACK 55

A FOREST

THE CURE 1980

"We paid for the second album ourselves. We did *17 Seconds* and 'A Forest' and then we had an identity... *17 Seconds* was, for me, when The Cure really started." (ROBERT SMITH)

In a sleeve with a moody, reverse image photo, 'A Forest' was a scary, hypnotic record (as was its source album, *17 Seconds*) which effectively launched The Cure's career, after some 18 months of minor cult status (though they didn't make much impression on the US charts until the *Disintegration* album in 1989.) 'A Forest' linked the new wave with the technology of the new synth pop. It's also a good example of a case where an obviously artificial-sounding drum machine is entirely in-keeping with the dream-like, even nightmarish atmosphere of the song – a real drummer would actually not have worked so well in this context.

'A Forest' starts with the drum machine and a lone guitar on the left, then the bass comes in at 0.12, with another guitar on the right. The guitars have a different sound from what had been considered the norm in rock in the previous decade. In the early 1980s the more innovative guitarists were turning their backs on the Fender/Gibson/Marshall sounds associated with rock/blues playing and striking out in new directions – even solidly 'rock' bands from the early Eighties, like Big Country and U2, were experimenting with guitar sounds. This coincided with a rise in the popularity of affordable and good quality Japanese-designed equipment (from companies like Yamaha and Roland), and in particular the proliferation of electronic effects units – phasing, flanging, and chorus effects were among the most influential on the music of the time (even bass players – traditionally conservative in tonal terms – started using them).

WRITER	Robert Smith / Lol Tolhurst / Simon Gallup / Mathieu Hartley
PRODUCER	Robert Smith / Mike Hedges
RECORDED	Morgan Studios, London
DURATION	4.54 (full length)
RELEASED	Fiction, April 1980
CHART	UK 30 US –

The guitars on 'A Forest' have a slow phase on them – which almost became a Smith trademark for a while. Because some notes are repeated, you can hear the signal changing as the phase sweeps through the frequencies. Listen for the echo on the voice – sometimes as many as four delays – and for the wind noise at 2.24. There's an out-of-tune synth that adds a sinister touch at 0.17 on the right, heard again at 2.28.

CREATIVE TIPS

Even if you usually record with a drummer, always consider the possibility that the mood and/or lyric content of a song might benefit from a drum machine.

'A Forest' is in A minor: the first sequence is Am C F Dm, but the bridge is a more harmonically disturbed B C F#m C B C F#m, which concludes with a chromatic slide to F and thence back to Am.

As for the lyrics... (adopts Germanic psychotherapist voice), "So tell me, Mr Smith, how long have you been having these nightmares?"... 'A Forest' is a dream narrative: the speaker sees a girl in verse 1, and hears her voice calling him in verse 2; he pursues her, and suddenly realises he's lost. The pay-off is, "The girl was never there – it's always the same / I run and then there's nothing / Again and again..." You can take this as a metaphor for failed relationships.

Listen for: the low, muted two-note guitar at 1.42; the chord spreads at 1.48 and 2.35; the distant, high synth line at 2.24; and the wonderful repeat echoes on "again" at 3.08-22 which terminate with the start of the guitar solo. The solo itself is scalic, and resolutely avoids any string-bending or pentatonic movement – instead it works with the echo and is played against an open string. The single version fades out on the solo at about the four-minute mark, whereas the full coda actually pulls the instruments out one at a time: at 4.10 the drums break down, and then out completely at 4.32, with the bass ending at 4.46.

LINKS

For a comparative guitar lead style, see track 48. On the first Cure album, Three Imaginary Boys, *Smith & Co did a punked-up cover version of Hendrix's 'Foxy Lady' – a bold move, musically and culturally, in those new-wave, anti-guitar-hero times.*

"the guitars had a different sound from what was considered the norm"

TRACK 56

CLUBLAND
ELVIS COSTELLO & THE ATTRACTIONS 1980

"I intended this to be a poisoned version of 'On Broadway', which the recording at least falls a long way short of. I think we improved upon it many times in concert, but the song says its piece and the record has its moments, particularly Steve's 'Rhapsody In Blue'." (ELVIS COSTELLO)

Elvis Costello emerged in the UK's new wave years (on the Stiff label) with a provocative press campaign – announcing Elvis Is King – and an engaging debut album, *My Aim Is True* (1977). He then formed the Attractions (Bruce Thomas, Pete Thomas and Steve Naive) and the quartet delivered *This Year's Model* (1978), a wickedly crafted mix of new wave aggression, sharp lyrics and 1960s beat-pop. Costello became a regular feature in the UK top 20 with singles like 'Watching The Detectives' – a brilliantly imagined filmic narrative set to a reggaeish beat, and 'Oliver's Army' – the only singalong ever to namecheck Checkpoint Charlie.

WRITER	Elvis Costello
PRODUCER	Nick Lowe / Roger Bechirin
RECORDED	DJM Studios, London
DURATION	3.42
RELEASED	F-Beat, December 1980
CHART	UK 60 US –

As the 1980s rolled on, Costello experimented with many styles. The most significant thing about his body of work, regardless of its commercial success, was that it showed a man besotted with popular song in *all* its forms, and ever curious. He said to me in 1996: "Broad musical tastes weren't in fashion in 1977. I knew if I went around saying I liked some of the music I liked I wouldn't get a hearing." He was, for example, playing covers of Bacharach songs long, long before the Bacharach revival, and records like *Get Happy* and *Almost Blue* consciously evoked 1960s soul and country respectively. A recording like 'Shipbuilding' did much to open people's ears to pre-rock'n'roll musical styles.

'Clubland', from the *Trust* album, shows how great the Attractions are as a band – surely one of the unsung combos of the post-punk era. There's piano and organ on the left, drums in stereo, toms on far right; a guitar on the left supplies toggle-switch feedback in the verses at 1.09-14, and at 2.56; the Jazzmaster guitar rhythm is to the right. There is an audible click noise on the left, which appears to be triggered by the drums through a reverb unit – they seem to have decided to use this as part of the percussion. Listen for the four-note guitar lick that punctuates the title in the chorus, reminiscent of the one in 'Born To Run', as both are drawing on Duane Eddy.

CREATIVE TIPS

"I've kept an open mind to the possibility that music isn't necessarily defined by the music of the moment." (Elvis Costello)

Harmonically, the song starts with a dramatic E6 Em6 change; the verse then uses a Bm G Em F# turnaround; the chorus changes key to B major. There's a clever sequence of bass guitar playing B F# four times under "the boys and girls, the Mums and Dads", where the third B in each case is under an E chord (ie making a second inversion).

The bridge after the second chorus introduces a bit of space. It has the 'Be My Baby' drum pattern and a great lead-up to the voice re-entry with a chopped high Em chord at 1.47. The sung bridge has a key-defying descending sequence: B A G F#m D E. Steve Naive's piano bit at 2.08-24 is pretty much over Bm, with two guitars audible, chords in the centre, notes on the left. Verse 3 is sparser in arrangement. On the chorus, notice how the drums go to a four-to-the-bar snare to drive it.

'Clubland' has an obscure but intriguing lyric about seedy goings-on around nightclubs. Listen for: the alliteration in the opening lines (backhanders, bevy, beauties); the four "going off" phrases that follow; the double entendre in verse 2 ("do the jerk"); and the marvellously facetious "The long arm of the law slides up the outskirts of town" – a line whose linguistic wit is miles ahead of 95 per cent of pop songwriters.

LINKS

For influences on Costello's songwriting... see most of the 1960s. For more toggle-switch feedback, see tracks 39 and 54.

TRACK 57

SPIRITS IN THE MATERIAL WORLD
THE POLICE 1981

"I went to every major record company with my songs, and they all said it wasn't commercial enough. That is what really made me feel a rapport with the punk movement. Although the music was a little shallow, the anger and the sense of wanting to revolutionise the music industry was something I felt strongly about. So The Police flew that banner for a while... We were energetic, loud and noisy... and as the punk bands fell by the wayside, for various reasons, we stayed and survived. (STING)

At the start of the 1980s The Police were virtually the biggest band in the world – a status they achieved with a series of catchy hit singles beginning with 'Roxanne' in early 1979. But their first three albums were wildly uneven: I can't think of another band with so much talent who were so erratic in terms of the strength of their songs. With some bands even their knock-offs are OK, but with The Police it was Grade A or zilch.

A significant change in the band's sound came with 'Invisible Sun', towards the end of 1981, which boasted a heavy riff and a heavy lyric about the 'troubles' in Northern Ireland. Sting, one of rock's more literate writers, was also reading Koestler's *The Ghost In The Machine* (a book about the complexities of the relationship between mind and body) – hence the title of their fourth album. The more thoughtful lyrics called for a more mature setting.

WRITER	Sting (Gordon Sumner)
PRODUCER	Hugh Padgham / The Police
RECORDED	AIR Studios, Montserrat
DURATION	2.58
RELEASED	A&M, December 1981
CHART	US 11 UK 15

In its own quiet way, 'Spirits In The Material World' was a revolutionary record, just at time when the materialistic 'Me' decade was getting started. It also happens to be one of the most rhythmically sophisticated records ever to make the Top 20. Though not as famous as the over-familiar 'Every Breath You Take', it strikes a deeper note.

The arrangement shows the increased discipline of the band's mature second phase: there are multiple vocal lines, with Sting singing in octaves; instruments include guitar, bass, drums, synth, and sax – the synth and guitars keep the beat, while the bassline is the usual touch of dark reggae dub, and the drums are off-beat during the verses. This creates of a floating sensation in the verse. The snare is brought in to give the chorus extra kick. Copeland's drums have a tight sound, different to the expansive, reverbed rock drum tone that was just developing via Gabriel and Collins' example.

The main riff is a plaintive Am9 Am G Em turnaround, with a chorus that revolves around D minor. After the bridge of Dm F G Am G F the synth takes the lead, which creates an extraordinary rhythmic sleight-of-hand. The synth rhythm changes according to how you hear it: it starts off sounding as though everything else is off-beat, then, when you become conscious of the backing, the synth changes to sounding off-beat itself. The effect is like one of those 3D images you are supposed to be able to see appear from a mosaic of small coloured squares.

Sting's English Literature background shows itself in the wordy vocabulary, with terms such as "subjugate'" "rhetoric" and abstract polysyllabic rhymes on "solution / evolution / constitution". There's a rueful joke on "there is no bloody revolution"... it's a song about how political revolutions will always fail if they do not involve a sufficient change of consciousness. We're still waiting for that.

Listen for: the burp of sax at the start; Sting's "Oh"; and the drum fill right on the fade.

LINKS

Contrast this song with Madonna's 'Material Girl'...

CREATIVE TIPS

Instead of four, try a three-chord turnaround and stretch out the first chord in the sequence by adding a note to it (like a suspended 4th, or 9th, etc)...

Sting on songwriting: "The ones that come quickly have already been written somewhere else. You just compile them. If you take, say, 'Every Breath You Take', which is probably my most successful song, it wrote itself. It's completely generic – a rhyming dictionary come to life. Yet there's something compelling about it that I can't explain."

"the arrangement shows the increased discipline of the band's mature second phase"

TRACK 58

HOUSE OF FUN

MADNESS 1982

"I listened to it, and I thought, 'Where's the chorus?'.... So they got 'round the piano, recorded [a chorus] once and we copied it and edited it onto the end of each verse... that's why it's got a slightly different beat – it's not totally in sync." (DAVE ROBINSON, STIFF RECORDS)

"We never thought of ourselves in any way as important. We were just having a good time and trying to make the most of what could really be a short career... We were just very fortunate. The longevity of the band is why it resonates. If we had just one hit, maybe we wouldn't have influenced anybody." (GRAHAM 'SUGGS' McPHERSON)

Madness were one of the UK's most successful singles bands in the early 1980s, racking up over 20 Top 20 hits. They were formed in London in 1978, originally as a four-piece called the Invaders, and then Madness after their line-up grew to seven. Like The Police, Madness had a musical link with reggae, in particular the uptempo form known as ska – Madness found their own pop variation on this, keeping the offbeat rhythms, with prominent piano and brass, and generating an increasing air of good-natured lunacy via the lyrics and the accompanying videos. As such they became an act whose appeal crossed many boundaries, and something of a British comic (and musical) institution.

WRITER	Mike Barson / Lee Thompson
PRODUCER	Clive Langer / Alan Winstanley
RECORDED	Eden Studios, London
DURATION	2.48
RELEASED	Stiff Records, April 1982
CHART	UK 1 US –

'House Of Fun' was their first UK number 1 (not to be confused with 'Our House', their biggest US hit), and is a fine example of their magic at work. Most bands set out with the intention of being taken as seriously as possible, so Madness's often-humourous writing and arrangements are hardly run-of-the-mill.

'House Of Fun' features a double-tracked vocal, backing vocals on the chorus, honky-tonk piano (left), organ (right), electric guitar (audible on the lead up to the bridge), bass, drums, and plenty of brass. The production sound is bright, with the drums to the fore, but relatively dry – the rhythmic sharpness of the song, coupled with the fact that so many of the parts are 'busy', means a long reverb would add confusion.

As much as any top-notch funk track, the rhythmic timing and inter-relationship of the parts is cleverly dovetailed so the track becomes a pulsating, whirling amusement ride. The idea of circus-type sounds is especially strong in the link at 1.29-37 after the second chorus, and in the diminished harmony of the slightly sinister bridge (1.38-51). Listen also for the backward cymbal, 'zzzzztt', at 1.39.

CREATIVE TIPS

With lyrics, find the poetry in the everyday, not on some far-flung mountain-top.... Bass players should study this song's bassline (by Mark 'Bedders' Bedford) for inspiration.

These arrangement details work with the harmony and lyrics. The intro and verses limit themselves to major chords only: the song starts in D major but adds the *b*VII C chord and then other non-key chords like B B*b*, F and E. These chromatic shifts help create the fairground colour. Minor chords are reserved for the chorus, which uses the technique of

repeating the same melody in different keys: chorus 1 is in E minor and F# minor; chorus 2 starts in F# minor. In many Madness songs, the bitter-sweet quality stems from the contrast of funny lyrics and jumping rhythms with minor chord progressions.

Lyrically, 'House Of Fun' is first-class – a witty, shrewdly observed tale of a teenager braving trial by public humiliation as he ventures into a chemist's shop/drugstore to buy a packet of condoms. The music evokes all his pumped-up nervousness and panic as various women walk into the shop. Unable to ask directly for what he wants, the boy only manages to give the impression that he is after balloons, and has to suffer the indignity of the store manager's response – "This is a chemist, not a joke shop". But on the chorus the song also archly cocks an eyebrow when it juxtaposes entry to the "house of fun" with "Welcome to the lion's den / Temptation's on its way'... We laugh knowingly with the young man, not simply at him – the basic impulse is sympathetic and humane.

LINKS

For other songs about the trials and tribulations of teenagerdom, see tracks 1, 7, 13, 39, 53, 61 and 65.

TRACK 59

FORBIDDEN COLOURS
DAVID SYLVIAN & RYUICHI SAKAMOTO 1983

"Ryuichi has a wealth of knowledge of music of all genres... he's one of the few people who can apply that knowledge just like *that*. You can be sitting in a room with him, working out an arrangement, and say, 'Elements of Debussy would be nice', and suddenly there they are; and then say, 'Not Debussy, Bill Evans', and there it is. That's very rare – and it all has his signature." (DAVID SYLVIAN)

"I have a kind of cultural map in my head, where I find similarities between different cultures. For example, domestic Japanese pop music sounds like Arabic music to me – the vocal intonation and vibrato. And in my mind, Bali is next to New York." (RYUICHI SAKAMOTO)

David Sylvian had some success with the group Japan in the early 1980s. His interest in the Far East eventually led him to team up with Ryuichi Sakamoto, formerly of the Yellow Magic Orchestra, for several projects, which included writing words to his theme music for the film *Merry Christmas, Mr Lawrence* (which starred David Bowie alongside Sakamoto himself).

The result, this memorable, beautiful single, in some ways anticipated the eclectic nature of popular music in the 1990s, combining as it does elements of Western harmony with some oriental touches. This seemed exotic in 1983, as did the Ferry-esque low-pitched vocal – very well sung by Sylvian.

Emotion in pop music is generally associated with singing high or loud, or both. Instead the vocal here is in a low register and restrained, yet expressive – the way he sings the first phrase, "The wounds on your hands never seem to heal", is superb. The subject matter is a love theme, yet the lyric is full of references to faith, and Christ in particular. "A lifetime away" is a good example of how lines can be interpreted literally or figuratively. And why does his love wear "forbidden colours"? There are a number of possibilities, including that (in the context of the film) the person could be an enemy.

WRITER	Ryuichi Sakamoto / David Sylvian
PRODUCER	Ryuichi Sakamoto / Shinichi Tanaka / Seigen Ono
RECORDED	poss Nippon Columbia Studios, Japan
DURATION	4.42
RELEASED	Virgin, April 1983
CHART	UK 17 US –

Faced with an apparently 'exotic' sound, it can a useful exercise to try working out what creates it. The instrumentation here is mostly synth keyboard, piano and strings, with Japanese percussion to give the 'wood' sound on the third beat. The intro fades in delicately, with synths playing a high figure in the centre of the mix, using two distinct tones; to this is added piano and string chords that come up in volume and then vanish; the percussion comes in with the main theme – a mostly pentatonic phrase over a decidedly Western progression of G*b*maj7 A*b* B*b*m. In terms of the vocal hook, the chorus is part of the verse.

At 1.48 there's a move to an E*b*m/A*b*m chord change for the bridge. The accompaniment here is mostly single notes rather than block chording. The next verse leads to a dramatic moment at 2.42 where the other instruments fall out and the strings take over in a sawing eighth-note rhythm, using close harmonies (listen to the internal parts here, they're beautiful); and these are thickened at 3.02. Listen for the use of inversions at the end of some of the choruses, heightening the emotional effect.

CREATIVE TIPS

Try pitching your lead vocal low rather than high, for a change.

LINKS

As an example of how flexible chord progressions can be, the main climbing sequence here is the same that drives Prince's carnal 'Little Red Corvette' (released around the same time), Kate Bush's 'Running Up That Hill' (1985, see track 68), and The Verve's 'This Time' (track 91). There's a re-recorded version of 'Forbidden Colours' on Sakamoto's 2000 album Cinemage.

"emotion in pop music is generally associated with singing high or loud, or both"

TRACK 60

WATERFRONT

SIMPLE MINDS 1983

"We wrote this song in Glasgow, and we took it around the world, and we found that this song is big enough to fill any stadium in the world." (JIM KERR)

"The musicians I work with build this ship, and it's my job to steer the ship into port. I'm the captain." (STEVE LILLYWHITE)

DA-DAH!... dum-di-dum-di-dum-di-dum-di-dum DA-DAH!... Liking this stuff is a guilty pleasure, really – like working in demolition and bringing down old power-stations or multi-storey flats. 'Waterfront' was the Minds' biggest single to this point, and pricked up the ears of a wider rock audience through its bombastic force. I'm not sure there's much of a song here, but there's one helluva noise, partly thanks to producer Steve Lillywhite (who was already associated with the burgeoning Big Drum Sound).

After a short period as a new-wave band (punk sympathisers with a Roxy Music bent), Simple Minds reinvented themselves as a stadium rock outfit with albums like *Sparkle In The Rain* and *Once Upon A Time*, for a short time rivalling U2 in the grand gesture stakes. They did this with a sound where the guitar was less prominent than in U2 (the main guitar part on 'Waterfront' is a slide phrase) and keyboards were to the fore. At the back by this stage was Mel Gaynor, a formidable exponent of the powerhouse hit-everything-harder-than-everything-else school of rock drumming (along with Matt Sorum, Cozy Powell and Michael Lee).

WRITER	Jim Kerr / Charlie Burchill / Derek Forbes / Mick MacNeil / Mel Gaynor
PRODUCER	Steve Lillywhite
RECORDED	London?
DURATION	4.39
RELEASED	Virgin, November 1983
CHART	UK 13 US –

This single is a milestone in terms of the pursuit of the Big Drum Sound – an atavistic resurgence based on a collective musicians' memory of what a Led Zep drum part was like. This, of course, was at a time when it was deeply unhip to like Led Zep, and shortly before the sampler came along to save you the trouble of getting your own drum sound together (see track 86). The pursuit of the Big Drum Sound gained impetus after Peter Gabriel's sessions for his third album (with Lillywhite and Hugh Padgham), and Phil Collins' 'In The Air Tonight': heavily gated snares, ambient miking of the kit, and recording in rooms with hard surfaces became popular recording techniques.

CREATIVE TIPS

Try writing a song where the distinction between verse and chorus is not obvious.

'Waterfront' is structurally clever, in so far as it blurs the distinction between verse and choruses: it starts with an instrumental chorus which has two sections – the first has each big DA-DAH! chord (it's a Dsus4), answered by a two-note slide phrase, then a four-note phrase. After this there is a quieter section implying a D-G chord change with lower-pitched melodies on synth. Verse 1 brings in vocals, then there's a bridge with ascending chords, then the first half of the chorus, verse 2, a full length chorus, a link section where the D pedal drops out, and then the chorus with both halves. Listen for the drum fill at 4.04, and the piano in verse 2.

Throughout almost the entire song there is a crotchet-quaver D pedal note in the bass (with a slight break around the 3.30 mark) which everything else sits over. During the verse there is a movement of 4ths underneath the melody – AD to BE to GC and back; the bridge has Dm7 G B*b* C over the D pedal.

Jim Kerr delivers this lyric as though it is Zen & The Art Of... oh I don't know... Flower

Arranging? Microphone Placement?... whatever. He's like a cork on the top of a tidal wave. A few vague phrases emerge – he's gonna walk on, or step on, up to the waterfront (wherever that is) now, and in one million years time. For what purpose we do not know. Whether Curtis Mayfield would have made anything of this exhortation to "move on up" is a moot point. Something is so close and yet so far (possibly another loose drumstick flying over his head).

The discrepancy between the size of the music and the vagueness of the lyrics is one of the things that irritated people about stadium-era Simple Minds. Stadium rock lyrics are an easy recipe – cook a few landscape generalities over a Big Drum Sound, season with a few "tonight"s, and gaze Messianically at the horizon (or the T-shirt stands at the back of the arena, whichever is further).

Still, there are moments when there's nothing like a bit of DA-DAH!...dum-di-dum-di-dum-di-dum-di-dum DA-DAH!...

LINKS

For more Big Drum Sounds, see track 71.

"like a cork on top of a tidal wave"

TRACK 61

THIS CHARMING MAN

THE SMITHS 1983

"We were against synthesisers, the Conservative government, groups with names like Orchestral Manoeuvres In The Dark, the English Monarchy, cock-rock guitar solos, and the American music scene at the time. We stood for the Englishness of The Kinks, T.Rex and Roxy Music, the arty quirks that kept those groups from being huge in the US. We were into the Rolling Stones, the MC5, the Patti Smith Group, Oscar Wilde... Morrissey and I wanted to be a modern-day Leiber & Stoller writing bubblegum tracks with intense lyrics."

(JOHNNY MARR)

When The Smiths appeared on British TV performing 'This Charming Man' in the winter of 1983, they looked like nothing else on the UK music scene. There had been three years of New Romantics, synth-pop, and guitar rock from the likes of U2, The Police and Big Country. Now there was Morrissey, careering around the stage in jeans with a bunch of gladioli hanging out of his back pocket, and wearing a pair of NHS specs. Marr and Morrissey were into 1960s pop and revered Motown writers Holland-Dozier-Holland.

The Smiths were in some ways akin to early R.E.M – both bands were arty, likely to appeal to students, had unusual lyrics, a touch of Rickenbacker jangle, an unconventional vocalist, and a healthy contempt for current chart formulas.

You could pick any number of Smiths songs to look at; 'This Charming Man' was their first hit, and one of the more imaginative responses to 1960s Motown (along with 'A Town Called Malice' by The Jam). It's pretty much a guitar, bass and drums rock record. The guitar is clean and bright, treble frequencies ringing out, which sharply differentiates it from the rhythm section. The production features a number of guitar parts – Marr (whose work with The Smiths made him one of the most important British guitarists of the decade) claims he put numerous overdubs on it, although this is not obvious to the listener. He told *Guitar Player* magazine in 1990: "There are about 15 tracks of guitar – three tracks of acoustic, a backwards guitar with a really long reverb, and the effect of dropping knives on the guitar – that comes in at the end of the chorus. People thought the main part was a Rickenbacker, but it's really a '54 Tele. I'm tuned up to F# and I finger it in G, so it comes out as A."

WRITER	**Morrissey / Johnny Marr**
PRODUCER	**John Porter**
RECORDED	**Matrix Studios, London**
DURATION	**2.40**
RELEASED	**Rough Trade, November 1983**
CHART	**UK 25 US –**

The guitar part is made up of single notes or thirds rather than chords – the chord-colour emerges from the totality of the music. The guitar plays a counter-melody throughout; Andy Rourke's bass on the verse does a Motown rhythm – think of 'You Can't Hurry Love' – and on the chorus ("a jumped up pantry boy") breaks into quick quarter-note walking lines, which increase the feeling of movement.

The song has a wonderfully evocative opening line – "Punctured bicycle on a hillside desolate" – and takes in colloquial turns of phrase like, "I haven't got a stitch to wear". Morrissey's lyrics are marked by a certain droll wit, much allusion and a deliberate avoiding of cliché. His melodies are diatonic and free of blues inflections – which is why the music sounds so un-American (and perhaps partly explaining the band's limited US success). This combination means that, like R.E.M in their own, rather more American way, The Smiths explored emotions that had rarely, if ever, been expressed in popular music. The melodies could also seem stiff at times, with an awkward relationship to the backing: here it involves a 5th from A to E with emphasis on E D C# – the 5th, 4th and 3rd of the scale.

CREATIVE TIPS

Lyrics can be made out of the most everyday phrases, instead of out-dated 'poetic' imagery... Morrissey on words: "It was always important to me to use lines that hadn't been said before, because it wasn't enough to use the usual pop terminology."

LINKS

On the original 12-inch of this song there's another version called the 'London mix' (as opposed to the 'Manchester') - one of the loveliest re-mixes I've ever heard. The single's bright, punchy dry mix is replaced by a muted one with more reverb, which brings out the sadness in the song; you can also hear more guitar parts and echo on the voice. (There are two other great tracks with it too, 'Accept Yourself' and 'Wonderful Woman'.) There's another version of 'This Charming Man', from a radio session, on the Hatful Of Hollow ***compilation.***

"his melodies are diatonic and free of blues inflections – which is why the music sounds so un-American"

TRACK 62

PERFECT CIRCLE

R.E.M 1983

"I was standing in the City Gardens in Trenton, New Jersey, at the back door and it was just getting dark. These kids were playing touch football, the last game before the dark came, and for some reason I was so moved I cried for 20 minutes... I told Michael to try and capture that feeling. There's no football in there, no kids, no twilight. But it's all there." (PETER BUCK)

"That song concerns my old girlfriend, and it was an intensely personal song to me. I really like that it can mean two different things... what I think about the song and what Peter thinks about the song. It's the exact same feeling but the details are different." (MICHAEL STIPE)

Rarely has a band's audience been so demarcated by a change of label. After five albums for IRS, R.E.M went to Warner Brothers for *Green* (1989) and its successors. Some R.E.M freaks think of the Warner period as "the later stuff" – good in parts but not necessarily The Real Thing; whereas most people think R.E.M fell out of the sky, fully formed, with 'Losing My Religion'. Needless to say, the former camp always hope to spread the Athenian gospel and convert the 'Losing My Religion'-ists to old glories like 'Perfect Circle', 'Cuyahoga', 'Wendell Gee' or 'Welcome To The Occupation'.

WRITER	**Peter Buck / Mike Mills / Michael Stipe / Bill Berry**
PRODUCER	**Mitch Easter / Don Dixon**
RECORDED	**Reflection Studios, Charlotte, North Carolina**
DURATION	**3.30**
RELEASED	**(album, Murmer) IRS, May 1983**
CHART	**not a single**

In 1980, Athens, Georgia, was a small but thriving university town full of students, some more into rock'n'roll than studying (as usual). Here Fine Arts student Michael Stipe met Peter Buck, guitarist and vinyl junkie, and Mike Mills and Bill Berry, who'd formed a rhythm section in Macon before enrolling at Georgia University, and together they formed a garage band playing covers. (Even at the time of *Murmur* they were still covering tracks like 'Born To Run' and 'In The Year 2525'.) They chose the acronym R.E.M (from rapid eye movement sleep) since it didn't pigeonhole them, and pressed up their own indie single, 'Radio Free Europe', which got them the deal with IRS. The debut album *Murmur* had a monochrome cover showing the kudzu vine, indigenous to the south, striking a low-key enigmatic note matched by Stipe's vocals (his voice blending in the mix) and his unorthodox lyrics. Fans nicknamed the album 'Mumble'. *Rolling Stone* called R.E.M "best new artist of 1983".

Murmur is a tentative sketch of their unique music: melodies that owed nothing to the *Billboard* Top 100, supported by chiming guitar and weird production touches. They were a refreshing contrast to the synth-driven pop of the early 1980s, or slick AOR, or punk's lack of mystery. If you need one over-riding reason to get *Murmur*, look no further than 'Perfect Circle' – their first stroke of genius and a song of entrancing majesty. It is a fine example of how music communicates by and through itself, rather than just through the lyrics.

CREATIVE TIPS

Generate a new emotion by using an unlikely instrument in a different context.

There are two honky-tonk pianos (one echoed to the left) – an instrument that normally calls up blues, rock'n'roll and saloon bar music, but R.E.M got something different out of it. The bass comes in half-way through the verse, then the drums on the chorus in stereo – snare on the left, reverb on the right along with the hi-hat. Buck enters with 12-string guitar in the chorus too.

The chorus is F C/E Dm C; the verse Dm D Dm G – the tonic major/minor contrast is important to the effect; the change to G instead of Gm implies a Dorian harmony.

Lyrically, this is typically inscrutable early Stipe, with memorable lines and others that stick out because they don't appear to make sense; phrases like, "Standing two shoulders high in the room" take on a mysterious power. He sings in an alarmingly passionless way, affected by the fact that the melody is in his lower register so he can't get a lot of power on the low notes. Yet that pitching is part of the effect. If this is a love song it seems to suggest a relationship quite above the normal banalities of pop lyrics; it suggests the unspoken connection between a couple who are in love, going out to meet mutual friends, but not wanting other people to know. It expresses sadness about human life, transience, the fragility of relationships, and and a deep, underlying compassion.

Listen for: Buck's picked guitar at 1.22; the 'wet' signal of a backward guitar at 2.32, also heard in the coda; the different piano sound at 3.18; and the slapping sound on the left in the chorus.

LINKS

For a later R.E.M song, see track 95

TRACK 63

RELAX

FRANKIE GOES TO HOLLYWOOD 1984

"I wanted to make the kind of records I heard in the discos I danced in at that time – funky, electronic sounds – while the musicians in the band were more rock-oriented." (HOLLY JOHNSON)

"We sold over a million 12-inch copies of 'Relax' in England alone, and that was unheard of at that point, so we knew we had a big market for 12-inch mixes – especially as ours were exciting." (TREVOR HORN)

WRITER	Peter Gill / Holly Johnson / Mark O'Toole
PRODUCER	Trevor Horn
RECORDED	Sarm West Studios, London
DURATION	3.53
RELEASED	ZTT, December 1983
CHART	UK 1 (1984; 5 in 1993) US 10

This is a record whose mechanistic ruthlessness mirrored the times and anticipated the ethos of much chart music in the 1990s. With its macho self-assertion, it's about as unerotic as a supposedly erotic record gets. But a combination of vulgarity, a brutally efficient production and a kerfuffle that saw it banned from BBC radio guaranteed its success. By July 1984 Frankie had the follow-up, 'Two Tribes', at number 1, with 'Relax' at number 2.

The track cost about £30,000 to record, and was the first release on the ZTT label, co-owned by Trevor Horn, co-founder of the Art Of Noise. Horn had seen Frankie performed 'Relax' on UK TV show

The Tube, and felt it could be a hit; but it went through several versions in the studio, as production and arrangement elements were assembled and then found wanting. One of the earlier, rejected versions used musicians from Ian Dury's outfit The Blockheads.

The track is held together by the sequenced bass, which sticks to the kick drum rigidly throughout, plus a stereo shaker/cabaza sound. The ethereal intro leads to a thumping quarter-note bass E that goes all the way through the sequence. With heavy bass boost, dominant synths, a little chorused guitar and plenty of reverb, it's a typical 1980s production. Notice the long delay on the lead vocal too.

CREATIVE TIPS

Another example of moving chords over a static root note for dramatic effect.

The stripping down of the lyric to virtually a single injunction was reflected in the music. Harmonically the song was certainly primitive, exposing a dumbing-down process that was to gather momentum in chart music. 'Relax' is basically a repeated chorus with various link passages, including a guitar that goes *booiiinnng* three times. The chorus puts Em-D-C-D over the E bass; the bridge is Em-D-C-A; the first chorus starts around the 30 second mark, and is succeeded by another, then a link, and a bridge built on a different bass note; at 2.00 there's a third chorus, not fully sung, followed by the link, and a fourth chorus with a partial counter-melody from the main vocal; this leads to a fizzy synth noise and then several large splash sound effects (in part sampled from the band jumping into a swimming pool). 'Relax' ends with a fifth chorus and a sudden stop.

LINKS

'Relax' helped boost the popularity of the 12-inch single (a genre pushed into the mainstream by New Order's 'Blue Monday' the year before), and alerted major record labels to the 'creative potential' (or should that be 'sales opportunities') presented by the idea of multiple alternate mixes – a form which more often than not led to ideas being stretched beyond their welcome. For an example of how well the extra space could be filled, see track 61.

TRACK 64

OVERGROUND

SIOUXSIE & THE BANSHEES 1984

"We've always wanted to hear our music classically and no bugger's ever taken up the initiative to do it, so we've done it ourselves... I really do like some classical music. It's much more powerful than The Clash can ever be... It's really emotive... powerful and aggressive and potent without needing guys with tattoos and muscles." (SIOUXSIE SIOUX)

Time has not been entirely kind to The Banshees' music. It has splendour, but a cold splendour – it's like a piece of ruby-encrusted gold made by a barbarous king a millennium ago and dug out of the permafrost: impressive, but not exactly essential for the home. Much of this has to do with the band's unrelenting Hammer Horror take on the darker aspects of the human condition, and refusal to have anything to do with the dominant emotions of pop. Thus the Banshees fell into the opposite sentimentality, forever in love with the transgressive. The Banshees are the anti-matter to The Carpenters.

They were a cheerful bunch who did songs about disembowelling horses, volcanic

eruptions, child abuse, voodoo dolls, Halloween and chopped-off heads. For all the instrumental exotica and power they tended to be emotionally one-dimensional, the icy hauteur of Sioux's voice only occasionally thawing, for the eroticism of 'Melt', for example, or strikingly on their celebration of self-pleasuring, 'Slowdive' (on a Jane Birkin-scale of 1-10, it scores 11... let's just say if *that's* faked, Sioux deserves an Oscar).

But, reservations apart, they created much hard-hitting and original music through the 1980s. They were assisted by two innovative guitarists in John McGeoch and John Valentine-Carruthers. Budgie was an inventive percussionist whose approach often drew on African rather than straight rock patterns. Steve Severin played functional bass like a guitarist and used chorus and flanging effects. He played bunches of straight eighths almost entirely without syncopation or common scales and fills – rather like Adam Clayton in U2.

WRITER	Siouxsie & The Banshees
PRODUCER	Mike Hedges / Siouxsie & The Banshees
RECORDED	Playground Studios, London
DURATION	3.51
RELEASED	Wonderland, October 1984
CHART	UK 47 US –

Despite the critical acclaim for their first couple of out-and-out punk albums, there's a strong case for saying the Banshees only really found themselves with their second line-up of Siouxsie/ McGeoch/Budgie/Severin – the band that recorded the powerful *Ju Ju* (1981). The main ingredients of their sound were flanged picked basslines, wiry guitar figures built on strange chords, and Sioux's dark imperious vocals. The albums *A Kiss In The Dreamhouse* and *Tinderbox* are both worth investigating.

'Overground' was originally a song on their debut, *The Scream*; the Banshees brought it back into their live set in the early 1980s with the addition of a string trio and amped it up into a pummelling piece of *theatre noir*. A thoroughly radio-unfriendly fade-in carries strings on the left, acoustic guitar on the right, and voice off-centre with reverb; at 1.15 electric guitars and drums make an explosive entry (listen for overdubbed Spanish guitar at 2.22); the coda sees a violent change of dynamics at 3.11; thereafter electric guitar is heard, followed by a single-note acoustic line on the right, and then another entering on the left.

'Overground' is built on a four-chord riff of A Dm B*b* C, played in 5/4 time with link passages in 4/4 on an A chord. The 5/4 time causes all kinds of strange effects with the vocal phrasing – almost as if there is a tension between the time signature and the melody.

'Overground' is about alienation. To be underground (as in the 1960s) is to be out of the mainstream, living a rebellious life. The protagonist is contemplating giving up life in "this nether world" and going up to "where the air is stale" and embrace the world of families and pleasantries. Abnormality is replaced by normality, the self is thrown overboard for the sake of identity. As usual the speaker cannot see the positive side of the world she fears; there's no sense of 'It is what you make it'. The pay-off line is "I'll be worse than me" – is that a threat or a promise?

CREATIVE TIPS

You can make a song exciting by dynamic volume changes... You don't always need to use a conventional drum set-up, as Budgie once remarked: "The first thing that went when I joined the band was the hi-hat... It slowly crept back in though."

LINKS

Successful songs in 5/4 time include Dave Brubeck's 'Take Five', Jethro Tull's 'Living In The Past', and Sting's 'Seven Days'

"The Banshees are the anti-matter to The Carpenters"

TRACK 65

HOW SOON IS NOW?

THE SMITHS 1985

"For the first time in too long a time, this is real music played by real people. The Smiths are absolutely real faces instead of the gloss and the pantomime popular music has become immersed in, as a matter of course. There is no human element in anything anymore." (MORRISSEY, 1984)

"I'm interested in melody, lyrics, and the overall song. I don't like to waste notes, not even one. Who was it said, 'The reason why all those guitar players play so many notes is because they can't find the right one'? I like to put the right note in the right place." (JOHNNY MARR)

One of the most fascinating musical spectacles is a band inspired to come up with something you would never have expected from them. Think of 'Marquee Moon', or R.E.M's epic 'I Remember California'. By the time they released *Hatful Of Hollow*, a stop-gap album of radio sessions and hitherto unreleased tracks, the Smiths had become one of the most successful and acclaimed rock bands in the UK, filling the hole left by The Jam. They had done this on the strength of a sequence of short, tight, witty songs that juxtaposed Marr's harmonic and melodic gifts with an infectious rhythm section and witty lyrics focused on the everyday realities of life. Then they unleashed this shimmering behemoth of a track.

The main hook is the tremolo guitar figure which opens it – a three-chord blues progression. Tremolo guitar (where the volume seems to fluctuate rapidly, creating a 'tremble' in the sound) was associated with late 1950s rock'n'roll and early 1960s surf guitar – neither of which genre was fashionable in the mid-1980s. It had been a long time since a record used tremolo in such a prominent way.

WRITER	Morrissey / Johnny Marr
PRODUCER	John Porter
RECORDED	Matrix Studios, London
DURATION	6.43
RELEASED	Rough Trade, January 1985
CHART	UK 24 (16 in 1992) US –

'How Soon Is Now' is also a brilliant essay in dissonance. Its main chord sequence is F# A B, with the chorus using A C G D B D E twice; over the top of the F# A B Marr overdubs a sinister two-note figure consisting of a third A C#, sliding down to G# B. Since the notes of F# are F# A# C#, you can see how dissonant a clash this is (next time you're near a keyboard try playing the triad with your left hand and the higher notes with the other). The G# B forms an Amaj9 and B6 over the backing.

Listen for how long these notes last, too. They also sound sinister because Marr has reverse reverb on them – the same effect used on voices in horror films like *Poltergeist* (remember the girl's voice coming out of the TV). This is also heard on the chorus chords. There is another high guitar line which ends with a dissonant little squeal, and a fourth which comes in just before Morrissey does his whistling.

Most of the time the song is kept going with the tremolo guitars and the rhythm section. Marr told *Guitar Player* magazine in 1990: "I wanted a very swampy song, a modern bayou song... I put down the rhythm [guitar] track on an Epiphone Casino through a Fender Twin Reverb without vibrato. Then we played the track back through four old Twins side by side:

CREATIVE TIPS

'How Soon Is Now' is someone jealously watching the scenario of 'I Saw Her Standing There' unfold. Take a famous song and write about the same situation from a contrasting perspective.

we had to keep all the amps vibratoing in time to the track and each other, so we had to keep stopping and starting the track, recording it in ten-second bursts." The slide part went through a harmoniser and the harmonics were doubled, with the guitar retuned so Marr could play them all at the 12th fret.

Lyrically, a lot of rock is a pantomime that doesn't deal with real emotions or situations (hence all those macho blues clichés). The Smiths overturned all that. 'How Soon Is Now' is a song about someone who always feels left out, the one who can't get the girl (or boy). Few songs have been written to the insecure and the shy – rock tends to do the opposite and focus on the loud and assertive.

This character is shy, and is told he "goes about things the wrong way" – a superb use of a common phrase; he goes to a club where he is told he might meet someone; he stands there, and then leaves on his own feeling worse. His friends say it will happen "now"– but as the title says, how soon is now...? Rock has been writing songs about dance-halls since the 1950s (think of 'At The Hop'), but a couple of lines here lift this into something else: "I am the son and heir of nothing in particular" – it's not just the language that's different, there's a deeper sense of alienation and resentment here than popular songs usually deal with.

LINKS

For other songs about dance-hall situations, see tracks 13 and 39.

> "few songs have been written to the insecure and the shy"

TRACK 66

FROZEN MOMENTS

ROY HARPER 1985

"My songs are my diary, and the love songs are a great part of the emotional journal... Sometimes I read through a lyric in my mind to relive a time, a circumstance, a terror, a passion, a desire.... A fleeting recollection of an attitude, a hope, a care... a secret longing." (ROY HARPER)

Ah, if only Jeff Buckley had done a cover of this... Roy Harper established himself as a singer-songwriter attached to the progressive rock scene of the end of the 1960s. While girlfriends listened to Joni Mitchell, Carole King and Cat Stevens, if boyfriend was into Neil Young, Hawkwind and Wishbone Ash he might also have had early Harper records like *Valentine* or *Stormcock*. Harper has always been something of an outsider, fiercely anti-establishment – given his upbringing and early experiences (death of mother in childbirth, brought up by Jehovah's Witness stepmother, spell in the Royal Air

CREATIVE TIPS

Try writing a song based around a single chord – change only the underlying bass note from time to time.

Force, discharged as insane, ECT treatment etc) this is unsurprising.

In the mid-1980s Harper's career was given a boost when Jimmy Page teamed up with him to record *Whatever Happened To Jugula?* (they were old acquaintances – witness 'Hats Off To Harper' on 1970's *Led Zeppelin III*). *Jugula* is an engaging album, one of Harper's own favourites, to which Page lends some impressively Crowley-esque guitar licks on tracks like 'Hangman'.

'Frozen Moment' is a beautiful glassy miniature, with a lyricism often eclipsed by Harper's role as angry outsider. The arrangement is very simple: two acoustic guitars, left and right; a synth that sometimes supplies a cello-like bassline, and a music-box sound. Harper occasionally adds a second vocal.

The song has two verses, no hook and no rhythm: it has the stasis of a James Brown track, except this is centred in a fixed harmony not in a rhythm. The whole point of the song is the evocation of a timeless moment – possibly a sexual encounter ("I still see you naked in my naked eye"). Harper does this with guitar parts that play almost the same notes throughout; the chord they imply is an A*b*maj7 (A*b* C E*b* G) with the major 7 chiming away at the top. The major 7 is in some ways the most human of chords because it reflects humanity's double nature – the contraries of human existence, sadness and joy – by virtue of being a major triad combined with a minor. A*b*major is A*b* C E*b*, and Cm is C E*b* G; overlay the two and you get A*b* C E*b* G – A*b*major7.

WRITER	Roy Harper
PRODUCER	Roy Harper
RECORDED	Jimmy Page's studio / Roy Harper's, Lytham
DURATION	3.15
RELEASED	(album, Whatever Happened To Jugula?) Beggars Banquet, February 1985
CHART	not a single

The melody comes and goes unpredictably. Towards the end Harper climbs upward and you can hear the echo on his voice. Every now and again the synth cello note introduces a low F, which turns A*b* major7 into an Fm9 chord (F A*b* C E*b* G) – always a beautiful chord, and here it intensifies the pathos of the moment. You can hear it at 1.01 and 1.38. The music box appears on the right at 0.55, 1.10, 2.25, and 3.06.

LINKS

For another song where the minor 9 chord is important, see track 92. Harper sang the track 'Have A Cigar' on Pink Floyd's Wish You Were Here *(1975); and you can glimpse him offstage (shaking a toy gorilla) in the Led Zeppelin film* The Song Remains The Same *(1976).*

"a beautiful glassy miniature, with a lyricism often eclipsed by Harper's role as an angry outsider"

TRACK 67

EVERYBODY WANTS TO RULE THE WORLD

TEARS FOR FEARS 1985

"I read *The Primal Scream*, and it seems very obvious to me that what he was talking about is that your upbringing affects your life. You live in the past all the time, because those things that [affected you] when you were young affect you now." (CURT SMITH)

Tears For Fears were certainly one of the more interesting bands to emerge during the new romantic/synth-pop era of the early 1980s. They took their name from Arthur Janov's book *Prisoners Of Pain*, which Roland Orzabal had read at 17 (Janov was a psychotherapist and proponent of the primal scream therapy which Lennon had experimented with in the early 1970s). The band got together in Bath: Orzabal on vocals, guitar and keyboards; Curt Smith on vocals and bass; with Manny Elias on drums and Ian Stanley on keyboards. Their first album, *The Hurting*, had yielded three UK hit singles. Their second album, *Songs From The Big Chair*, produced three big hits in the US in 1985, including this track.

There is an astonishing self-assurance about this record. It was recorded in three days – quick by their standards – and the last track done for the album. Orzabal's half-finished song didn't sound any good to him, but it came together quickly at the finish. Smith described it as like American "drive music" (which is in fact what it became, thanks to US FM radio play).

WRITER	**Roland Orzabal / Ian Stanley / Chris Hughes**
PRODUCER	**Chris Hughes**
RECORDED	**TFF studio, Bath**
DURATION	**4.05**
RELEASED	**Mercury, June 1985**
CHART	**US 1 UK 2**

It has a sparse arrangement, but plenty of reverb and a meaty snare drum. The reverb goes to the left, and a guitar chord is added on the right in the chorus. The vocal also doubles on the chorus, and the melody is played on keyboard in the middle. Verse 2 brings in a busy tonic pedal note on the left, and at 1.11 the bubbling high synth sound heard at the start of the record re-appears. The second chorus has guitar fills in thirds; power chords on the bridge make an effective contrast and a break from the shuffle 12/8 rhythm.

Written in E*b* major, the intro and verse have a pedal note with a third changing above it. The chord sequence moves II III IV III II III IV V I – an unambiguous progression rising briefly, falling, and then rising again with a feeling of inevitability. The melody itself makes strong use of 5th intervals.

The lyric reflects the acquisitive nature of the 1980s, while satirising it at the same time. "Turn your back on Mother Nature", they sang; nothing lasts forever, so seize the day. Everybody can't rule the world, of course. But irony in pop music means having your cake and eating it: half your audience likes a song for its ironic attack on something; and the other half misses the irony and likes it because it seems to be in favour of the subject. This happened with 'Born In The USA' and 'Money For Nothing' – was the latter a dig at that materialist culture or a celebration of it? The music industry has an endless ability to co-opt your song to mean what capitalism would like it to mean in order to shift more units. "So sad they had to fade it" is a good dig at DJs and MTV. "Welcome to your life" is a strong opening line.

CREATIVE TIPS

Find a chord change over a static pedal note.

Listen for the first solo, in 3rds and 4ths (2.31-48) – an inventive break that owes nothing to blues/rock tradition. Here was a guitarist (Neil Taylor) justifying his keep. Listen also for:

the counter-melody at 1.52 on "So sad they had to fade it"; at 3.00, the guitar figure that started the song, played up an octave; the exuberant vocal on "one headline" at 3.06; and the fine second guitar solo.

LINKS

There was another version called 'Everybody Wants To Run The World', used as a theme for the Sport Aid *charity event in 1986. Co-writer and producer Chris Hughes was formerly producer (and drummer) for Adam & The Ants.*

TRACK 68

RUNNING UP THAT HILL

KATE BUSH 1985

"It's very much about two people who are in love, and how the power of love is almost too big for them. It leaves them very insecure and in fear of losing each other. It's also perhaps talking about some fundamental differences between men and women." (KATE BUSH)

After the artistically successful but under-selling *The Dreaming* (1982), Kate Bush found renewed success with her fifth album *Hounds Of Love*, and the first of several singles from it, 'Running Up That Hill' (her first hit in the US). The song was originally titled 'A Deal With God', but Bush bowed to record company advice that having the word God in the title would damage air-play in certain countries. (Actually, 'Running Up That Hill' is a better title – metaphorical and more suggestive.)

A range of new musical approaches provide a touching, troubled setting for a striking lyric about wanting to save a relationship by changing places with the other person. Unlike so many love songs that reach the charts, this one does nothing to dilute its sense of conflict and pain. In almost every way, the distance between this song and 'Wuthering Heights' (track 51) is enormous. The degree of progression in Bush's music is unusual in popular musicians, and not driven by fashion or style-hopping but always in an integral relationship with its emotional core.

The first thing that strikes you is the up-front power of 'Running Up That Hill', with its bold galloping drum rhythm that never lets up, and the thunderous fills that punctuate the record's closing minute (at 3.03, 3.39 and 3.57). Notice there are no hi-hats or cymbals – this is the stripped-back drumming pioneered by Peter Gabriel (with whom Bush has worked over the years). Bush said of the album in 1989: '... particularly in the production, I wanted to try and get across a sense of power... and the kind of power I didn't find in a lot of females' music."

WRITER	Kate Bush
PRODUCER	Kate Bush
RECORDED	Abbey Road Studios, London
DURATION	5.02
RELEASED	EMI, August 1985
CHART	UK 3 US 30

'Running Up That Hill' comes in with a breathy minor 3rd (C E*b*) sustained throughout the song, supported by an unflinching C in the bass. Over this we hear the first chord change – A*b* B*b* Cm A*b* – which for the first few lines of the verse becomes A*b* B*b* Cm Gm/B*b*. The first inversion Gm (heard at 0.29, 0.32, 0.37) is very expressive, giving the simple changes the dignity of an Elgar progression (as would be apparent if there were ever an orchestrated version). For all its brash rhythm and exotic synth-derived phrases, there is something quintessentially English about this song. Notice also that the chords on the intro have a bar each, but on the verse they start to have only two beats each: this quickening of the rate of harmonic change is an important feature. The chorus melody is notable for the leaps between the notes.

Listen for: what sounds like a sampled mandolin – the brittle swishing noise audible at 2.24-34 and on the chorus; the build-up at 2.50; the 'telegraph' guitar figure at 3.23; the heart-breaking peal of voices at 4.14, and the massed vocals (through a harmoniser) at 4.34, spreading her voice several octaves up and down. The drastic changing of the pitch is a musical equivalent of her changing places with someone else – a transposed voice expresses the wish of a transposed perspective.

CREATIVE TIPS

For more urgency in a chord sequence, double the rate of harmonic change.

LINKS

See tracks 60 and 63 for sounds that continue through a record almost unchanged. Some of the progressions here are the same as track 59.

"the degree of progression in Bush's music is unusual"

TRACK 69

19

PAUL HARDCASTLE 1985

"One can only imagine the situation if I hadn't had my own recording studio and gone to an A&R guy and said, 'Look, I've got a great idea for a new record. It's about Vietnam, and it's gonna go N-N-N-N-N-N-N-Nineteen....' I'd have been told, 'Get out, you're mentally ill'." (PAUL HARDCASTLE)

This track won an Ivor Novello songwriting award in 1985, and was the best-selling single around the world that year. Its success had a profound effect on the mainstream development of technology-based recording, essentially because of its dependence on a recording device called the sampler – a key component of the digital revolution in music-making (particularly in the UK at first), comparable in its influence to the electric guitar and the multi-track recorder in previous decades. Unfortunately, in my view, this has led into something of a creative cul-de-sac in terms of songwriting – with a few exceptions, some of which are in this book. On the whole, *Inside Classic Rock Tracks* concentrates on more traditional song-creating techniques, but I want to examine why '19' made such an impact.

The song itself originated when Paul Hardcastle video-taped a TV documentary called *Vietnam Requiem* (directed by Couturie and McCord, hence their credits). He recorded the dialogue onto a Revox reel-to-reel tape with the idea of using this to make an unusual record. But when it came to finding a way of emphasising his song's core message – that the average age of the combatants in Vietnam was so young – nothing he tried for a chorus seemed powerful enough. The answer came when he hired an Emulator 1 sampler and sampled parts of the spoken words: by triggering the samples from his keyboard, he found the stuttering "N-n-n-n-nineteen", which became the record's hook.

WRITER	Paul Hardcastle / Bill Couturie / Jones McCord
PRODUCER	Paul Hardcastle
RECORDED	Leytonstone / Soundsuite Studios, London
DURATION	6.07 (3.39, edit)
RELEASED	Chrysalis, April 1985
CHART	UK 1 US 15

This was arresting because it was one of the first times the public had heard a voice chopped up like that. In 1965 Roger Daltrey stammered his way through The Who's 'My Generation' – the stammer sung in real time, a brilliant device to express the splenetic inarticulacy of the teenager. On '19', some 20 years later, the mechanical effect of chopping up a human voice was entirely appropriate to the lyric of this song. The triumph of machine over man in music paralleled the reduction of the individual to a statistic in high-tech modern warfare. What happened then of course was, as with all imitation, the effect became redundant by thoughtless repetition and misuse. By the 1990s pop hits routinely sampled and chopped up the singer's voice, regardless of creative justification or lyrical context. What in '19' is a fine means-to-an-end became a routine gesture of dehumanisation.

For the '19' rhythm track, Hardcastle used a Roland TR-808 Rhythm Composer – a sophisticated early programmable drum machine, and another digital device central to much dance music of the last 20 years – but the part itself is simple: he confessed he was in too much of a hurry to program something more complex. Using a collage technique, the track incorporates drum machine, bass synth, synth chord pads, a high synth melody, sound effects, spoken dialogue, and Janice Hoyt on vocals.

CREATIVE TIPS

Hardcastle on demos: "I used to do demos on a little portastudio and think, 'Yeah, great'. But when you do them again in the studio, the initial idea's been lost... and half the vibe... The best way to make a record is when you get initially excited about it, when you're adding bits and pieces, and it sounds great."

The song structure is loosely verse and chorus, but with considerable variations dictated by the spoken text extracts he wanted to fit in; notice how verse 3 strips everything back to voice and drums. Harmonically, '19' has two sections in a phrygian E minor: one is four bars, going from Em to a D over an E with a keyboard melody on top; then there is a three-note bass riff, which takes a bar, first heard at 0.47 – and using the same notes as Bjork sings on the verse of 'Army Of Me' (track 86). Towards the end, orchestra stabs hit F and B together – creating the dissonant augmented 4th interval (see Metallica for another instance of this).

The lyric surely makes this one of the greatest protest songs of the 1980s. '19' evokes the horrors of the war, providing chilling statistics to a dance beat. Key words leap out – it was probably one of the first times the public heard the phrase "Post Traumatic Stress Disorder"; notice the reference to the Purple Heart medal towards the end, and the way the following "Saigon" is pitch-shifted upward and sped-up, suggesting the hysteria of the war-makers. It's an example of a record where the sound communicates as much as the words themselves.

Listen for: the orchestra strikes at 1.11, 2.39, 3.05; the scream at 1.30, preceded by a laser noise; and the fragment of military trumpet in G major whose gung-ho nature contrasts ironically with the track.

LINKS

There were a number of different mixes of '19', including longer ones with more graphic content for the 12-inch format, and foreign language versions. Hardcastle has actually had ten other singles in the UK Top 60 (I wonder how many you can name...), as well as numerous re-mixes and tracks released under various pseudonyms. He also now writes film and television music.

KISS

PRINCE & THE REVOLUTION 1986

"'Kiss' doesn't sound like anything else... I have no idea where it came from. They're gifts. They aren't conscious efforts – you just have to get them out. Nothing in it makes sense. Nothing. The hi-hat doesn't make sense..." (PRINCE)

Minimalist. Deconstruction. Helium. The first three words that spring to mind listening to Prince's 'Kiss'. While many chart acts at the time were heading for ever bigger productions, Prince took a sideways step and came up with this ear-arresting confection. Let's apply these three words, one at a time, to the analysis...

First, minimalist. Here is the opposite to an everything-plus-the-kitchen-sink arrangement. Not so much a *wall* as a shoebox-of-sound. The first verse is carried with little more than a drum machine, lead vocal and a single synth part that sketches in the chords. Notice the dryness of the sound (a stylistic forerunner of much 1990s dance music), with the tight, probably gated snare drum augmented by a low 'crunch' noise spread left and right, along with the hi-hat and cymbal.

WRITER	Prince & The Revolution
PRODUCER	Prince
RECORDED	Paisley Park, Minneapolis
DURATION	3.40
RELEASED	Paisley Park, April 1986
CHART	US 1 UK 6

When the song reaches the first hook, backing vocals join in, before the ringing guitar chord (an allusion to Jimmy Nolen's famous phrase in James Brown's 'Papa's Got A Brand New Bag') and the "kiss" Prince squeezes into the gap. As the song proceeds other instruments are added – a second synth in verse 2, the lead guitar with wah-wah during the break – but the instrumentation remains slight. It is this sense of what is missing that piques the listener's ear.

Second, deconstruction. One of the reasons Prince can be so minimal about the arrangement is because the underlying form is one that is instantly recognisable to the audience: the 12-bar blues. In blues and rock'n'roll, the '12-bar' takes the following form: four bars on chord I, two on chord IV, two on chord I, and then one each on V, IV, I, and V, making 12 in all. Prince expands/deconstructs this by first doubling the length of chord I from four to eight bars, and doubling its second appearance from two to four bars; his last line (where the hook is) comprises two bars on V, and two on IV repeated. It's a clever variation on the 12-bar – people unconsciously know what chords go where in such a familiar song form, so Prince is able to imply them.

Third, helium. Another arresting feature is the heady falsetto in which Prince sings this; the odd occasion he comes out of falsetto is quite a shock – as at 1.27 and 3.21. The timing of the vocal shows he is thinking as much about the rhythm of the phrases as their melodic relationship with the underlying harmony – such rhythmic phrasing was taken to absurdly mannered extremes by Michael Jackson.

CREATIVE TIPS

As the cliché goes, less is more – sometimes it's what's not there that counts.

LINKS

Tom Jones had a hit with a more traditional production of this song with Art Of Noise in 1988. For influences on Prince, see track 32 - and Little Richard, and Sly Stone.

TRACK 71

CHINA IN YOUR HAND

T'PAU 1987

"What I can't stand is huge great pompous theories from artists and journalists on pop music, because, for crying out loud, we're not doing anything important, we've got no deep and meaningful reason for doing what we do – we just enjoy it... They try and find the gravity and credibility behind everything, and there isn't... Why does everyone have to analyse it?"

(CAROL DECKER)

Ladeez'n'gennelmen... a big hand for The Power Ballad... This was T'Pau's second single: the first, 'Heart And Soul', reached number 4 on both sides of the Atlantic. With her Nicole Kidman red curls and office-wear suit, Carol Decker was a Cilla for the 1980s – the girl next door from Shrewsbury. 'China In Your Hand' is a gift for any singer – a real belter (I mean, just think of the devastation that would have resulted if Whitney Houston had dropped this on us... oh no, let's not...). To her credit, Decker sticks to the melody and doesn't try to show off with unnecessary vocal decoration. Yes, I know it's pompous and a bit silly... but it makes you want to go and have a relationship crisis just to savour that whoops-there-goes-the-floor drum sound.

'China In Your Hand' was produced by Roy Thomas Baker, who had worked with Queen (see track 44) and so knew a thing or two about knob-twiddling for Stadium Excess. In contrast to the Spector wall-of-sound, which depended less on reverb and more on having a barrage of instruments, big 1980s productions tend to have few instruments and tons of reverb. The mix gives us piano, synth, and pizzicato strings on one side; lead vocal, bass and drums in the middle; and a stereo echo takes the keyboards to the opposite side. The chorus has a single-note guitar phrase doubled at an octave – a technique Queen used for 'Who Wants To Live Forever'. Listen for the double-tracked vocal on the chorus.

WRITER	Carol Decker / Ron Rogers
PRODUCER	Roy Thomas Baker
RECORDED	Los Angeles
DURATION	3.43
RELEASED	Siren Records, October 1987
CHART	UK 1 US –

From the drums, you'd think this had been recorded at Headley Grange (where Zep did 'When The Levee Breaks'): it's not really Bonham's drum sound, but rather The Idea Of Bonham's Drum Sound – an entity which haunted studios in the 1980s, coming from 'Kashmir', via Simple Minds and Phil Collins. It became a mad competition to see who could get a drum sound that caused objects to fall off mantelpieces during a tom fill. I mean, the bass drum alone here sounds like ten firms of furniture removers are having difficulty shifting a mahogany wardrobe in each of the ten houses on either side of you. 'China In Your Hand' is probably one of the last great exercises in the Big Drum Sound before it was replaced by the Big Boom-Boom of the drum machine.

Structurally, the song throws in a nice false ending, with the return of the sax and vocal ad libs on the coda. Sax solos – which were revived in pop largely thanks to Raphael Ravenscroft's licks on Gerry Rafferty's 'Baker Street' in the late 1970s, and reinforced by hits from Hazel O'Connor, Spandau Ballet, George Michael and the like – have a coded meaning in this sort of context, along the lines of, "We're more sophisticated than them yobs who'd have stuck a guitar solo in here".

CREATIVE TIPS

Try a false, early ending and then come roaring back when your listener is not expecting it.

The title is cleverly ambiguous: lots of people idly musing on bus journeys enjoyed the realisation that "china" had nothing to do with the country, and this was not a disguised anthem for Mao Tse-tung. The lyric (allegedly inspired by Mary 'Frankenstein' Shelley) is actually fairly incomprehensible in the verses. What appears to be a sci-fi scenario about a child in the form of a man sweeps by with words like "prophecy" and "fantasy" flying in the wind, scrambling the radar of comprehension like so much tin foil. But the chorus is direct and smart, reversing the common notion that it's great to get what you want.

The drums are held back until the first chorus. But you know they're coming. The dynamics are as contrived as a ride on the Big Dipper, but it works regardless. Also listen for: the 1.50 fill into "them"; 2.56 drums fills; and the sax player's lovely choice of notes on the III-IV change, at 2.38-40. Decker's vocal fill at 3.22 – "You shouldn't push too hard" – is irresistibly 1960s in its melodrama, hinting at the pop roots of this song; and there's a lovely blues phrase at 3.45. Notice how Decker pronounces the "d" in "land" and "hand" as a "t" – it sounds like she's singing about 'China In Your Hat'.

LINKS

I have heard at least one version of this on a compilation in which the last minute inexplicably turns into mono - so purchase carefully. T'Pau got their strange name from a minor character in **Star Trek** ***- and apparently (trivia fans) the Trek fan lobby consequently persuaded the programme to name one of their space-ships the USS Decker in response.***

"probably one of the last great exercises in the Big Drum Sound before it was replaced by the Big Boom-Boom of the drum machine"

TRACK 72

WITH OR WITHOUT YOU

U2 1987

"I just started writing with the echo and it all happened... Parts that would have sounded at best bland without the echo suddenly sounded amazing... "

(THE EDGE, ON HOW HIS GUITAR STYLE EVOLVED)

This was one of a number of tracks from U2's fifth album, *The Joshua Tree*, which propelled the group to the position of World's Biggest Rock Band. U2 were one of the few rock bands who played as though music could change the world, and whose lyrics reflected social, religious and political themes. In this sense, although they don't sound like them, they are heirs to The Who; there are other resemblances too – notably that both were formidable live acts. Bono's voice has some of the power, projection and tortured reaching-after-selflessness of Daltrey. And both bands had a guitarist with an immediately recognisable style.

At the close of the 1980s, U2 acquired a reputation for being musically overblown – the band later made energetic attempts to deconstruct their own version of stadium rock, which led to the more experimental, ironic 1990s albums. But 'With Or Without You' demonstrates that even at the height of their stadium phase, their sense of arrangement was far ahead of most rock bands.

WRITER	Bono / Edge / Adam Clayton / Larry Mullen
PRODUCER	Daniel Lanois / Eno / Steve Lillywhite
RECORDED	Windmill Lane Studios, Dublin
DURATION	4.57
RELEASED	Island, March 1987
CHART	US 1 UK 4

To appreciate the skill of this track you first have to look at the musical building blocks. When it's not hovering on a D chord, 'With Or Without You' comprises a single four-bar sequence of D A Bm G (I V VI IV) – a sequence that has been used on many hits, including Men At Work's 'Down Under', The Police's 'So Lonely', and 'Since You've Been Gone' by Rainbow, to name but three. U2's arrangement has two major elements that make it different: first, this progression is subjected to a dynamic in which the song starts quiet and slowly builds to a roaring climax, dies away, and then has a partial recovery; secondly, at no time are these chords fully articulated – 999 bands out of 1000 would have had a couple of acoustic guitars merrily strumming their way through these changes. U2 avoid this. Instead, the chords are implied in the musical space between the bass root notes and the Edge's guitar parts, none of which are straightforward chords.

The song opens with a minimal drum-beat playing eighths, and on the right a high rippling triplet D major arpeggio, which continues throughout. Dry on the left (and reverbed/treated on the right) is a high sustained guitar part created by a gizmo known as the 'Infinite guitar', invented by Michael Brook (with whom Edge had worked on the soundtrack of *Captive*). As Edge explained: "It has a similar effect to the E-Bow, but the disadvantage of the E-Bow is that it's either on or off, whereas this gives you all the mid-points between no sustain and infinite sustain, and different levels of 'emergence' of the note."

CREATIVE TIPS

Take a simple chord progression and find a way of implying the chords, not actually playing them.

At 0.09 the bass enters in eighths, in time with the kick drum. At this point the arrangement has a vertical quality – with something low, something very high and not a lot in the middle; towards the end of the first verse another instrument appears in the centre at 0.58; then a handclap at 1.09 is immediately followed by some startling 'treated' guitar on the right from 1.13-19; the drums get heavier at 1.45, on the link into verse 3; at 1.52 we have the first appearance of the Edge's high-string guitar riff – a 5th opening to a 6th – with lots of delay (his trademark sound); at 2.06 the first hint of backing vocals come in for "give yourself" – these can be heard again at 2.32 where the lead vocal is answered by the guitar.

Bono's passionate delivery of the title is supported by tougher drums, and then at 3.03 the song peaks with a bursting out of emotion that can't be kept in any longer. At this point there is an increase in 16th-note rhythms – on guitar, cymbals and tambourine. A couple of Bono's vocal phrases appear to be double-tracked here to thicken them out, since they are competing with a dense backing. At 3.38 the music dies back to what it sounded like during the intro. Bono's falsetto at 3.48 is supplemented at the lower end by what sounds like a bass synth doubling the bass guitar (see at 3.53). There is a certain nobility about the way the music picks itself up for the coda, recovering some of its intensity with the re-appearance of the Edge's main riff.

LINKS

For implied rather than played chords, see track 70. For a later U2 song, see track 99.

"999 bands out of 1000 would have had a couple of acoustic guitars merrily strumming these changes"

TRACK 73

TOWER OF STRENGTH

THE MISSION 1988

"I'm of the old school I suppose – if you can sit down with an acoustic guitar, sing it and strum it, then it's a song; you don't need drum machines and sequencers, though obviously we'll use them to embellish the song."

(WAYNE HUSSEY)

Goth was a funny mixture of rock, nouveau hippies in black nail varnish, tarot cards and too much exposure to the *Rocky Horror Picture Show*. In record sales it amounted to Not A Lot, but it was a fine excuse to dress up once new romanticism was a thing of the past. In fact, perhaps this was the last rock audience that actually did dress up. The chief bands were The Mission, who formed out of the ashes of the original line-up of goth pioneers Sisters of Mercy, along with All About Eve, and the Fields Of The Nephilim – the last of whom came on like escapees from a spaghetti western, and kept flour manufacturers' shares up by regularly dusting the stuff all over themselves.

The Led Zep revival was in full swing by 1988: heavy rock bands seemed intent on re-

CREATIVE TIPS

For a taste of the mystic East, an open tuning will yield octave scales over a droning accompaniment – the poor man's sitar.

writing large swathes of Zep's back catalogue (Whitesnake were one notable example). The Mission loved Zep too – their single 'Severina' had lifted the intro of 'Achilles Last Stand'. And 'Tower Of Strength' (nothing to do with Frankie Vaughan's jaunty 1961 hit, in case you wondered) was a rather good take on a Zep-like slice of Turkish Delight – its authenticity helped no end by getting none other than Zep bassist John Paul Jones to write the terrific string part and produce it.

'Tower' starts with exotic percussion – tablas and so on – and massed acoustic guitars, most likely in an altered tuning because they have a droning quality (with octaves moving up and down but other strings remaining the same). Bass and drums don't come in fully until about 1.20. The chords move across the basic three-note riff. At 2.20 we get Jones' string break – listen out for the way he harmonises his initial melody. The song is finished off with some powerful drum fills (a minor outbreak of war at 2.48), and choked lead guitar at various points.

WRITER	Wayne Hussey / Craig Adams / Mick Brown / Simon Hinkler
PRODUCER	John Paul Jones
RECORDED	The Manor Studios, Oxfordshire
DURATION	4.33
RELEASED	Phonogram, January 1988
CHART	UK 12 US 126

'Tower' is basically an over-wrought hymn of adoration to the singer's main squeeze, set to an intoxicating rhythm. You only have to hear the line "You lift me up..." to know exactly where the lyric's going; "Salvation lies just a touch away", sings Hussey in his characteristically histrionic style. Lyrically, all very un-Zep. I mean, adoration? Nah... they'd be writing songs about abusing groupies with goldfish... or something.

LINKS

Cliff Richard has never done a cover version of this. In case you wondered.

TRACK 74

DESPERATE PEOPLE

LIVING COLOUR 1988

"Be real with the people you're working with. If things bother you, don't just let it sit there and eat away at you. Have the courage to speak up. If there's something you don't agree with - if you don't like the producer, or the record label - don't, just for the sake of a little fame, sacrifice essentially who you really are, because who you are is gonna come out and bite you." (VERNON REID)

CREATIVE TIPS

Great arrangements benefit from attention to detail... If you're playing a riff why not fool with it, just once?.. And tempo changes can enhance the excitement of a rock song.

Formed as a three-piece in New York in 1984, it was as a quartet that Living Colour came to prominence with this fine debut album. Guitarist Reid was invited to play on Mick Jagger's album *Primitive Cool* and Jagger got so fired up by Living Colour that he helped with the production of their album once they'd got a record deal. The band had their biggest UK hit in 1991 with 'Love Rears Its Ugly Head';while their best-selling US hit was 'Cult Of Personality', from the debut album *Vivid*.

There was always more musical intelligence in Living Colour than most comparable bands from the late 1980s, and *Vivid* shows there's nothing like a touch of soul to make hard rock groove a little. It remains an effective cross-fertilisation of heavy rock and funk – a style that requires considerable musical technique.

Living Colour had a way of throwing in the odd accent or beat here and there that would make you sit up and take notice, lifting the material above the average – and the individual bandmembers had the chops to pull it off. Funky basslines and soul-influenced vocals were matched with a heavy rock drum sound and the squalling lead guitar and heavy riffs of guitarist Reid.

Reid could play Hendrix-style 'Little Wing' fills, bassy riffs, dive-bombing tremolo notes, squealing harmonics, and throw in a few jazz chords for good measure – he soon found himself featured in the US guitar press as a fretboard hero. He was also tagged as the first black guitarist to draw Hendrix comparisons since Ernie Isley – but as Reid famously commented at the time, whenever people sought to make this an issue: "It's not odd that black people play rock'n'roll – what's really odd is that people think it's odd."

WRITER	**Vernon Reid / Cory Glover / Will Calhoun / Muzz Skillings**
PRODUCER	**Ed Stasium**
RECORDED	**Skyline Sound on Sound / Right Track Studios, New York**
DURATION	**5.36**
RELEASED	**(album, Vivid) Epic, September 1988**
CHART	**b-side of 'Middle Man', May 88 US – UK –**

In 'Desperate People' they had a killer song and arrangement. Opening on feedback imitating a siren, the song begins like a whirlwind with two bars of fast triplets, only to suddenly drop to a medium-paced sledgehammer riff at 0.55; the main riff (B E G A) is used for the verse and the hookline; the bridge chords are the same as the intro but at a different tempo – they show a good use of inversions, E/B B B/G D/A D. The song ends with a jazzy chord echoed back and forth, left and right.

Like much of *Vivid*, the lyrics of 'Desperate People' couldn't have been further from the usual Satan Ate My Troll of 1980s HM. It's an address to someone who is floundering in a drug habit, the lyric proceeding by a series of neat reversals: the subject is crying in the sunshine and laughing in the rain, and has a life like TV; the bridge tells them they need help, but first, "You have to help yourself".

As on Van Halen's debut, there are minimal overdubs. The guitar is recorded in stereo to spread the sound out (especially noticeable on the solo), and the bass is bright. Listen for: the great kick drum pattern under the main riff; the snare drum going four-to-the-bar on the coda; the strong vocals on the bridge; the brilliant reversed accent before the solo at 3.51, where once and only once the band do a wrong-foot slam; and the echo at the end of the solo (4.36), which is first left then right, pealing down.

LINKS

For another rock band recorded with minimal overdubs, see track 52.

"a way of throwing in the odd accent or beat that would make you sit up and take notice"

TRACK 75

I WANNA BE ADORED

THE STONE ROSES 1989

"When we'd finished recording, Leckie comes up to us and says, 'Listen, this is really good. You're going to make it'. And I remember thinking, 'I know'. It could've been even better. Mani and Reni didn't get their thing down as heavy as it was in rehearsals. I think Leckie had listened to 'Waterfall' and thought it sounded like Simon & Garfunkel, so he's turned the bass and drums down. He's gone for that Byrds, Sixties thing. But Mani was the best white bass player I'd heard, and I wish that was more audible on the record." (IAN BROWN)

In between The Smiths and Britpop was Manchester – and, in particular, The Stone Roses. The Stone Roses were prime under-achievers who took the torch of guitar rock from The Smiths, held it aloft for their acclaimed debut, *The Stone Roses*, and then made it burn a different colour for their sprawling, belated follow-up *The Second Coming*. John Squire is a guitarist who has never fully realised his potential: on the first album he did some fine 1960s jangle, and on the second he showed he could play heavy 1970s rock lead with a bit of soul (he is in fact one of the few guitarists, along with the likes of Slash, who actually picked up anything of Jimmy Page's lead style – as opposed to those who simply copy Zep riffs).

'I Wanna Be Adored' is highly imaginative in terms of the atmosphere it creates: it fades in to a chilling soundscape, a subterranean vision like something out of William Blake – some hidden god of unreason moving wheels in clouds; the bass enters at 0.40, closely followed by a doomy chugging riff on guitar, then another guitar high up, playing pentatonic echoed figures that ripple and scurry like silver salamanders over black rock; the bass drum enters on the beat at 1.13; the background noise fades at 1.30 as the main theme appears on doubled guitars at contrasted octaves; acoustic guitars enter on the left at 2.21.

WRITER	**John Squire / Ian Brown**
PRODUCER	**John Leckie**
RECORDED	**Battery Studios, London / Rockfield Studios, Wales**
DURATION	**4.50**
RELEASED	**Silvertone, May 1989 (12-inch)**
CHART	**UK 20 (1991) US –**

Harmonically, the song has two sections: the first is a four-bar D G D Em progression; the second is an eight-bar bridge moving from D to C and back at about 3.04-24 (with more prominent cymbal work). It's in E minor – an especially potent key on the guitar because of the low E and other available open strings.

I wonder how many people first hearing this song thought the key line was, "I don't need to save my soul / He's already in me"? Had it been so, the band would have given rock music one of its greatest spiritual songs: 'I Wanna Be Adored' would have been a substitute for the ghastly sentimentality of most religious popular music – a Gnostic evocation of the *strangeness* and *otherness* of God. Sad to say, the line is actually, "I don't need to *sell* my soul" – so we're once more (as The Stones would put it) dancing with Mr D.

The generally minimalist lyric leaves it up to the music to work on the imagination. Vocally, there's a case for saying that Ian Brown was always the weakest link in the band – this is painfully apparent on 'Tears', where his vocal adds almost nothing to an otherwise fine track. Here, notice he is sharp on "adored" at 3.38-40.

Listen also for: the return of the guitar runs at 3.33, and the flourishes at about 3.45, and

at 4.24 there's a fine slowing up, with feedback. There's some excellent drumming too: the double snare-drum at 1.29, and the bass drum thereafter, the off-beat snare at 2.12, 2.20, and 2.46, and the hi-hat work in verse 2 at 2.35.

LINKS

Although first released (on 12-inch EP) in 1989, 'I Wanna Be Adored' didn't chart until the 7-inch version was issued in 1991. There is an early version on Garage Flower *(1996) and a re-mix on* The Stone Roses - The Remixes. *Producer John Leckie worked as a tape-operator for Phil Spector on George Harrison's* All Things Must Pass *(see track 33), and has gone on to work with, among others, Radiohead.*

CREATIVE TIPS

One way of getting more inspiration from something you've already recorded is to listen to it backwards – you might want to use this as a piece of music in itself and maybe sing over it... or if you listen to a backward lyric the nonsense syllables can sound like words – these might suggest a new lyric... or the backward music might give you an idea for a new chord progression... The Stone Roses used these techniques with a number of tracks ('Don't Stop' is 'Waterfall' backwards, for instance).

"prime under-achievers who took the torch of guitar rock from The Smiths"

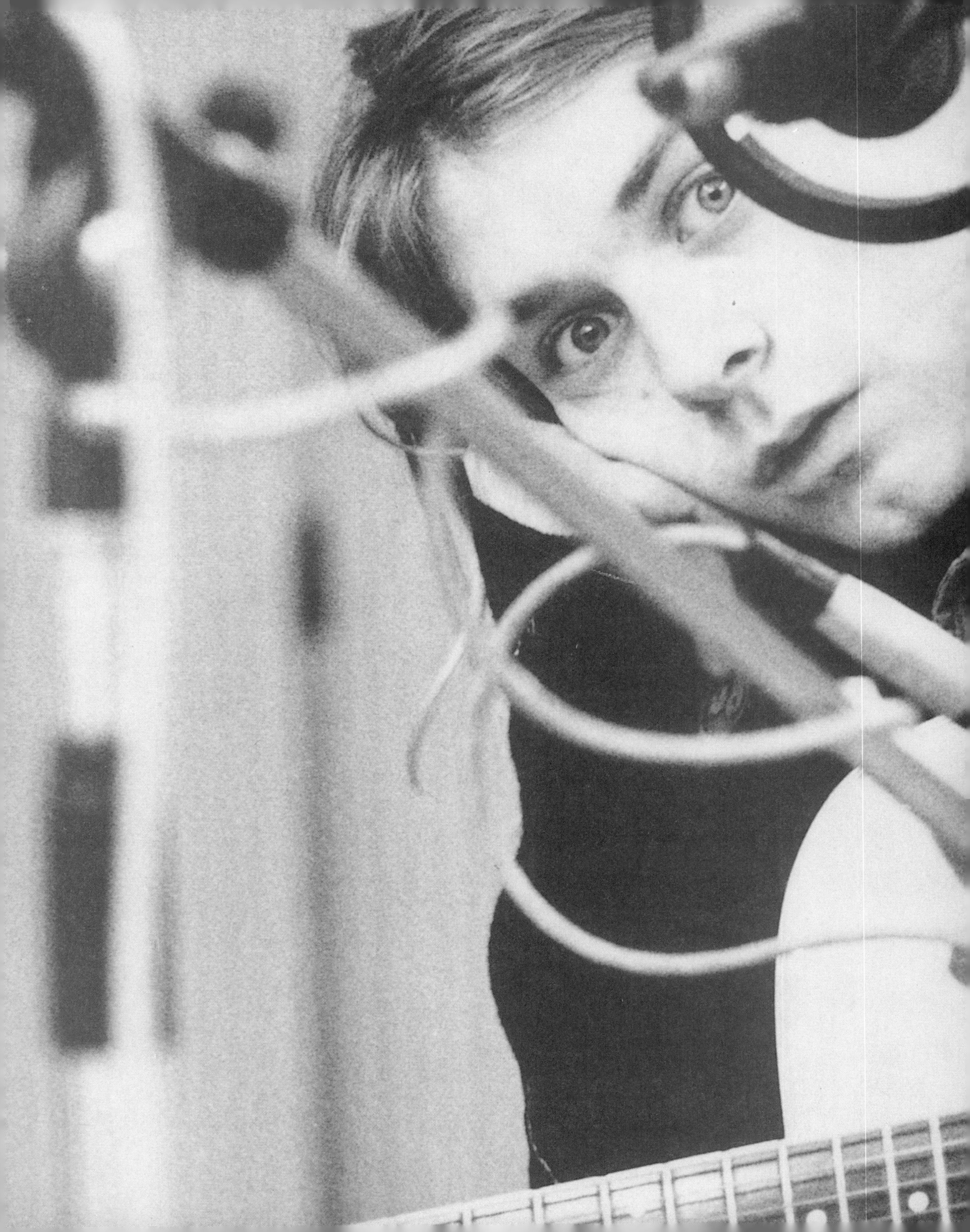

76	The La's	*There She Goes*
77	Metallica	*Enter Sandman*
78	Nirvana	*Smells Like Teen Spirit*
79	Madonna	*Erotica*
80	Bruce Springsteen	*If I Should Fall Behind*
81	Suede	*Animal Nitrate*
82	Grant Lee Buffalo	*Fuzzy*
83	Beck	*Loser*
84	Soundgarden	*Fell On Black Days*
85	Duran Duran	*Thank You*
86	Bjork	*Army Of Me*
87	Jeff Buckley	*Last Goodbye*
88	Tori Amos	*Not The Red Baron*
89	Dodgy	*In A Room*
90	Radiohead	*Let Down*
91	The Verve	*This Time*
92	Madonna	*Frozen*
93	Catatonia	*Road Rage*
94	Gomez	*Get Miles*
95	R.E.M	*At My Most Beautiful*
96	Garbage	*The World Is Not Enough*
97	Goldfrapp	*Lovely Head*
98	Queens Of The Stone Age	*Better Living Through Chemistry*
99	U2	*Beautiful Day*
100	Radiohead	*Everything In Its Right Place*

TRACK 76

THERE SHE GOES

THE LA'S 1990

"Modern studios – we just don't mix. They put noise reduction on everything and it takes away the hiss and that; it also taps some other frequency where all the ambience and harmonics are – you're left with the bare bones." (LEE MAVERS)

"When he came in that day, Lee just said he had something new while we were jamming. With the intro riff it was immediately obvious – I just thought, 'That is fantastic'. You could tell it was a great song. Everything else just followed." (PAUL HEMMINGS, GUITARIST)

If the stories are true it would seem we are lucky to have 'There She Goes' at all. It was written by Mavers in 1987, and apparently recorded more than once by the band, but never entirely to the satisfaction of the notoriously perfectionist singer-songwriter. The sessions for the band's first (and only) album were also protracted and difficult – songs were recorded repeatedly at Mavers request, but still fell short of his standards. In the end the label put out what they had, regardless – Mavers has claimed that half the album is based on demos and guide vocals.

Ironically, despite his pivotal role, Mavers wasn't the band's original frontperson. The La's were formed in Liverpool in 1984 by Mike Badger, but he was ousted in 1986 by Mavers, who took charge of the band's creative output; but Mavers proved increasingly hard to please, and to work with, and ultimately stifled the band's career. Since then there have been rumours of Mavers recording, but nothing more concrete. John Powers, who played bass in the band, went on to form Cast, whose hits like 'Walk Away' in some ways continued the La's sound (though Mavers has been reportedly scathing of his efforts).

WRITER	Lee Mavers
PRODUCER	Bob Andrews / John Leckie / Mike Hedges / Steve Lillywhite
RECORDED	Chipping Norton / Devon / and London (1988-89)
DURATION	2.41
RELEASED	Go! Discs, November 1990
CHART	UK 13 (59, 1989; 65 1999) US 49 (1991)

CREATIVE TIPS

Unexpected leaps add vitality to a melody.

Whatever Mavers misgivings about this recording, 'There She Goes' is undeniably a piece of sublime guitar-driven pop. It was eventually a hit on its re-release at the beginning of the 1990s, though its spirit and feel are very 1960s – it might be compared to 'Jesamine', though it's not as innocent. (Mavers has been quoted as saying the band's influences were as much Beefheart and Bo Diddley as The Beatles and Merseyside.) Visually, The La's themselves might have been mistaken for a lost incarnation of The Yardbirds onstage.

'There She Goes' starts with a chiming stereo guitar figure, and gradually more guitars enter until drums, bass and acoustics come in and widen out in the stereo image. The droney effect of the main riff depends on the repeated D, and the chiming effect of E D E D E D on the top two strings, one open, one fretted. The guitar also uses thirds on the top two strings, which is reminiscent of The Smiths. There is a delightful 'bloom' of reverb at 0.13 seconds. Listen for the backing vocal in verse 2 which echoes the verse lines, then harmonises low in the mix. The bridge hits an E minor chord and a variation on the main guitar figure. About 1.16 there's an electric guitar playing the main riff,

and a slight hint of castanets. At 1.42 the vocal lines multiply – there are three separate vocal parts on the coda.

The song is squarely in G major, with a main change of G D Cadd9, and an Am appearing in the third line. The bridge is remarkably good, not only for its dramatic Em start, but the change in rhythm for the G D C D, and the build-up to the last verses.

'There She Goes' has an unusual melody, notable for its range and interval leaps. On the surface it's an entranced love song, expressing the self-transcending feelings of love. But is the drug experience a metaphor for love, or the other way around? The trance-like feeling is partly created by musical effects such as the droning guitars and repeated D of the riff, but also the fact that the lyric uses eight rhymes on the 'ane' sound (nine if you count the approximation "name"). So, in its own way, 'There She Goes' is a lesson in a degree of musical stasis.

LINKS

American band Sixpence None The Richer covered this in 1999 (and had more success in the US than The La's version did), prompting a third release of the original single. The La's album was remastered in 2001.

> "a piece of sublime guitar-driven pop"

TRACK 77

ENTER SANDMAN

METALLICA 1991

"I always find that the first song you write for an album has a certain magic – and that was 'Enter Sandman'. This song just has such a feel to it that we felt it should be the first new thing people heard. It's one of the easiest songs we've ever written. If you're gonna narrow it down, it's about nightmares from a little kid's point of view..." (LARS ULRICH)

From Ye Booke Of Eternal Darknesse, Cacophonies chapter 3, verse 666 and following... In the beginning, there was the heavy rock of Zep, Purple and Sabbath. Of these three Sabbath became the hoary grandfathers of Heavy Metal. In the late 1970s the New Wave of British Heavy Metal (NWOBHM) – Iron Maiden, Def Leppard, Saxon, Judas Priest *et al* – took up the legacy of pentatonic minor riffs. Thence a third generation of headbangers was spawned in America – Anthrax, Slayer, Megadeth and Metallica – whose brand of heavy rock was often detuned riffery that owed less and less to the blues-based hard rock of the late 1960s/early 1970s, and was often played at lightning speed. When the dust settled, Metallica

(formed in San Francisco in 1981) emerged as kings of the pack. They will go down as possibly the most important HM band of the genre's twilight years.

Metallica are to HM what the stealth bomber is to aviation: darker and meaner than anything else. They discovered that slowing the tempos raised the megatonnage of the payload. They jettisoned the more cartoony aspects of earlier versions of HM and played up the existential despair. They popularised a new harmonic vocabulary for HM, using a *b*5 and *b*2 in the natural minor scale (E F G A B*b* B C D); in came the 'scalloped' power-chord with its thumping top and bottom-boosted EQ; and along with the carpet-bombing riffage, they also had a maniacal sense of arrangement.

WRITER	**James Hetfield / Lars Ulrich / Kirk Hammett**
PRODUCER	**Metallica / Bob Rock**
RECORDED	**One On One Studios, Los Angeles**
DURATION	**5.25**
RELEASED	**(US) Electra; (UK) Vertigo, June 1991**
CHART	**US 16 UK 5**

The whole pantomime of HM has little to do with any recognisable world of human experience – but it's a vicarious thrill to ride the back of this particular beast. Earlier Metallica albums are more thrashy, frenetic, with epic, convoluted songs. With their eponymous, plain-sleeved fifth album (also known, in Beatles/Spinal Tap fashion, as 'The Black Album') they cut the waffle and perfected their style, taking head-banging to new levels of Germanic precision (and in the process going to number 1 on both sides of the Atlantic). Ever since then they've been trying to escape the black-hole event horizon of their own darkness.

'Enter Sandman' starts with a cleanish guitar arpeggio and one cat-spit of wah-wah, before the drums and bass enter, followed by the riff. Listen for the guitar on the opposite side to the riff, which initially is changing from an E5 to A5 chord; both guitars play the riff at the end of this long build-up. Heavy damping of strings and boosting of certain frequencies means the riff sounds as though your speakers are about to disembowel themselves. That's the intention. The verses use a semitone E-F shift, and the chorus goes up to F# C-B (another tritone) for "Exit light – enter night". The guitar solo is a good one, but should be compared with Cobain's on 'Smells Like Teen Spirit', which is musically more integral to the song. Listen for the guitar's tremolo arm gargling on the last note of the solo.

CREATIVE TIPS

There is a masterful arrangement stroke with the unexpected re-entry of the rhythm section at 4.28, two riffs earlier than you expect... Remember that in rock and pop, four of anything is very predictable – so mix it up: repeat something three times instead of four – which moves the track along quicker – or add an extra couple of beats to a bar, to break things up.

The famous 'Enter Sandman' riff uses variations of the fabled tritone interval of E/B*b* – known in medieval church music as the 'devil's interval', and central to 1990s HM (for proof that this interval can be as erotic as diabolic see Led Zep's 'Dancing Days'). 'Enter Sandman' took its place in the pool of guitar riffs that people tend to play in music shops, joining a select group that includes 'Smoke On The Water' and 'Sweet Child O' Mine'.

James Hetfield has a style of singing that suggests he is about to shape-shift into a wolf at any moment. Lyrically, 'Enter Sandman' is a paean to Things That Go Bump In The Night, or at least (since Metallica are a *post-modern* HM band) Things That Kids *Think* Go Bump In The Night. There's a kitsch bridge section where the band quieten down and we hear a preacher reciting a prayer on one side of the mix and a child giving the responses on the other. The pay-off line is the bit about the beast "in your head" – the Sandman figure is really in the imagination. Hetfield's vocal seems to delight in terrorising this poor little kid who wants to go to sleep. But it's OK, she'll probably grow up to be an Eminem fan, and then the shoe will be on the other foot.

Listen for the glee with which Hetfield sings "exit light". It must also be said that Lars Ulrich is the Stewart Copeland of HM drumming: this man not only knows how to lay down a titanic beat, but also has a great line in off-beat drum strikes.

LINKS

For more heavy rock, see track 84.

T R A C K 7 8

SMELLS LIKE TEEN SPIRIT

NIRVANA 1991

"Everyone has focused on that song so much. The reason it gets a big reaction is people have seen it on MTV a million times – it's been pounded into their brains. But I think there are so many other songs I've written that are as good, if not better – like 'Drain You'." (KURT COBAIN)

Greatest rock record of the Nineties...? Next question...? Nirvana were at the heart of a seismic shift that rippled out of Seattle in the late 1980s. At that time US rock was predominantly a kind of hard rock/glam hybrid typified by Guns N' Roses, Poison, Motley Crue and others, and rock guitar was going through an especially technically-obsessed phase. Part of this was the generation-lapse fall-out from Van Halen's tapping in 1979, which upped the *ante* for what you had to do to be considered a gunslinger on the guitar block. Hence Vai, Satriani, Gambale, Malmsteen et al – an awful lot of widdling but nothing that connected to the mainstream. On the other hand there was a thriving US underground scene with bands like The Pixies, who influenced Cobain.

WRITER	**Kurt Cobain**
PRODUCER	**Butch Vig / Nirvana**
RECORDED	**Sound City Studios, Van Nuys, California**
DURATION	**4.58**
RELEASED	**Geffen, November 1991**
CHART	**US 6 UK 7**

Nirvana sparked a musical revolution by taking The Pixies' punk/garage sensibility and combining it with HM's riffage. Thus was born grunge. On *Nevermind* Nirvana gave grunge a pop edge by focusing its rage and power into verses and choruses, with memorable tunes. Cobain linked this musical force to his own angst, and accidentally wrote an anthem for the so-called 'blank generation', announcing in a maelstrom of self-loathing, "Here we are then / Entertain us".

Nirvana's sound has an imploding nuclear intensity – as can be heard on tracks like 'In Bloom' and 'On A Plain'. 'Smells Like Teen Spirit' has a clever arrangement, with powerful dynamics (something Nirvana intuitively grasped, and which always seemed to escape Oasis). The verses are sinister and quiet, the choruses raucous, exploding into thrashed guitar, wild drums and doubled-up vocal. The verse is actually the same chord sequence as the chorus but on the verse you only get the bass playing steady eighth root-notes to suggest this – the chords are implied, not stated. Instead the guitar plays only a 4th (C-F) with slight chorus effect pitch wobble (and it may be double-tracked – in other words recorded twice). These two notes are hit more frequently as the chorus is approached, during the "hello" repetitions.

Time to nail one myth about this chord sequence. Discussing the band Boston in *The Rough Guide To Rock* (1996), Charles Bottomley claims: "Listening to the heavenly 'More Than A Feeling' so affected one Kurt Cobain that he sold it to the Nineties generation under the title of 'Smells Like Teen Spirit'..." But in fact the chords of these songs are not the same: 'More Than A Feeling' (see track 47) goes G C Em D (I IV VI V), whereas, if anything, 'Teen Spirit' is closer to a key-striding sequence like G-C-A-D – all major chords... But even that isn't it. Cobain's twist of genius was to dislocate this sequence by forcing the second two chords a minor third away from the first two: F B*b* Ab D*b*. Cobain himself confused the issue by talking about the Boston track – and the band were even known to (mischievously) launch into 'More Than A Feeling' before playing 'Teen Spirit' live...

CREATIVE TIPS

Use dynamics to make a song exciting... Get something new out of a familiar chord pattern by dislocating it.

One of the most arresting moments on the track is the "yay" that leaps out of the mix at 1:32 and 1.36, eclipsing the noise of the band. It uses a guitar technique called a unison bend: a note is held on the second string, and then on the third string, two frets higher up, a note is bent up a tone so the two strings sound at roughly the same pitch. On top of this goes Cobain's voice. The interjection is so abrupt as to jump out of the speakers.

As for the guitar break, Cobain crafts it out of the verse melody instead of using familiar bends. This is what makes it an era-defining solo – it's an anti-solo, with no guitar clichés in it. The same approach can be heard on Radiohead's 'Paranoid Android'. There's no showing off.

Taking its memorable title from a teen-marketed brand of deodorant, there's an enormous amount of frustration in the song's lyrics – sexual and otherwise (see "a mosquito / my libido") – as well as an offhand, bleakly resigned attitude best caught in, "I found it hard, it was hard to find, oh well, whatever, nevermind".

LINKS

Tori Amos's cover version, apparently loathed by Nirvana, is worth a listen for its sheer chutzpah and leap of imagination - obviously no-one could improve on Nirvana's rock arrangement, so Amos goes the other way and turns it into a torch ballad... Nirvana producer Butch Vig went on to form and play drums with Garbage (see track 96).

"focusing grunge's rage and power into verses and choruses, with memorable tunes"

TRACK 79

EROTICA
MADONNA 1992

"Art and music can never be too permissive, especially as they're an alternative to the reactionary attitudes of Reagan and the moral majority."
(MADONNA)

CREATIVE TIPS
Dissonance can be sexy.

Early in 1992, after nearly 30 international hits in just nine years, Madonna signed a new seven-year contract with Warner Brothers. Exhausted after the *Blonde Ambition* tour, she proceeded to throw herself into making films, recording a new album, and publishing a book called *Sex*. In October that year, three years after her last album, Madonna released what was in effect a double album, *Erotica*. It acknowledged recent developments in dance music, house, rap, and hip-hop – she was determined to move with the times, using new technology, like the ubiquitous sampler, as she went. Madonna's music thrives on a tension between its dance axis and its pop side, and the title track of *Erotica* shows that her best music often results when she brings these two into a creative balance.

The reputation of this single was probably affected by the adverse reaction to her endeavours at this time. She was suffering in part from over-exposure (in some senses quite literally) and a double album didn't help. 'Erotica' was seen as the record of the book, and suffered as a result.

Co-producer Pettibone's comment on the album serves as a good introduction to the single: "Pretty dark, introspective, with an R&B edge... The techniques I used are like the ones used in the Seventies – we went for the dirty rather than the clean sound everyone goes for nowadays". The song's production shows fine attention to detail, with a hypnotic groove and a sample from Kool & The Gang's 'Jungle Boogie'. The arrangement is sparse in the vein of 'Justify My Love', but more upbeat – there's more going on than you would think.

It starts with vinyl crackle and a low two-note bass riff. It clings seductively to its key chord of F# minor, though when the keyboard comes in it implies a D chord over the F# bass. The pre-chorus ("Give me love, do as I say") uses a D-F#m change, with the bass moving too. Essentially the song is mostly two chords with a third B minor hinted at towards the end (4.22 and 4.42) and an E over F# thereafter.

WRITER	Madonna Ciccone / Shep Pettibone
PRODUCER	Madonna / Shep Pettibone
RECORDED	Mastermix / Soundworks Studios, New York
DURATION	5.18
RELEASED	Maverick, October 1992
CHART	US 2 UK 3

Most of the vocals used, according to Pettibone, were from Madonna's original demos: over a large part of the song she does a spoken dominatrix rap about the pleasures of S&M, complete with a naughty implied rhyme (what could rhyme with "truck"?). She sings on the chorus (note the minor 9th), and at times there's a nice use of simultaneous spoken and sung phrases: for instance the slowed-down voice for the phrase "I'm not going to hurt you", and the coda, where she gets in some middle eastern-sounding scales, which take on a subversive power.

Listen out for: the jumpy funk guitar riff and the whirling sandstorms of strings in the background; every now and then a dissonant E# (it's E# rather than F because of the key) sounds a single bell-like note, very high up, against the F# minor chord (at 0.50 and 1.37, for example) – the same as had been used in 'Justify My Love'; there is a low-level scratching noise that moves from left to right and back, throughout; and notice the deep bassline (either a five-string bass or a convincing sample) putting some extra-low-end on the record.

LINKS

The album version is slightly longer than the single – the latter has the edge. For a later Madonna song, see track 92.

> "Madonna's music thrives on a tension between its dance axis and its pop side"

TRACK 80

IF I SHOULD FALL BEHIND

BRUCE SPRINGSTEEN 1992

"I think all the great records and all the great songs say, 'Hey, take this and find your place in the world. Do something with it, do anything with it. Find some place to make your stand, no matter how big or small it is." (BRUCE SPRINGSTEEN)

In Springsteen's career, commercial and critical acclaim have not always coincided. The bombast of his *Born In The USA* period turned many people off, even if they knew who he was before. In the 1990s he has achieved critical acclaim with albums like *The Ghost Of Tom Joad*, in which he relates himself deliberately to a folk tradition of American songwriting, and his one-man-and-a-portastudio album *Nebraska* has been favourably re-assessed. This change of style is reflected in the thinner, more nasal timbre of his recent singing (as here) in contrast to the soulful funkster of the second album and the Presley/Orbison butch vocals of *Born To Run* and *Darkness On The Edge Of Town*.

Popular music overflows with songs about the difficulties and disappointments of love, but has immensely fewer songs which convincingly describe the time when the romantic dream stops and the process of loving really begins. An example that should be better known is Paul McCartney's 'Maybe I'm Amazed', to which he gave one of his best-ever vocal performances on the mid-1970s live Wings album. Though not as openly passionate or secure in its belief, 'If I Should Fall Behind' is a song worthy to set beside it.

WRITER	**Bruce Springsteen**
PRODUCER	**Bruce Springsteen / Jon Landau / Chuck Plotkin**
RECORDED	**Thrill Hill Recording (BS's home studio), New Jersey**
DURATION	**2.55 (studio) 4.32 (live)**
RELEASED	**(albums, Lucky Town, In Concert) Columbia, 1992**
CHART	**not a single**

One of the marks of a top-flight songwriter is the ability to write a great song with a handful of chords – here Springsteen uses only I, IV and VI. But, like Dylan, Springsteen has sometimes seemed indifferent to the sonic aspects of making records, and this song is a case in point. The studio version has a 110bpm tempo, with a country-ish backbeat, synth pad, acoustic guitars on both sides – understated and workmanlike, it doesn't quite get to grips with the emotion in the songwriting.

Springsteen seems to have felt he could get more out of the song, making significant changes for the live MTV *In Concert* version, changing the key from D to E major and slowing the tempo to 102bpm. He sings the first verse with no percussion, just guitar and a synth. Verse 2 brings in the rest of the band and the last verse has the populist touch of mandolin-type strumming. The drums fall out for the last verse and re-enter for a repeat of the last lines. The live version puts a harmonica break before the bridge, and that's where you feel the difference in emotional depth. In recent years the song has become something of a concert set-piece, in which members of the band get to sing a line or two, as can be heard on Springsteen's *Live In New York City*.

'If I Should Fall Behind' has a magnificent lyric. A couple stand on the verge of marriage, facing the anxieties of commitment. Whereas romantic songs stress the similarities of lovers, this one embraces difference: in verse 2 Springsteen sings with a hard-won maturity, "But each lover's steps fall so differently". In the bridge the song addresses the fact that everyone "dreams of a love lasting and true" but that dream doesn't always survive contact with reality. Instead, we can at least "make our steps clear so the other may see". The last verse evokes

CREATIVE TIPS

Consider the possible effect of tempo, arrangement and key changes on a song... Write about real relationships, rather than idealised ones.

Biblical imagery of a river in the valley ahead, the oak tree, the path of life and the threat of mortality – "Should we lose each other in the shadow of the evening trees"...

The beauty of the hook, "If I should fall behind, wait for me" is in the way it describes human frailty, recognises it, and tries to support it through the promise of marriage. It also portrays marriage as a journey, not a destination, thus neatly avoiding a negative reaction of envy from the listener.

LINKS

In 1994 'If I Should Fall Behind' appeared on the B-side of 'Streets Of Philadelphia', Springsteen's biggest international hit since 1984's 'Dancing In The Dark'. For an early Bruce song, see track 43.

> "the ability to write a great song with a handful of chords"

TRACK 81

ANIMAL NITRATE

SUEDE 1993

"You recreate yourself as an outsider. Because you know you're not going to have fun as the centre of the gang, you're immediately drawn to people like David Bowie. When you live in an environment where there is nothing elegant, nothing lasting, you're bound to be drawn to someone like that."

(MATT OSMAN, BASSIST)

Suede emerged in 1992, had hits with 'Metal Mickey' and 'Animal Nitrate', then a UK number 1 debut album, which also won the 1993 Mercury Music prize, and even prompted brief talk in the music press about a glam revival. 'Animal Nitrate', their third single, sounds like Bowie circa 1972, and in a way like the last pop record in history. Suede made the right glam moves in terms of the bisexual 'are they/aren't they?' game – witness the two people kissing on the cover of their debut album, and the naked figure on the cover of the follow-up, *Dog Man Star*.

WRITER	Brett Anderson / Bernard Butler
PRODUCER	Ed Buller
RECORDED	Master Rock Studios, London
DURATION	3.24
RELEASED	Nude, February 1993
CHART	UK 7 US –

Of course the main reason Suede resemble glam-era Bowie is Brett Anderson's voice. Notice that it has a metallic, hysterical quality, as if on the verge of losing its grip on pitch and breaking upward. Aside from echo and double-tracking, this was probably achieved by taking part of the signal and feeding it through a harmoniser set an octave up

and then combining the higher notes with the straight vocal.

'Animal Nitrate' comes in on a bed of simmering feedback. The intro guitars chords have phasing added – the acoustic guitars give themselves away by their high, rattly noise – then there is a burst of parallel lead lines. Once the track is fully underway it's clear the guitars are substantially layered. Note the lead guitar playing the delightful chromatic lick on the chorus is unusually far forward in the mix.

Harmonically, the verse has a B minor feel as it works down the Bm A G Em sequence. By contrast the chorus is in D major, with D G D G Bm A G, but ends on a startling, unrelated C. The bridge/guitar break proves more adventurous, and has a chromatic chord shift as a surprise link back to the chorus.

CREATIVE TIPS
There's a time and a place for everything – especially handclaps.

Lyrically, it's a song about physical abuse, the title punning on the drug amyl nitrate. Details are less clear. Who is the person being talked to? Are they male or female? At first the chorus is, "Oh what turns you on", and later it becomes, "What does it take to turn you on / Now your animal's gone". Is the speaker seeking a relationship with this victim who is sexually repressed by their experiences?

Listen for: Butler's Mick Ronson-like single-note guitar fills in the verse, especially after the first two lines of lyric; the distorted chord at the end of chorus 2; and the sublime pop moment when the handclaps are introduced into the final choruses starting at 2.25. Careful listening reveals a cleaner lead guitar underneath the distorted one.

LINKS

For the originator of this style, see track 39. In America the band had to be called London Suede, to avoid confusion (and litigation) with another act.

TRACK 82

FUZZY
GRANT LEE BUFFALO 1993

"I don't believe any of us are going to find redemption in the government and those systems. We're going to have to find it in ourselves, and that's why we turn to the arts, to music, for some sort of inspiration, some sort of light."

(GRANT LEE PHILLIPS)

In the same year that Suede paid homage to glam-era Bowie with 'Animal Nitrate', this record paid homage to T.Rex... But how? It's partly a matter of the double-tracked vocal on the chorus, where Grant Lee swoops up into falsetto, and also the way he sings along with the guitar break; 'Fuzzy' even has a gentle rock'n'roll shuffle rhythm, such as Bolan might have used; and there is a distinct attempt to imitate the Bolan warble at 4.09.

CREATIVE TIPS
When recording with several acoustic guitars, try detuning one of them to get a deeper tone.

The other connection is the guitar break: here two fuzz-tone guitars panned left and right are playing roughly the same line but they deviate at various points, for example 2.38-40 – they don't maintain the strict symmetry of a harmonised line as found on mid-1970s Queen or Boston records. This deviation is the natural consequence of double-tracking a lead guitar part without listening to the first take at the same time, and then deciding to keep both of them. It is often more expressive than strict twin lead.

The production has beautifully-recorded acoustic guitars, tuned below concert pitch, and one of them in an altered tuning (possibly dropped D). Bass and drums come in on the chorus and continue through verse 2, where there's a slide guitar at the end of the first line. The bass and drums drop out for verse 3.

Harmonically 'Fuzzy' is... well, slightly fuzzy. It appears to be in D*b* but the hook word falls on an emphasised G*b*m, so there is a sense of moving between these two chords as potential key centres.

This is one of those lyrics that is easy to misunderstand: the hook, "I've been lied to", could also be "I'd like to" or "I would've liked to". An arresting line opens verse two: "The world is small enough for both of us"; another good one, in verse 3, is: "We water like a dead bouquet / It does no good, does it dear?". The lyric mentions returning home, possibly after a lovers' quarrel. The song ends with "We've been lied to" – by romantic love?

Listen for the excellent high guitar lead at 4.35.

WRITER	Grant Lee Phillips
PRODUCER	Paul Kimble
RECORDED	Machine Elf Studios, Los Angeles / San Francisco
DURATION	4.55
RELEASED	(album, Fuzzy) Slash, September 1993
CHART	US – UK –

LINKS

As well as being the title track of the band's debut album, 'Fuzzy' was actually released twice as a single – in 1991, on the Singles Only Label run by Bob Mould of Hüsker Dü/Sugar, and again in 1993 – but failed to chart either time. For more glam guitar, see tracks 38, 39 and 42.

TRACK 83

LOSER

BECK 1994

"You can do this stuff in the convenience of your home and you're not spending tons of money. You can play all the parts yourself and put them together like a composer would have done 200 years ago... What I've done has grown out of embracing limitations. It's about this marriage of lo-tech and hi-tech, trying to find the soul in the technology and use it as an instrument." (BECK)

If Nirvana are the blank generation's Beatles, is Beck their Dylan? As a child, moving between relatives in Los Angeles, Kansas and Europe, Beck Hansen was introduced to the music of Leadbelly, Woody Guthrie and Mississippi John Hurt, alongside industrial post-punk noise core. He tried and failed to make it in New York, then moved back to LA where he cut some independent singles that gained record company interest. His debut album, *Mellow Gold*, was a lo-fi collection of demos which caught people's ears because of the diverse mix of sounds; its follow-up, *Odelay*, was a huge hit. Beck established a reputation for being able to juxtapose musical styles (on 'Tropicalia', for instance, the Latin 'easy listening' music is deliberately at odds with the lyric). This reflected the increasingly eclectic nature of music-making in the 1990s – which in turn stemmed from a growing

awareness of, and curiosity about, the history of popular music, the availability of that history on CD, and, of course, the technology to pilfer it ('Loser' acknowledges sampling Dr John's 'I Walk On Gilded Splinters').

The approach is a montage of various pieces taken from different styles: tremolo guitar has a 1950s/surf connotation (we last encountered it on The Smiths' 'How Soon Is Now?'); the sitar guitar is 1960s pop; the drums and bass are hip-hop; the slide guitar is from country blues; and the vocal on the verse is a rap.

'Loser' is essentially in a blues-inflected D major. In the production, there's a drum loop, bass, and vocals in the centre. The instruments are brought in one at a time: you hear a slide acoustic guitar phrase in what is probably open D tuning; then drums enter, then bass, then another guitar on the left just as the vocal starts. On the left you can hear two distinct guitar sounds – one is the tremolo guitar effect, the notes cutting in and out rapidly; the other is the sitar guitar, which makes a high-pitched twangy tone meant to approximate an Indian sitar (you can also hear it on tracks as varied as Diana Ross & The Supremes' 'No Matter What Sign You Are' in the 1960s and Gomez's 'Hangover' in the 1990s).

WRITER	Beck Hansen
PRODUCER	Beck / Tom Rothrock / Rob Schnapf / Karl Stephenson
RECORDED	Rob's House / Karl's House / Beck's four-track
DURATION	3.55
RELEASED	Geffen, March 1994
CHART	US 10 UK 15

At certain points these instruments are dropped out of the mix: before the first chorus a voice says "cut it" (at 1.06), and for a second everything stops; on the last bit of verse 1 at 0.57, the left channel guitars drop out. Verse 2 starts with a drum and bass combination, then the slide lick re-enters, and then there's a section where there's tremolo guitar and drums but no bass. The bridge section after chorus 2 features a burst of chopped-up voice (2.25), several voices droning on a single note (2.32), and some backward voices probably taken from the chorus (2.38). Right on the fade there is a brief moment of distorted electric guitar.

Lyrically, the verses are stream-of-consciousness raps – reminiscent of a less-gravelly Tom Waits in their surreal allusions to low-life goings-on. The arresting chorus hook-line, "I'm a loser, baby, so why don't you kill me?", is in keeping with the negative self-loathing lyrics of much of the grunge/slacker genre – though with an edge of black humour.

CREATIVE TIPS

Beck on lyrics: "I like to approach lyric-writing as if I don't know English and I'm feeling my way around it – I like the language when it's awkward."

LINKS

For a similar montage approach, see song 94.

"Beck established a reputation for being able to juxtapose musical styles"

FELL ON BLACK DAYS

SOUNDGARDEN 1995

"It usually works like this: I come up with a riff that I think is totally retarded. And then Chris [Cornell] composes some incredible melody that makes it work. He has a great ear for that. I can write something that is very obtuse, rhythmically and harmonically, and he'll still come up with a melody for it."

(KIM THAYIL)

Soundgarden came to prominence as part of the Seattle grunge scene, and this track was on their fourth and most successful album, *Superunknown*. 'Fell On Black Days' is that rare beast – a heavy rock song that manages to express emotions grounded in reality. In contrast to 'Enter Sandman', which is exploding all over you, 'Fell On Black Days' is like feeling the vibration from a nuclear device going off underground: you can't see the damage but there's a rumble afoot. Though Soundgarden's music has a line of ancestry that goes back to Black Sabbath, the loping introverted feel of 'Fell On Black Days' reminds one of a heavier Free.

WRITER	Chris Cornell
PRODUCER	Michael Beinhorn / Soundgarden / mixed by Brendan O'Brien
RECORDED	Bad Animals Studio, Seattle
DURATION	4.38
RELEASED	A&M, January 1995
CHART	UK 24 US –

There are many fine points in the writing and arrangement that establish this song's stature. The production creates a dark, slow-burning setting: the initial guitar is panned right to one side with hi-hat opposite to balance the stereo image; listen for the way drums and voice come in together; there's careful layering of multiple guitars with some subtleties of harmonising – in the verses the same part of the melody is backed by a different chord each time.

It is notoriously awkward to write melodies over heavy riffs, but 'Fell On Black Days' manages it. Lyrically, it's a song about depression and ill-fortune, a zillion miles from something like Ozzy's rabid "Finished with my woman 'cos she couldn't help me with my mind" on 'Paranoid'. Everything seems to have gone wrong for the protagonist, and the vocal delivery varies from a numb bewilderment to protestation. In verse 3 there's a sense that he wants to get away: "So don't you lock up something that you wanted to see fly / Hands are for shaking" and the understated "I sure don't mind a change" – both of which imply some hideous inevitability to what is happening.

Listen for the major 7 chord at the end of each verse just before the chorus – major 7s are rarely used in heavy rock because they are deemed too 'sweet', but when their emotive appeal is successfully linked up to the power of heavy rock the effect is tremendous. The 6/4 time signature also makes a pleasing change from rock's standard 4/4. Other highlights are: the bass going down to the really low register on the first "How would I know?", and from then onwards; the extreme wah-wah break; the singer's shift up to a higher range for "I sure don't mind a change"; and the guitar harmony line towards the end of the song.

LINKS

There's a history of slightly 'alternative' American rock bands being accepted more readily in the UK than in the States, particularly in their early days - cf Television, Pixies, Throwing Muses, and Pearl Jam, as well as Soundgarden themselves.

CREATIVE TIPS

Soungarden's Ben Shepherd discussing their mixing engineer (and Pearl Jam producer) Brendan O'Brien: "He has an approach to mixing which creates a great sound – for a start, he never mixes loud, everything's always quiet, and that's something we believe: if a record sounds powerful when it's quiet, then it'll sound great loud."

TRACK 85

THANK YOU

DURAN DURAN 1995

"Most bands started out playing other people's songs... we never really did that – we just jumped in at the deep end and started finding out how to write ourselves ... It's taken us 15 years to get around to putting together a collection of other people's songs that inspired us in one way or another... We were always fans of the David Bowie covers album, *Pin Ups*, and the Bryan Ferry album, *These Foolish Things*, which came out in the early 1970s when we were kids... artists whose writing you liked and here they were introducing their audience to some of their influences... but they very much made the songs they covered their own." (NICK RHODES)

Now here's a turn-up for the books, and a treat for the ears. During the late 1980s and early 1990s, Led Zeppelin's star was once again firmly in the ascendant. At the time of writing (2001) they are second only to The Beatles in terms of album sales. Duran Duran chose this track as the title song for their own album of cover versions (which they recorded in various studios as they toured the world), and the track was also included on a Zep tribute album, *Encomium*, the same year. Of course, covering Zep songs is a little like doing Beatles tunes – great fun at parties but usually regrettable in the cold light of morning. And of all the bands to attempt it... Duran Duran? The new romantics bunch? 'Rio' and 'The Reflex'...? Surely this would be not so much physical graffiti as tangible vandalism.

Sometimes a cover works by going to the opposite of the original (like Cocker's 'With A Little Help From My Friends' or Hendrix's 'Watchtower' – see track 21); sometimes a performer expresses something revealing about themselves in their choice and interpretation of a well-known song (see Joplin's 'Little Girl Blue', track 28); and sometimes a performer stays relatively true to an original and yet places its beauty in a new frame. This version of 'Thank You' falls in the last category. It's delightful, largely because the 'who-would've-thought?' quotient is so high. Here 'Thank You' takes on an elegiac quality for anyone who loved it first time round: the Durans' cover is beautiful in its own right and, like good art criticism, gives the original back to us, only more so.

WRITER	Jimmy Page / Robert Plant
PRODUCER	Duran Duran
RECORDED	London / France / US...?
DURATION	4.32
RELEASED	(album, Thank You) Parlophone, March 1995
CHART	not a single

The band take an ambient approach: the tumbling echo suits the lyric, whose images Plant borrowed from early 1960s pop songs like 'Stand By Me', with its mountains crumbling into the sea. There's a lot of reverb and depth, so this track really benefits from headphone listening. The Durans slow the tempo to 70bpm, compared to the original's 75-77; the original organ sound, Page's Fender 12-string and Jones' Motown-influenced bassline are all replaced; the vocal has phasing on it to make it sound 'smoky'; there's a distant synth pad, vocal echo, two acoustics and an electric in the middle of the mix.

Simon Le Bon does a commendable job of finding a new way to sing this – he does so by phrasing noticeably late, after the beat (obvious on the "kind woman" line). He also puts a conspicuous vocal 'blue' note on the word "by" (as in "days gone by").

CREATIVE TIPS

Try structuring a song in three sections of equal importance, instead of the usual verse, chorus and bridge.

'Thank You' is a song of three sections: the D-C-G/B sequence we have already heard in 'More Than A Feeling'; the "kind woman" section runs Bm-E-Bm-E-A and temporarily establishes A as the new key; and the C straight afterwards ("little drops of rain") is a shock return to D via its *b*VII, although the ear isn't secure about this until the D is landed on.

Listen for: the high motif that comes in on the bridge (just before "kind woman"); the pre-echo in the hallucinatory last verse, where you hear Le Bon's phrases before he's actually sung them; at 3:02 there's a spine-tingling high note as the rhythm is picked up; the final section has deep notes in the synth, possibly backwards; and the bassline creates more inversions. Page's original mock-flamenco guitar break is replaced with a mellow backward solo. The final irony, or rather a wheel turned full circle, is that the 1980s Big Drum Sound, which stemmed partly from Bonham, returns to its source.

LINKS

The original of 'Thank You' can be found on Led Zeppelin II (Atlantic, 1969). Check out those Bowie and Ferry covers albums if you haven't already.

"Le Bon does a commendable job of finding a new way to sing this"

TRACK 86

ARMY OF ME

BJORK 1995

"Music is about freedom of expression and being able to say whatever enters your mind. We have language and daily communication with people where we always have to be logical and functional... Music's been the only abstract area – and it's been this way ever since the monkeys decided to become men; it's where you hear five notes and they make you cry, or you hear two notes and you laugh your head off. Music's supposed to express things you can't even express with your best mate." (BJORK)

Bjork was one of the most innovative musicians of the 1990s. Born in 1965, she released her first record at 11, and was a member of Iceland's top band, The Sugarcubes, before embarking on a solo career in 1992. 'Army Of Me' (which featured in the film *Tank Girl*) was her sixth UK Top 40 single, and was taken from her second album *Post*.

It is a typical 1990s record in the way it uses a collage technique. There's a minimalist lyric, in which the speaker tells a persistently whining acquaintance to get a grip, because, "I won't sympathise any more", leading to the threatening hook, "And if you

complain once more / You'll meet an army of me". Bjork has explained that it's about anger toward self-pity, but the exact situation is left unspecified: it could be a lover talking to a partner, or taking place in a work environment, or it could be an ironic exposure of such a threatening attitude. The rest is up to the listener.

As in many of her other songs, the lyric doesn't use rhyme. Bjork is an inventive lyricist – take the lines from 'Hyperballad', where she lives on a mountain and every morning, "I walk towards the edge / and throw things off like / car-parts, bottles and cutlery / or whatever I find lying around".

WRITER	**Bjork / Graham Massey**
PRODUCER	**Nellee Hooper / Graham Massey / Bjork**
RECORDED	**Compass Point Studios, Bahamas**
DURATION	**3.54**
RELEASED	**One Little Indian, April 1995**
CHART	**UK 10 US –**

Harmonically, 'Army Of Me' is also unusual. The verse melody has a Phrygian flavour, with the 2nd, 3rd and 7th notes of the scale lowered, making the melody sound fresh. The scale is C Phrygian: C D*b* E*b* F G A*b* B*b*. The verse is based on a Cm chord, though there's no particular chord that fits over the three-note chorus motif, D D*b* C.

Of the song's creation, co-producer Graham Massey (ex-808 State) has been quoted as saying: "We'd come up with this rock-monstery groove, which obviously triggered something off in her mind in regard to the lyric, and then it became a solid thing rather than just a riff." Notice the phrase, "*We'd come up with*". 'Army Of Me' is in fact indebted to a drum loop created from the opening seconds of Led Zeppelin's 'When The Levee Breaks'. To my mind there is a significant difference between the plagiarism of old – say The Beach Boys re-doing Chuck Berry's 'Sweet Little Sixteen' as 'Surfin' USA', or Led Zep themselves pinching from Willie Dixon (with attendant settlements) – and the digital copying of an actual performance. On the drum loop here you even get the reverb from the original recording.

One of the more original parts of the arrangement on 'Army Of Me' is the wriggling electric worm of a bassline, played on a synth, along with various other percussive bangs. In the last verse, where the drums drop out, you can hear the synth sound being EQ'd – the manipulation of EQ (tone) is a 1990s mixing technique that's often used as a substitute for harmonic interest.

CREATIVE TIPS

Location can influence a recording: working in the Bahamas allowed the ever-experimental Bjork to record her vocals on the nearby beaches – "I had a microphone with a very, very, very long lead... I would take my shoes off in the middle of the song, and stick my toes in the water. Then I would run and hide behind a tree and sing the quiet bit of the song there, and then run fast down the beach in the action part of the song... It was brilliant. I was just goose-pimply all the time."

LINKS

'When The Levee Breaks' is in fact (along with James Brown's 'Funky Drummer') one of the most widely sampled drum breaks ever - used by the earliest underground sampling pioneers, (in)famously rapped over by The Beastie Boys on their appropriately named 1986 track 'Rhymin & Stealin', and used (at various tempos) by countless acts since. It's become almost a standard on drum-loop CDs, and something of a cliché through over-use - which is another problem with sampling. For the original, and still best, see Led Zeppelin IV *(Atlantic, 1971).*

"a typical 1990s record in the way it uses a collage technique"

T R A C K 8 7

LAST GOODBYE

JEFF BUCKLEY 1995

"I daydream thinking about great songwriters. I was brought up with all these different influences – Nina Simone, Nusrat Fateh Ali Khan, Patti Smith – people who showed me music should be free, should be penetrating, should carry you." (JEFF BUCKLEY)

"There is no 'good' singing, there's only 'present' and 'absent'. That's it... It's the balls. Just the utter deathlessness, fearlessness..." (JEFF BUCKLEY)

WRITER	Jeff Buckley
PRODUCER	Andy Wallace
RECORDED	Bearsville Studios, Woodstock, New York
DURATION	4.33
RELEASED	Columbia, April 1995
CHART	UK 54 US –

Obituaries often err on the side of over-valuing the talents of their subjects. For once they didn't have to worry. Jeff Buckley was a huge talent and his death a real loss to music. There's little doubt that his debut album, *Grace*, which garnered a brace of favourable critical views on release, will become as legendary as the work of his tragic singer-songwriter father, Tim Buckley, who died of an accidental heroin overdose in 1975.

Jeff was just eight when his father died (having spent very little time with him), and he always resisted people's attempts to draw similarities between his music and that of a man he never really knew. Jeff absorbed an enormous range of musical influences, from classical to rock; he studied briefly at LA's Musicians Institute, played in a few bands, and did a cover of one of his father's songs at a tribute concert in 1991, reputedly stealing the show.

His first recording was a live EP of two covers and two originals with just an electric guitar, released on the Big Cat label. He signed to Columbia, put a band together and was allowed plenty of time to make *Grace* – an album which showcased his distinctive songwriting and remarkable voice. He could roar in best rock fashion or sing in a high falsetto, and employed a complicated phrasing and decoration more common in soul singers than rock vocalists. His singing was as unpredictable as it was expressive – he was a tightrope-walker, ever ready to take vocal risks, and usually pulling them off.

'Last Goodbye' is typical of the verve with which Buckley approached his music, opening up the possibilities of what could be done as a singer-songwriter, and making many other male performers look pedestrian. This applies to his songwriting craft as well as his bravura vocals.

The track starts with distant echoed and reverbed slide guitar in stereo, plus bass. We then have guitars on both sides, possibly in an altered tuning, along with drums and bass. Violin is added in the second and third verses. Sections are linked by feedback/howlround. After verse 3 we get a sensuously curvy string part.

The structure is complex: slide intro – band in / riff – verse 1 – link – verse 2 – riff – verse 3 – string break – bridge – verse 4 (with a different chord sequence) – link – verse 5 – coda; and it has an adventurous harmony to match.

Rarely has a song about splitting-up managed to look backward with such regret and, at the same time, forward with such anticipation. The music is alive to the myriad possibilities

CREATIVE TIPS

Male singer-songwriters should look at their melodies, to see if they are making as much use of their vocal range as they could be. (Then again, there aren't many Jeff Buckleys around.)

that lie all around you at such a moment of farewell. Maybe he didn't know her, he concedes – but maybe she didn't know him either.

Listen for: the hi-hat opening on the second appearance of the riff; Buckley's vocal taking off in verse 3; the drum fill into verse 4, and out of it into the link; and the four stray piano notes at the end.

LINKS

His posthumous collection of demos and out-takes, Sketches (For My Sweetheart The Drunk)*, was in part produced by one of Buckley's own many influences, Tom Verlaine of Television. Ironically, Buckley himself also re-inspired some of those whose work he'd admired, including Page & Plant; and Soundgarden's Chris Cornell paid tribute to him in 1999 with a song called 'Wave Goodbye'.*

> "opening up the possibilities of what could be done as a singer-songwriter"

TRACK 88

NOT THE RED BARON

TORI AMOS 1996

" 'Not The Red Baron' holds so much compassion for the boys as they're going down in their planes... At that point I didn't want to kick 'em in the nuts any more... Yet this song really became about, 'devils with halos and beautiful capes, taking them into the flame.' And I saw these lovely women ushering the men with the tears to their next place. Always connected to fire, always all of us trying to find our own fire." (TORI AMOS)

Tori Amos emerged as one of the most gifted, if troubled, female singer-songwriters of the 1990s. The Kate Bush comparisons were too easy and did little service to either artist: Amos is altogether brasher, more confrontational, less reserved (there is an obvious English/American contrast). Kate Bush plays piano the way Peter Green used to play guitar (see track 25); Amos wants to be Van Halen and Led Zep rolled into one (and on one song, 'A Northern Lad', even admits that, "sometimes you go too far / When pianos try to be guitars").

On the downside, despite her quirky originality, there is a two-dimensionality about at least part of her work. It's an obsessive pushing of certain buttons, both in herself and her audience, a wilful lyrical obscurity, and a tendency to be hag-ridden by conflict with her parents' Christianity. But when her craft opens up enough she is capable of songs that avoid clichés of lyric, arrangement and form, and reach deeper emotions.

Boys From Pele was her third album, a post-relationship *Blood On The Tracks*-type record which, unlike Dylan's (but like Bush's *The Red Shoes*), is uneven and too long. 'Caught A Lite Sneeze' is the stand-out track, but I have chosen 'Not The Red Baron' as a song which is more innovative and composed in a manner different to anything else in this book, with the exception of the Roy Harper track (66).

'Not The Red Baron' is piano and vocal with the added sound effect of a radio broadcast. As it fades in you hear Tori say, "What language? No, Dutch" – she and her engineer are listening to a radio and have landed on a station they can't identify. Meanwhile the piano plays a complex, unpredictable sequence of chords which changes at a kaleidoscopic rate. The production sound is intimate; there is little sense of an acoustic 'space' in which the music is occurring – Amos' voice is dry and close-up in the mix when she starts singing at 1.31.

WRITER	Tori Amos
PRODUCER	Tori Amos
RECORDED	(album) Church, Wicklow & Cork, Ireland / New Orleans
DURATION	3.49
RELEASED	(album, Boys For Pele) WEA, 1996
CHART	not a single

The song does not have a conventional verse/chorus structure – it's almost as if she is singing a new melodic phrase for each line of lyric. This blurring effect is aesthetically very pleasing – all too often it is easy to hear the joins between the sections of a song. This is different.

The important harmonic fact here is the rate of chord change – virtually one chord per beat – with a strong onward movement. The rate of chord change is too quick for the ear to identify every one. Bewildering at first, this increases the beauty of the music, and it means you can listen many times without ever getting to grips with it. You wonder if she worked these sequences out in advance, or if some of this is maybe improvised.

Amos's lyrics are often obscure, combining whimsy with tough talk. Sometimes this mixture works, sometimes it doesn't. She has a pathological tendency to hide behind metaphor, as anyone who has interviewed her will know. 'Not The Red Baron' alludes to the World War I flying ace (and sworn enemy of Charlie Brown's dog Snoopy in the doghouse fantasy sequences in the *Peanuts* cartoons – hence their mention in the lyrics). The phrase "another pilot down" evokes loss, along with the mention of hell, with cartoon devils and capes. Verse 2 refers to films, to Judy Garland and Jean Harlow. But where is the "there" of the last couple of lines? As for the final image – the girls with "the prettiest red ribbons" – it could be interpreted as a lover who is the pilot, shot down by the lure of another woman – the one with the red ribbons with whom the speaker cannot compare. Or is she the pilot...? Whatever its meaning, the amount of emotion Amos compresses into this image, and the last chord, is amazing.

CREATIVE TIPS

Use your intuition. "I'm always trying to push the boundaries of form, but I don't analyse it when I'm writing. To me it's about a visual symmetry and that's how I can write from an emotional level – knowing instinctively, the craft of sensing when a melody doesn't work." (Tori Amos)

LINKS

See tracks 51, 66, and 68.

"a pathological tendency to hide behind metaphor"

TRACK 89

IN A ROOM

DODGY 1996

"When our first album came out in 1993, I think some people thought we were taking the piss. We were writing songs the traditional way, with harmonies, choruses, middle-eights and proper instruments. Now, of course, the whole idea of proper songwriting has come round again... Songwriting is an open book there to be read. So many great records have been made, and I'm not scared to listen to them." (NIGEL CLARKE)

This track could be subtitled 'Homage to Keith Moon'. What struck me most on first hearing this was the magnificent drumming – all scampering toms and unpredictable cymbal crashes. OK, it's more grounded than Moon, but nevertheless, in 1996, 'In A Room' (lifted from their UK Top Ten album *Free Peace Sweet*) was water in a desert of drum machines (often programmed by people who couldn't think beyond four quantised kick-drum beats and eight hi-hats). Here, ecstatically, the spirit of The Who mugs The Hollies – and you breathe a sigh of relief to find a rock record that understands dynamics.

'In A Room' comes in with off-centre strummed acoustic on an Am-G-D riff – if it was Townshend playing the riff, the chords would have been harder and hit about a 16th earlier. Then it adds electric guitars, with horns under the solo that make it sound like *Quadrophenia*-era Who. The Hollies touch comes with the harmony vocals on the chorus. And note the handclaps on the riff after the first chorus.

WRITER	Nigel Clarke / Matthew Priest / Andy Miller
PRODUCER	Hugh Jones
RECORDED	poss Rockfield Studios, Wales
DURATION	4.18
RELEASED	A&M, May 1996
CHART	UK 12 US –

The bridge section ("I've thrown away the key") pulls out the drums and takes the dynamics down. It contrasts with the song's G major/Dorian A minor tonality by going to A major via Bm and E. This is followed by a scampering drum fill and a guitar solo that enters cleverly with a pre-bend (where a note that has already been bent up is let down). The solo is well-constructed, consisting of only about four phrases. Horns re-appear on the coda as the instruments pile on, including a sustained guitar lead.

If you can stop air-drumming for a minute (put down those pencils) and listen to the lyrics, you find 'In A Room' is a song of domestic drama in which depression leads to the protagonist saying, "If we are together again / Surely this will never end". The line, "I'm waiting for you behind the door" makes an ominous close to the chorus. In the bridge the emotion becomes introverted despair: "I've thrown away the key / I'm gonna lock myself in for good / No-one can reach me / No-one hears my voice any more".

Listen for: the blues lick on verse 2; the first blast of horns on the solo; the dramatic F chord that ends it; and the bass fills on the last chorus/coda at 3.44, wandering into the upper register. And of course, the star of the show, drummer Matthew Priest.

CREATIVE TIPS

Do the unexpected at the start of a guitar solo... And get a good drummer.

LINKS

This was released at the height of Britpop, whose best-known exponents were Blur and Oasis. The same year, Dodgy opened for The Who on tour. And see track 13.

TRACK 90

LET DOWN

RADIOHEAD 1997

"Andy Warhol once said that he could enjoy his own boredom. 'Let Down' is about that. It's the transit-zone feeling. You're in space, you are collecting all these impressions, but it all seems so vacant. You don't have control over the earth anymore. You feel very distant from all these thousands of people that are also walking there." (THOM YORKE)

Beauty is a revolution whose time can never pass. Radiohead have had a ton of critical bouquets lavished on them. When they are as good as this they deserve them all. This song has 40 years of rock music behind it – it knows exactly what it is doing, and all the artistic choices it has refused, and, like the walker in Robert Frost's 'Stopping By Woods On A Snowy Evening', knows what it is to have many miles still to go.

WRITER	Thom Yorke / Ed O'Brien / Phil Selway / Colin Greenwood / Jonny Greenwood
PRODUCER	Radiohead / Nigel Godrich
RECORDED	St Catherine's Court, nr Bath
DURATION	4.58
RELEASED	(album, OK Computer) EMI, July 1997
CHART	not a single

After their highly successful rock album *The Bends*, the band found even more acclaim with *OK Computer*, a recording which stretched the boundaries of rock by embracing new technology, though not in a reverential spirit. Radiohead know you might as well mess with the knobs and buttons and push the gear to its limits, and then see what you get.

It is fashionable to decry Radiohead as no more than prog-rock reborn. This is musically unfair – even if the lyrics and the sleeve of *OK Computer* do have a faint whiff of prog's Us versus Them misanthropy (and how keen they are to remind us that we are sleep-walking consumers, even as we put our money down for their latest CD or video).

'Let Down' is a classic example of how to write an emotional rock song that avoids cliché. If there are any sonic precedents for it, they perhaps lie in the more ambient guitar areas of U2 – though this is not stadium rock.

It was recorded at 3am in the ballroom of a mansion near Bath. Before the drums and bass enter you can hear three distinct parts: two guitars (one high, one low) and what could be a glockenspiel. These generate a texture like spun light. Acoustic guitars on both sides lend support. The drums don't settle onto a straight rock rhythm until verse 3, and drop out at various points. The echo on the centre guitar has plenty of regeneration, and builds up the high frequencies. A strong eighth-note rhythm leads from the bridge to the last verse – random bleeping from ZX Spectrum computers announce its arrival. The last verse has one electric guitar on the left, with acoustics more audible, and only one vocal on the right. The computer bleeps are juxtaposed with acoustic guitar on the coda – the organic is pitted against the inorganic nature of the electronic pulsing.

CREATIVE TIPS

Take a piece of equipment... and mess with it.

Listen for the harmony vocal in the centre on the word "reaction". The lead vocal is double-tracked, one voice each side, placed right out at the edge of the stereo image, reinforcing the alienation. Notice that there is no big finish.

'Let Down' is a song that uses travel to articulate an obscure feeling of loss. Because of the way Yorke sings it the words are not particularly clear: the opening verse talks about transport, motorways, tramlines, flying and a sense of alienation that flows from being on the

move; the chorus focuses on the image of an insect, of being "crushed like a bug in the ground" (as memorable as Ashcroft's cat in the bag in 'The Drugs Don't Work').

The tension in the track results from a struggle on the part of the speaker to resist the obvious emotion, hence verse 1's comment about "sentimental drivel" and feeling "hysterical and useless". The song climaxes with a question about place and its relationship to being: "One day you'll know where you are". As Radiohead expert Mac Randall put it, "'Let Down' is a victory – a victory over the very emotionlessness it depicts."

Listen for: the cymbal crash that signals a pick-up in the drums (1.49), lifting the track to a new dimension; Yorke's harmony vocal on "reaction" (2.00); and his melisma on "ground" on the left at 2.18; the texture at 2.48; the entrance of the bleeps with an ascending guitar line at 3.29, along with heavier drums; Yorke making the words "floor collapsing" sound like an obscenity; his entrance into falsetto at 4.10, and his held note through the chorus.

This is sublime. It would be tragic if, in their desire to move forward, Radiohead failed to see that creating music of this beauty is always as revolutionary as anything that sets out to be 'shocking'.

LINKS

For a later Radiohead recording, see track 100.

"this song has 40 years of rock music behind it"

TRACK 91

THIS TIME

THE VERVE 1997

"I realised I wanted to write great songs, songs that felt up there with The Beach Boys, Bacharach and The Byrds. Especially Burt Bacharach... this was when that whole easy listening thing was kicking off, a lot of people listening to songs like 'Wichita Lineman' or 'Superstar' by The Carpenters... [these songs] had a clarity and a purity that you wanted to hold onto." (RICHARD ASHCROFT)

With their third album, *Urban Hymns*, The Verve turned in one of the biggest-selling records of 1997. From it came the big singles 'Bittersweet Symphony' and 'The Drugs Don't Work', as well as lesser hits 'Lucky Man' and 'Sonnet'. The band's previous album, *A Northern Soul*, had been something of a critical fave, if more modest seller, and yielded the single 'History'.

'This Time' is a song about missed opportunities, looking back on a life, and the desire to transcend this feeling of waste and regret. While beautiful, there is a case that it could have

been better – a criticism you can make of many 1990s recordings. (Another common problem highlighted by *Urban Hymns* is the excessive length of modern albums – a symptom of the CD-age.) It is worth pinning down how and why this track could be better.

First, the melody is unnecessarily linear. Ashcroft spends too much time singing on the note A, which deprives the melody of a lovelier curve and more interest. It makes me wonder how much of this was generated in the studio and how much of the melody was worked out before the backing track was recorded. Secondly, the whole song is based on a single four-bar ascending progression of Fmaj7 G Am G/B C – with C as the 'home' key chord the music never gets to settle on.

The lyric talks about rising up to the light: if so, C major represents the goal it only momentarily touches for two beats, and from which it then falls back. The appeal of the chord sequence would have been enhanced by giving the listener a break from it – easily achieved by adding another four-bar progression and building some tension before the return to the verse. In this respect compare 'From The Underworld' (track 19) where there is a break from the three-chord change.

WRITER	Richard Ashcroft
PRODUCER	Youth / The Verve / Chris Potter
RECORDED	Olympic Studios, London
DURATION	3.50
RELEASED	(album, Urban Hymns) Hut, September 1997
CHART	not a single

'This Time' (which apparently had a working title of 'Discordant') is a complex arrangement in terms of the number of parts; the net result, oddly enough, is akin to the delicate funk groove of 'Still Water' (track 31). The initial ten seconds have no established root note, as the guitar plays a six-note phrase, which returns at about 2.30; the drums have a distinct stereo delay, evident on the bass drum; an ascending wah-wah guitar plays percussively on one side, and another guitar adds a descending octave phrase doubled by a high line of some kind. After the first chorus there is a piano, then a mellotron phrase enters at 1.35, just off-centre; the lead vocal is answered by another on the second chorus; and high strings emerge on the coda.

The mix is constructed from all these fragments, then stripped back to its percussion base at the end, with the intention of creating a piece with a trance element – you can feel this during the three-voice phrase, "There is time".

CREATIVE TIPS

Enhance the power of a progression, riff, or melodic hook by giving your listener a break from it.

LINKS

The songwriting royalties to The Verve's huge-selling 'Bittersweet Symphony' famously ended up going to The Rolling Stones' publishers because it used a sample of an orchestral version of a Stones track. Despite the argument that the fragment was small, was heavily overdubbed with dozens of new parts, and in the end barely audible (and the band had apparently received clearance to use it in the first place), Ashcroft ultimately had to surrender 100 per cent of his copyright on the track. Harsh, but yet another object lesson in the dangers inherent in sampling.

"Ashcroft spends too much time singing on the note A, which deprives the melody of a lovelier curve"

TRACK 92

FROZEN

MADONNA 1998

"I'm always searching for something new and edgy and undiscovered... I love to work with the weirdos that no-one knows about, the people who have raw talent and who are making music unlike anyone else out there." (MADONNA)

"Calculated is very much the wrong word. We listened to very little outside music – in fact I'd mention something and she'd say, 'I don't want to hear it'." (WILLIAM ORBIT)

Forget all that messing around with musicals about South American dictators and their preposterous wives, this was Madonna's best ballad since 'This Used To Be My Playground', though more adventurous in its arrangement. As with 'Erotica', she has enough of a pop sensibility to keep the song commercial while taking onboard the latest production tricks. The song is also blessed with some fetching 'Eastern' string flourishes, courtesy of arranger Craig Armstrong.

'Frozen' unthaws from the absolute zero of silence (metaphor patent pending) with said mournful strings, and a sinister bleeping synth: by the late 1990s bleeping synths were the very essence of grey futurity. (You can almost imagine *2001*'s computer HAL... "Hello, Dave... Would you like me to play the new Madonna single, Dave...?"). The strings and synth make a combination of old and new, traditional and modern instrumentation, in keeping with the overall tenor of an album (*Ray Of Light*) that tries to express a spiritual perspective without rejecting the dance-floor – you can be fairly sure Madonna is not about to take up anything that involves strict puritanism. For which, all say Amen.

WRITER	**Madonna / Patrick Leonard**
PRODUCER	**Madonna / Patrick Leonard / William Orbit**
RECORDED	**Larrebee Studio, Los Angeles**
DURATION	**6.12**
RELEASED	**Maverick, March 1998**
CHART	**US 2 UK 1**

There's some quasi-Indian percussion (first heard at 0.18) and a drum loop in verse 3, with the bass drum on the first beat. For much of the song the drums come and go – it's interesting here that the drum part has been dislodged from its usual position at the centre of the mix, as the predictable rhythmic chassis onto which everything else is bolted for the ride. Instead, it often feels more like an instrument that is added to the mix, as though the pulse of the music is kept by something invisible.

CREATIVE TIPS

Instead of building an arrangement from the drums upward, try adding percussion later to emphasise the more dramatic moments in a song.

The lyric is addressed to someone else, and speaks of them being emotionally closed; she is trying to get them to open up. The line "Love is a bird, she needs to fly" is clichéd – but the video has some impressive imagery to distract from any lyrical shortcomings.

Harmonically, 'Frozen' is in F minor – a key which some composers associate with cold and bleak experience. The chord progression is based on I-VI-VII-I, which is also the basis for 'Running Up That Hill' and 'Forbidden Colours'. There's also a Fm B*b*m G*b* A*b* phrase, and an Fm B*b*m D*b* A*b* section. To get the Eastern phrasing, the strings use the harmonic minor on the first and third phrases of the bridge (at 3.19 and 3.37), where an E natural is heard.

Also listen for: the first drum fill at 0.53, the second into the chorus, and the third in the chorus in stereo; at 1.53 the drum fill is 'squeezed' with extreme use of EQ, making it sound as though the drum is underwater because of the initial cut in high and mid-frequencies (such

EQ sweeps are a common feature of 1990s dance mixes). Listen for the string line on "give yourself to me", which has a lovely rising curve and continues on to harmonise the next "mmm-mmm" sequence; and on chorus 4 (about 4.45) where Madonna harmonises her lead vocal in fourths.

LINKS

Co-producer William Orbit had actually been remixing Madonna tracks since 1990's 'Justify My Love', before he was invited to get more involved on this album, Ray Of Light. ***If you get bitten by the strings, try Samuel Barber's 'Adagio'; if you like the Turkish Delight facet of 'Frozen', try Transglobal Underground, and also tracks 45 and 73. If F minor is your thing, go to tracks 96 and 97.***

> "tries to express a spiritual perspective without rejecting the dance-floor"

TRACK 93

ROAD RAGE

CATATONIA 1998

"I don't think about singing, exactly, but I suppose I must subconsciously recall those great singers, how the voice breaks or shudders or holds a note or belts it. What makes me tingle. Cry. Shout. Then I howl it out and go dizzy and cross-eyed." (CERYS MATTHEWS)

WRITER	Cerys Matthews / Mark Roberts
PRODUCER	Tommy D / Catatonia
RECORDED	Monnow Valley Studios, Wales
DURATION	5.09
RELEASED	Blanco Y Negro, April 1998
CHART	UK 5 US –

This was the fourth shot in an impressive opening salvo on Catatonia's number 1 second album, *International Velvet*. This is 1960s pop re-styled for the 1990s and sung in a lascivious homegrown style – like Cilla and Carol Decker, Cerys Matthews is something of a girl-next-door. The bittersweet is always close to the heart of pop, and certainly to the pop single, and Cerys's backing vocal refrain of "It's not over" articulates that bittersweet emotion – especially the higher up it is pitched – and is beautifully harmonised on the second chorus.

'Road Rage' has no intro – we're straight in, with a trip-hop, echoed drum pattern that runs through the verse. The other initial instrumentation is stereo synth and prominent bass – listen for the funk phrase at 0.22. The chords on the verse are

CREATIVE TIPS

Use transposition to freshen up the later verses, not just the last chorus where it has traditionally been used.

implied rather than fully stated; the guitars shove their way in at 0.40 for the pre-chorus ("You should be making it..."); the lead vocal is doubled, and there's a touch of harmony. Notice the drop in volume from the bold chorus for verse 2. When the guitar solo comes in it is played on the low strings, like a Duane Eddy melody. Listen for the la-la's under it.

'Road Rage' is a virtuoso performance in transposition, yet carries this off as lightly as a feather. It runs through a staggering *nine* keys: the guitar is detuned a semitone at the start, so it begins in A using I-III-IV-V; the pre-chorus goes via C#7 to a new key of F# minor; the first chorus is in F# major – its chord II (G#m) is chord VI of the key in which verse 2 starts (B major). The second pre-chorus is in G# minor, the second chorus in A*b* major, verse three in D*b* major, the third pre-chorus in B*b* minor, and the song ends in B*b*.

Cerys writes songs that have the reality quotient of The Smiths. Who else would call a song 'Lost Cat', or 'Londinium', talk about "industrial cleavage", play with the phrase "London just sucks ... the life out of me", and insert a dodgy pun about "custard's last stand" at the end of 'Valerian'?

'Road Rage' is shaped around a 1990s catchphrase for the irrational, and occasionally fatal anger manifested by frustrated drivers. The line, "You should be making it easy on yourself" is a witty and ironic allusion to the Walker Brothers' 1965 hit – presumably she means you could be making it easy on yourself by getting back together, not splitting up.

Listen for: the male voice "ah" at 0.30; the drum fill at 3.02; the change of ambience at 3.11 (possibly an edit); the echo feedback at 4.25; and, at 4.47, how the guitar breaks out into its own counter-melody. The third chorus pans Cerys' chant from left to right and back; the fourth and fifth chorus are an ecstatic mix of hooks, with the guitar melody, lead vocal, and those exquisite "it's not over"s.

LINKS

For other songs with numerous key-changes, try our old friends at Motown, Holland-Dozier-Holland – for instance, on 'I Hear A Symphony', by The Supremes, and 'I'm In A Different World' by The Four Tops.

> "a virtuoso performance in transposition... it runs through a staggering *nine* keys"

T R A C K 9 4

GET MILES

GOMEZ 1998

"Someone once asked me how we mix so many different styles up in one song, and I told him, 'Well someone will start playing a country guitar line, and Blackie [Paul Blackburn] will come in with a funk bassline, Ian [Ball] refuses to play anything but loud psychedelic rock, and Olly [Peacock] will kick in with a mellow jazz groove or some crazy nine-beats-per-second vibe." (TOM GRAY)

"I think anyone who's into music these days has that kind of aesthetic, putting it all together and seeing what happens." (BEN OTTEWELL)

Gomez's debut album *Bring It On* won the Mercury Music Prize in 1998, and the band were enthusiastically embraced by many listeners as offering a way forward from the seeming impasse of UK popular music at the end of the 1990s: from backward-looking Britpop on the one hand and mechanistic dance on the other. Gomez fitted the requirements: they came on like a garage version of The Band – organic, eccentric, rootsy, and lo-fi, yet willing to add hi-tech elements. In 'Get Miles' they were even singing about getting out of the city.

WRITER	Ian Ball / Paul Blackburn / Tom Gray / Ben Ottewell / Olly Peacock
PRODUCER	Gomez
RECORDED	"On Merseyside" (mostly in a garage in Stockport)
DURATION	5.14
RELEASED	(album, Bring It On), Hut, December 1998
CHART	not a single

A five-piece from the north of England, each member brought a diverse mixture of musical enthusiasms to the band's writing. They seemed to operate with no prior musical conceptions about what goes with what – anything with anything else was the order of the day. To add to the appeal, this blending of styles was carried out in a suitably lo-fi environment: much of the album was recorded (often in adverse weather) in a garage on a four-track recorder, with an assortment of other gear – some of which worked if you talked nicely to it.

To top it all off, the band had the sit-up-and-take-notice voice of Ben Ottewell – a grizzled, deep, blues-soaked malt of a voice that surely must have originally belonged to some poor individual in the Deep South (and I don't mean Sussex). One can only guess at the motivation of the mischievous sprite that swapped two voices in the night, leaving some bewildered American with a Stockport accent.

'Get Miles' is mostly still the original four-track recording (and the performance was apparently only the second time they'd played the song through), with tuba parts and bass added later, once the original was transferred to 16-track. It starts with a synth octave, before bringing in drums, percussion and wah-wah guitar; bass comes in 0.37 with a sustained note on the left, which cuts out when the vocal starts. Most of the song is harmonically carried on the tension between Dm7 and D. The unpredictable element is the tuba that comes in toward the end. Listen also for the echoed guitar lick that flickers like a butterfly across the stereo image at 2.28.

If Gomez illustrate the rewards of musical eclecticism, their style also hints at the potential risks. First, they must be cautious not to rely too much on Ottewell's bear-howl blues-singing

CREATIVE TIPS

To create classic funk tension, put a major chord over a pentatonic minor bassline of the same root note – for example, strum a D major chord (D F# A) over a bass line that uses D F G A C.

to carry the emotion of their music. Second, eclecticism cannot by itself nourish the wellspring of musical creativity – that must come from the pressure of personal feeling and experience. A large record collection is a useful source of ideas, but not a substitute.

LINKS

A reverb-heavy mix of part of the coda of 'Get Miles' returns as 'The Comeback', the last track on the album. For a similar musical approach see Beck, track 83 (Gomez wrote the track 'Whippin' Piccadilly' after seeing Beck at Manchester University).

"anything with anything else was the order of the day... this blending of styles carried out in a suitably lo-fi environment"

TRACK 95

AT MY MOST BEAUTIFUL

R.E.M 1999

"The elements in our songs are always the same, going back to *Murmur* – the difference is how it's mixed, how it's arranged. Typically, in the past, we'd have 30 tracks of stuff, but the guitar and the drums would take the front seat and everything else would sound interesting but indistinct, occurring somewhere underneath. The difference with *Up* is that the underneath stuff now becomes the stuff on top. And the drum machine takes precedence over the drums." (MICHAEL STIPE)

Courtesy of its continued high placing in critics' polls, The Beach Boys' *Pet Sounds* (1966) continued to grow in reputation through the 1990s, leading to a re-assessment of the band in general, and ultimately the issue of the landmark *Pet Sounds Sessions* box-set. 'At My Most Beautiful' is a tribute to that sound, at once conveying something of R.E.M *and* Brian Wilson. In other words, it's not so much like The Beach Boys that it's a pastiche, but sufficiently like them to be a musical homage.

Its chart success is touching – I can't think of another recent single whose charms were seemingly too fragile to survive the rough and tumble of the Top 20, but somehow it did.

There is a God... and She, too, loves Brian Wilson, and evidently wishes that Gold Star Studios had not been demolished, and that *Smile* had been completed...

Guitarist Peter Buck supplies the patented Hal Blaine snare-fills that punctuate the song. On the right you can hear bass harmonica (also featured on 'The Boxer'), with quarter-note piano chords and bass. There's a strummed guitar in the middle, and stereo backing vocals courtesy of Mike Mills – who has a singularly plaintive voice for backing vocals (there is no truth, by the way, in the rumour that the reason Mills' vocals are always in the background on R.E.M records is because they either refuse to give him a microphone or they keep him lashed to the studio back wall so he has to sing from there). On the left are tubular bells and sleighbells, with their reverb signal audible on the right. An organ fills out the sound on the chorus, and sawing cellos give the coda that 'Good Vibrations' edge.

WRITER	Peter Buck / Michael Stipe / Mike Mills
PRODUCER	Pat McCarthy / R.E.M
RECORDED	Seattle / San Francisco / Athens, Georgia
DURATION	3.34
RELEASED	Warners, March 1999
CHART	US 4 UK 10

The key is F major: the intro has Fmaj7-D-Gm, going to an unexpected D major; the verse uses a I-III-IV-II progression; and the chorus a II III IV V climb. The verse also has an F/A (F with an A bass) – neatly observed, following the example of Wilson's fine use of inversions on *Pet Sounds*.

The title could almost be Morrissey – except Stipe has something less witty and more heartfelt in mind, namely that being in love finds him at his best. This is a tender love song that includes references to leaving messages on answerphones (with a pleasing note of self-deprecation as he refers to reading bad poetry down the phone), and knowing obsession – it's about the ennobling effect of love, yet is aware of its playful narcissism: "At my most beautiful, I count your eyelashes secretly". Stipe's choice of notes is typical of him – it worries away at that obsession with the 1-4-3 of the scale (also all over the *Green* album). Listen for Mills singing major 7th chords on the verse at 1.46 and 1.53.

LINKS

For an early R.E.M track, see song 62.

CREATIVE TIPS

Mike Mills: "Around the time of Document we caught ourselves repeating ourselves. We really made some breaks about that time, writing and playing on different instruments, consciously using different tempos and keys. We'd swap instruments... Peter would try to write on mandolin, or piano and on the organ rather than use it as an embellishment. We'd sit in the studio and instead of bass, drums, guitar, we'd have mandolin, organ, bass, or mandolin, guitar, organ."

"it's not so much like The Beach Boys that it's a pastiche, but sufficiently like them to be a musical homage"

TRACK 96

THE WORLD IS NOT ENOUGH

GARBAGE 1999

"People are so determined to be Luddites that they don't realise technology is so sophisticated now it allows you unbelievable spontaneity. We can go anywhere in the world, sit on the tour bus or in this hotel room, and make studio-quality recordings. ProTools – everybody's scared of that, but it frees you up to try things there's no way you could have dreamt of doing even five years ago." (SHIRLEY MANSON)

By this time we all know what to expect of a Bond song. The trick is how to update the formula without breaking it: the song has to suggest sex and violence in equal measures; it has to purr in your ear but shoot the person hiding outside on the balcony without missing a beat, then purr in your ear some more. If it succeeds, you can listen to it on a grey and cold afternoon yet smell the popcorn and the cheap perfume, see the floor-lit red plush, feel like hiring a tuxedo and driving round town, and find white cat-hair has mysteriously appeared on your sleeve.

After some indifferent songs by other artists on the latter-day Bond films, Garbage came closer than most with 'The World Is Not Enough'. So how was it done? Vell, before I haf you killed in a suitably unpleasant manner, my friend (and such a shame, so close to the end of the book), let me explain...

WRITER	**David Arnold / Don Black**
PRODUCER	**Garbage**
RECORDED	**Metropolis Studios, London / Armoury Studios, Vancouver**
DURATION	**3.57**
RELEASED	**Radioactive, November 1999**
CHART	**UK 11 US –**

It's written in the 'Bond key' of F minor, and there are several harmonic reminiscences of earlier Bond songs: the intro and chorus use a I IV V progression (Fm B*b*m C), which is the same as 'Thunderball', except that was in B*b* minor. The middle-eight at 2.40 uses the IV-V minor key chord change (B*b*m to C) that can be heard in the bridge of 'You Only Live Twice' (on that tune's "don't think of the stranger" bit). Composer David Arnold – himself an avowed John Barry fan – cleverly ends this middle-eight with a Cm instead of C, and for the coda comes up with a splendid Fm B*b*/D D*b* change over a persistent F bass.

To update the song we get a chugging dance rhythm, and on the verse a drum loop that still seems to be carrying vinyl crackle from wherever it was sampled (unless of course the crackle has been deliberately added later – another ironic twist in the rather pointless 'let's make digital dirtier' trend). Notice the use of synths in a similar fashion to 'Frozen' and the backward noises during the middle-eight.

CREATIVE TIPS

For a minor key song with a more exotic harmony, try adding a major form of chord V – so in A minor use chords Am C Dm E F G... To increase the effect, try an Am to Fm or Am to C#m change.

The orchestral instruments provide the traditional touches: listen for the stabbing brass on the intro and chorus, the harp flourishes (0.25, 2.00), and the slinky if intermittent strings. A chromatic four-note string phrase crawls like some deadly spider over the mix at 0.51, while on the chorus the strings support the melody. The guitar, an early Bond signature, is present too in the little motif that preludes each chorus, and in the low-string phrases heard in the chorus itself, and on the coda (starting 3.25).

Shirley Manson's vocal delivery should be compared with that of Bassey: Bassey takes her phrases early, Manson sings more languidly, behind the beat – try imagining Bassey singing this and you'll hear the difference. The lyric plays the usual games, mixing "kiss" with "kill", and leaving you unsure whether it's about Bond or the villain, since half the phrases usually fit both.

LINKS

Don Black also wrote the words for several of the early Bond theme songs, including 'Thunderball' and 'Diamond's Are Forever', the music for both of which was composed by John Barry (see track 12).

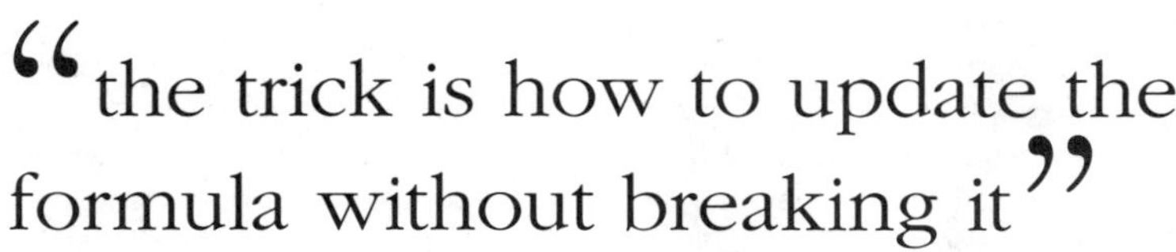

TRACK 97

LOVELY HEAD

GOLDFRAPP 2000

"We decided that we didn't want to sample anything – everything had to be written and played by us or people we brought in. No beats, no loops, but a concentration on melody and experimenting with sounds. We made lots of rules for ourselves about what was and wasn't allowed." (ALISON GOLDFRAPP)

WRITER	Alison Goldfrapp / Will Gregory
PRODUCER	Alison Goldfrapp / Will Gregory
RECORDED	Home Studio / 'The Bungalow'
DURATION	3.46
RELEASED	Mute, May 2000
CHART	UK – US –

Goldfrapp's debut album *Felt Mountain* has enjoyed considerable critical acclaim. Let's look at why this might be, and how much of it is deserved. The sleeve-notes state: "Will thanks Sergio Leone", and the sound of 'Lovely Head' is indeed like a Spaghetti western soundtrack colliding with... yes, again... John Barry's 007 soundtracks. It continues the revival of interest in 1960s film soundtrack music, as popularised in the early 1990s by groups like Portishead. But, as with Gomez, the danger is that this stuff just originates out of peoples' record collections and not from a deeper source as well. This is not a crude polarity between music inspired by other music (bad) versus music inspired by 'life' (good). Much music that *seems* original, that *appears* to come out of nothing except a writer's experience, often turns out to have been partially cloaked in an infatuation with someone else's music. There's a lot of conscious and unconscious emulation among the greats of popular music, as this book shows – but if you've put in the work, and you've got talent, the end result comes out as yours regardless (see tracks 6 and 7 in this respect). All the same, there must be that personal drive pulling everything together.

After a strange, disconcerting noise at the start (like a clarinet being garrotted), 'Lovely Head' cuts to an undeniably cinematic entrance, complete with whistling and strings; then we

CREATIVE TIPS

If you use a four-chord sequence, break from it into something else in order to 're-charge' it for a return... Compare the middle-eight's role in 'Stoned Love'.

get light percussion, bass, occasional harp glissandi, and a harpsichord figure. Engaging as this vibe is, it really doesn't go anywhere. At 1.16 there's a bizarre solo section, which could be a theremin or a heavily distorted voice; this returns at the coda, where there's also tympani. The arrangement disguises the repetitive nature of the progression – but herein lies the slightly unsatisfying nature of the song. As with The Verve's 'This Time', it feels under-composed, not helped by an obscure lyric.

The reason is that the whole song is an eight-bar four-chord sequence of Fm E B*b* B*b*m7*b*5 / D. The F minor and E major chords are connected by what is known as a 'false relation' (the A*b* in F minor becomes a G# in E major) – although only a semitone apart, the chords are distant. The change from E to B*b* is also an angular change – remember the E-B*b* tritone interval in 'Enter Sandman'. These musical effects, added to the arrangement and the breathy, languid vocal, create the air of frigid mystery. The song would have been stronger if there had been another musical section, enabling there to be a refreshed return to the main theme.

Listen for the vocal gasp at 3.25, and the hint of a B in the strings against Fm in the harpsichord at the end (F-B is another tritone interval).

LINKS

If you like this, try French pop, Air, Ennio Morricone, Portishead, and tracks 12 and 96.

TRACK 98

BETTER LIVING THROUGH CHEMISTRY
QUEENS OF THE STONE AGE 2000

"We don't have any [writing] habits. Sometimes the song will be all done, complete. But we also collaborate on stuff, or things happen just jamming in the rehearsal room and we end up chasing it down till it's done. It's a real good habit not to have any songwriting habits, because as soon as you start to work a certain way that's asking for writer's block. Keep the avenues open and there's always gonna be a different street to turn down." (NICK OLIVERI)

Whither rock in the 21st century? Has everything been done that can be done with the raw charge of guitars, bass and drums? I don't think so – and to judge from their album *Rated R*, neither do Queens Of The Stone Age. It's loud, hip, poetic, funny and unexpected by turns, and makes current UK big names like Travis and Coldplay seem pedestrian. Above all (thank Jim Marshall) the Queens don't sound defeated even before they've left the starting blocks. It's 42 minutes of varied rock, from the sheer punk buzz of 'Feel Good Hit Of The Summer' to the neo-T.Rex riff of 'Quick And To The Pointless', handclaps and all.

CREATIVE TIPS

When mixing, deconstruct the sound, if only briefly... Move stuff in and out, or left and right... An unexpected moment of silence, or some other break, throws quite a spanner into the works.

'Better Living Through Chemistry' has an impressive dignity about it that is also possessed by 'Fell On Black Days'. It has moments that seem like Radiohead – the melody that follows the guitar riff on the verse, for example – and others that make it seem Crosby, Stills, Nash & Young have gate-crashed a Nirvana recording session.

It starts with a conga link from the previous track, which adds an unexpected exotic twist;

the congas are dry on the right, with their reverb to the left, where guitar riff 1 comes in. The mix here is unusual: guitar 1 is dry, but doubled by a much higher instrument, possibly a keyboard; at various times the band is squeezed into one channel and the voice is likewise moved off-centre.

The song structure is conga intro / guitar riff 1 / verse 1 / heavier chorus (guitar riff 2) / long pause with feedback (at 1.36). The bridge section starts at 2.14 with riff 3, and at 2.52 we get riff 4 and a solo, quickly faded away under the harmony vocals, which are especially touching. At 3.18 the guitars return, with the rest of the band, compressed into the right channel and then spreading out; at 4.06 riff 2 and riff 1 return to introduce another verse (with an extra voice interjecting lines from the right) and chorus, and we already have a feeling of having been on a journey; riff 2 functions as the coda.

This is a track with oodles of power that unexpectedly backs off into other textures. It understands that rock is often most effective when it has dynamics and deviates from its power into surprising lulls before roaring back.

WRITER	Joshua Homme / Nick Oliveri
PRODUCER	Chris Goss / Joshua Homme
RECORDED	Sound City Studios, Van Nuys, California
DURATION	5.48
RELEASED	(album, Rated R) Interscope, June 2000)
CHART	not a single

LINKS

See tracks 78 and 84.

"it's loud, hip, poetic, funny and unexpected by turns"

TRACK 99

BEAUTIFUL DAY

U2 2000

"Success for us was a bit of blind faith and ignorance. We wrote songs because we couldn't play other people's songs. We could hardly play our own instruments. This was a band that could not form an E chord." (BONO)

Widely seen as a return to form by U2, 'Beautiful Day' comes on like vintage wine. Here is a band bringing all their experimentation in the 1990s to bear on a more traditional rock song, with explosive effect. If U2 never recorded another track this would be a fitting farewell, because it gathers together all the threads of their music. It has the ambient element which featured on their earliest albums, the full-on rock of their 1980s output, a chiming delayed guitar riff, and roaring vocals.

Reverbed electric piano and a sustained string patch introduce the song. The production is quite dry, especially on the voice, which is upfront. The rhythm is carried initially by the eighth-note bass (typical of U2) and the drum/beatbox for the verse. The vocals on the chorus are interesting: Bono delivers the main tune in quite a restrained manner, but the backing vocals off to one side have a loud, bellowing quality – as if his old vocal style has been pushed into the background.

WRITER	Bono / Edge / Adam Clayton / Larry Mullen
PRODUCER	U2 / Daniel Lanois
RECORDED	Windmill Lane Studios, Dublin
DURATION	4.06
RELEASED	Island, October 2000
CHART	UK 1 US 61

Harmonically, the verse and chorus both use the same A Bm D G / D A turnaround, in which the chord changes are not always one to a bar. The bridge ("Touch me") heightens the emotion with its F#m G D A progression; and there's a second bridge – Em D Em G D Em G D A – which suggests the key of D major rather than the home key of A major. There's a sudden, low-key ending, with the regeneration of a signal drifting back and forth across the stereo image.

'Beautiful Day' – which comes off the *All You Can't Leave Behind* album – has a typically 'fuzzy' U2 lyric, operating in an ambiguous subject area between religion and romance. The verses talk about grace and salvation, and there's an ambiguity about who is being addressed – is the speaker the "you", or someone else? Note also the darkly witty "you've been all over and it's been all over you". The second bridge section has an impressive bird's-eye 'flying' sequence, taking in Noah, the flood, the rainbow, the dove of peace, China, canyons, the sea, the Bedouin fires, and the oil fields.

CREATIVE TIPS

Make a turnaround more interesting by not allowing the chords to change after each bar.

Bono saves his best line till last – "What you don't have, you don't need it now" – as the band turn up the heat. The lyric doesn't tell you how to pull it all together, but there are so many suggestive images that it's enough.

Listen for: Edge's patented echoed arpeggio at 0.29 (parts of this signal seem to be echoed and moved across to the opposite side, overlaying the string sound); Bono's Sam Cooke phrase at 1.50; the F#m chord at 1.55 on "Touch me"; the exhilarating link at 2.08 after bridge 1, with a modulating two-note electric phrase; and the break in eighth-note rhythm at 2.15, where the bass plays a G under the Em chord, implying a chord change that isn't there.

LINKS

For an earlier U2 song, see track 72.

"if U2 never recorded another track this would be a fitting farewell, because it gathers together all the threads of their music"

T R A C K   1 0 0

EVERYTHING IN ITS RIGHT PLACE

RADIOHEAD 2000

"*Kid A* was our first attempt at working on songs from sounds in the studio. We wanted to understand more about some of the modern ways of making music, such as samplers and sound modules... We still love to play live; it's just that we needed to find some more colours to play with. Also, we're not 'players', so the machines are beguiling because they're constructed for duffers such as us." (COLIN GREENWOOD)

Kid A was a brave album to make, but definitely the right one. Few albums in recent years were so anticipated as the follow-up to *OK Computer* – or received with as much confusion and disappointment. From the worst reviews, you would imagine Radiohead had released an album devoid of anything resembling music. *Kid A* is in fact an album of idiosyncratic but beautiful music – very much a record for headphone listening, so sounds buried low in the mix (like the squalling midgets in 'Kid A') can be enjoyed.

WRITER	Thom Yorke / Ed O'Brien / Phil Selway / Colin Greenwood / Jonny Greenwood
PRODUCER	Radiohead / Nigel Godrich
RECORDED	Paris / Copenhagen / Gloucestershire
DURATION	4.10
RELEASED	(album, Kid A) EMI, October 2000
CHART	not a single

It grew out of the ambient side of their music, the interest in sound textures, and the specifics of a track like 'Fitter Happier'. Some of *Kid A* is lovely, even if it does not express all of Radiohead's virtues as a band (ie their gift for melody and explosive dynamics).

'Everything In Its Right Place' is dominated by the electric piano that opens it, and there's an electronic bass drum pulse throughout. The piano sound becomes more synthy as the track progresses, with emphatic EQ applied to the main keyboard toward the end, as the song crescendos at 2.50. It's a dry production, overall, though the vocals towards the end are distanced with reverb, then sampled, cut up, pitch-shifted and distorted.

Initially the song appears formless, with no traditional verse/chorus sections. It is actually based on three two-bar phrases: the first (which we'll call A) consists of the chords C D*b*maj7 and E*b*6, a bar of 4/4 followed by a bar of 6/4. (The song actually starts two beats before the first bar-line.) This is heard six times. Then comes section B (at 0.35) which is F C D*b*maj7 and E*b*6, again 4/4 and 6/4, four times; then another four of section A; then section C (at 1.14), which puts the 6/4 bar before the 4/4, and goes D*b*maj7 C E*b*. This is followed by repeats of sections B and A, eight more of C, and then a coda entirely made up of A. The sustained note C is crucial, because that's the note Yorke continues to sing in both sections. The song is nominally in F, but never really settles there, undermined by both the D*b* and E*b* chords.

The lyric amounts to only a couple of lines: "Yesterday I woke up sucking a lemon", part of which is sampled for the intro, and "There are two colours in my head / What is that you tried to say?". The cutting up and displacement of the sampled voice reflects the refusal and failure to communicate, presumably because of a feeling of alienation – the song's theme.

CREATIVE TIPS

Try omitting the bass where you would normally expect it.

LINKS

Thom Yorke has been quoted as saying the band's biggest influence while recording Kid A *was the Talking Heads album* Remain In Light *(produced by Brian Eno in 1980). For an earlier Radiohead song, see track 90.*

appendix 1

100 TRACKS LISTED BY TRACK NUMBER

*The **bold** number on the left is the track number, and on the right of the title is the page where you'll find that track.*

100 TRACKS LISTED BY TITLE

appendix 2

The number to the right of the title is the page where you'll find the track.

appendix 3

LIST OF FEATURED ARTISTS

The number to the right of the artist denotes the page where you'll find their featured track(s).

GENERAL INDEX

In this index, as throughout the body of the book, single 'quote' marks are used to denote a song title, while album titles are in *italics*. Numbers here are page references.
Bold type means the track is one of the book's 100 featured songs.

index

acknowledgements

I would like to thank everyone at Backbeat - Pen, Phil, Nigel, and Tony - for their help in bringing this idea to fruition, and Paul Quinn for editing the final text. **RR**

Editorial Sources

The artists' quotes and facts & figures used in the book were drawn from a number of sources – we would gratefully like to acknowledge the following publications, journalists and websites:

Guitar Player, *Acoustic Guitar*, Seth Rogovoy, *Berkshire, Eagle*, *Guitar World*, *Guitarist*, *In His Own Words* (Omnibus Press), Michael Watts, *Making Music*, *Melody Maker*, *Mojo*, *Melody Maker*, *NME*, *Playboy*, *Las Vegas Style*, Black Rock Coalition, Colin Devenish, Joe Smith's *Off The Record – An Oral History Of Popular Music*, *Sonicnet*, Paul Cashmere, *Timdog*, *Radioundercover.com*, *The Psychedelic News*, *Classicrockpage.com*, Chris Welch, Steve Escobar, Billy Walker, *Sounds*, *5years.com*, Tony Stewart, *Rootsworld.com, Record Collector* , *JamMusic Vox*, John L Walters, *Independent* , *Lexicon*, Jim Walsh, *St Paul Pioneer Press, Record Mirror, Q Magazine, UniVibes, Sound On Sound*, Mark Cunningham, *Good Vibrations – A History of Record Production,* Martin C Strong, *Great Rock Discography, Guinness Book of British Hit Singles, Billboard Book of USA Top 40 Hits, Virgin Encyclopedia of Popular Music, Uncut, Toronto Sun, Too Much Joy, MTV,* Ernest Hardy, *Los Angeles Weekly, DotMusic*, Andrew Harrison, *Mixmag*, Larry Flick, *Billboard, spinwithagrin.co.uk*

Mucical Sources

The following albums were used as listening references in the compiling of this book:

The Everly Brothers – *Golden Years Of...* (WEA)
Roy Orbison – *Best Of...* (Sony)
The Tornados – *Telstar: The Original Sixties Hits Of...* (Music Club)
Dusty Springfield – *Goin' Back: The Very Best Of...* (Phonogram)
The Beatles – *Please Please Me / 1962-66* (EMI)
Phil Spector – *Back To Mono* (ABKCO)
The Beach Boys – *Summer Dreams / Beach Boys Greatest Hits / Smiley Smile / The Pet Sounds Sessions* (all Capitol)
Burt Bacharach – *The Look Of Love: The Classic Songs Of...* (Polygram)
Burt Bacharach & Hal David – *Connoisseur Songbook Series*
Bob Dylan – *Greatest Hits* (CBS)
John Barry – *Thunderball: Original Soundtrack* (EMI Manhattan) / *Themeology: The Best Of...* (Columbia)
The Who – *Meaty Beaty Big & Bouncy* (Polydor)
The Marvelettes – *Compact Command Performances* (Motown)
Four Tops – *Anthology* (Motown)
Pink Floyd – *Piper At The Gates Of Dawn* (Columbia) / *Relics / Ummagumma* (Harvest)
The Herd – *An Anthology* (Music Club)
Love – *Forever Changes* (Elektra)
Jimi Hendrix – *Electric Ladyland* (Polydor)
The Rolling Stones – *Singles Collection: The London Years* (ABKCO)
The Casuals – *The Very Best Of...* (Spectrum)
Fleetwood Mac – *Greatest Hits* (CBS)
Glen Campbell – *20 Golden Greats* (EMI)
Janis Joplin – *I Got Dem Ol' Kozmic Blues Again Mama!* (CBS)
The Supremes – *40th Anniversary Box-Set* (Motown)
James Brown – *The Ultimate Collection* (MCA)
George Harrison – *All Things Must Pass* (Apple)
Mountain – *Flowers Of Evil* (BGO)
Rod Stewart – *Every Picture Tells A Story* (Polygram/Mercury)
Marvin Gaye – *What's Going On: Deluxe* Edition (Motown)
T.Rex – *The Slider* (Edsel)
David Bowie – *The Singles Collection / The Best Of David Bowie 1969-74* (EMI)
Focus – *Moving Waves* (Blue Horizon) / *Hocus Pocus: The Best Of Focus* (EMI Holland)
Roxy Music – *Street Life: 20 Great Hits* (EG)

Bruce Springsteen – *The Wild, The Innocent & The E Street Shuffle* (CBS)
Queen – *Sheer Heart Attack* (EMI)
Led Zeppelin – *Physical Graffiti* (Swansong)
Alan Stivell – *A Dublin / E Dulenn* (Fontana/Dreyfus)
Boston – *Boston* (Epic)
Television – *Marquee Moon* (Elektra/asylum)
Sex Pistols – *Never Mind The Bollocks* (Virgin)
Abba – *Gold* (Polar/Polydor)
Kate Bush – *The Kick Inside / Hounds Of Love / The Whole Story* (EMI)
Van Halen – *Van Halen* (Warner Bros)
The Jam – *Greatest Hits* (Polydor)
The Clash – *London Calling* (CBS)
The Cure – *Standing On The Beach: The Singles* (Fiction)
Elvis Costello – *Trust* (Fbeat)
The Police – *Ghost In The Machine* (A&M)
Madness – *Divine Madness* (Virgin)
Simple Minds – *Glittering Prize 81–92* (Virgin)
The Smiths – *Hatful Of Hollow* (Rough Trade) / *The Singles* (WEA)
R.E.M – *Murmur* (IRS) / *Up* (Warners)
Siouxsie & The Banshees – *Twice Upon A Time: The Singles* (Wonderland/Polydor)
Roy Harper – *Whatever Happened To Jugula?* (Beggars Banquet)
Tears For Fears – *Songs From The Big Chair* (Phonogram/Mercury)
Prince – *Parade* (Paisley Park)
T'Pau – *Bridge of Spies* (Siren)
The Mission – *Children* (Phonogram/Mercury)
Living Colour – *Vivid* (Epic)
U2 – *The Joshua Tree / All You Can't Leave Behind* (Island)
The Stones Roses – *The Stone Roses* (Silvertone)
The La's – *The La's* (Go! Discs)
Metallica – *Metallica* (Vertigo)
Nirvana – *Nevermind* (Geffen)
Madonna – *Erotica / Ray Of Light* (Maverick)
Bruce Springsteen – *Lucky Town / In Concert* (CBS/Columbia)
Suede – *Suede* (Nude)
Grant Lee Buffalo – *Fuzzy* (Slash)
Beck – *Mellow Gold* (Geffen)
Soundgarden – *Superunknown* (A&M)
Duran Duran – *Thank You* (Parlophone)
Bjork – *Post* (One Little Indian)
Jeff Buckley – *Grace* (Columbia)
Tori Amos – *Boys For Pele* (WEA)
Dodgy – *Free Peace Sweet* (A&M)
Catatonia – *International Velvet* (Blanco Y Negro)
Radiohead – *OK Computer / Kid A* (EMI)
The Verve – *Urban Hymns* (Hut)
Gomez – *Bring It On* (Hut)
Goldfrapp – *Felt Mountain* (Mute)
Queens Of The Stone Age – *Rated R* (Interscope)
Various Artists – *The Godfathers Of Britpop* (Polygram) / *Motown Chartbusters Vols 1& 5* (Motown) / *Hitsville USA 1959-71* (Motown) / *Shades Of Soul* (Global) / *Encomium* (Atlantic) / *The World Is Not Enough* (Radioactive)

Rikky Rooksby is a guitar teacher, songwriter, and music journalist. He is the author of *How To Write Songs On Guitar* and contributed a chapter on rock'n'roll to *Classic Guitars Of The Fifties*. He has also written *The Complete Guide To The Music Of Fleetwood Mac* and *The Complete Guide To The Music Of Madonna*, 14 *Fastforward* guitar tutor books, four of the *First Guitar* series, transcribed and arranged two dozen chord songbooks including Bob Dylan, Dire Straits, Eric Clapton, The Stone Roses, Travis, and *The Complete Beatles*, and co-authored *100 Years 100 Songs*. He has published interviews, reviews, articles and transcriptions in magazines such as *Guitar Techniques*, *Bassist*, *The Band*, *Music Collector*, *Encore*, *Sound On Sound*, and *Making Music* where he writes the monthly 'Private Pluck' guitar column.